Dreams Do Come True—West Coast
LIST OF PARTICIPATING B&B INNS:

Below is a list of inns that are accepting the *Dreams Do Come True* certificate. Please contact the B&B in advance for availability, rates, reservations, cancellation policies, and other B&B requirements, terms, and conditions.

BRITISH COLUMBIA, CANADA

Lakeside Illahee Inn | *Vernon, BC*
Not valid July–August
Will offer a room upgrade
See listing on page 35

CALIFORNIA, USA

Historic Sand Rock Farm | *Aptos, CA*
Valid anytime. *Will offer a room upgrade*
See listing on page 56

Alpenhorn Bed and Breakfast | *Big Bear Lake, CA*
Valid Monday–Thursday (except holidays)
See listing on page 58

Brannan Cottage Inn | *Calistoga, CA*
Valid weekdays only,
November 1–March 31; Sunday–Thursday
See listing on page 59

Chelsea Garden Inn | *Calistoga, CA*
Valid Monday–Wednesday,
November 12–April 15
(based on roooms priced $195 or higher)
Will offer a room upgrade
See listing on page 59

Olallieberry Inn Bed and Breakfast |
Cambria, CA
Valid October 2011–December 20, 2011;
Sunday–Thursday nights
(excluding holiday periods)
See listing on page 62

Country Inn B&B | *Fort Bragg, CA*
Valid anytime. *Will offer a room upgrade*
See listing on page 72

American River Inn | *Georgetown, CA*
Valid Sunday–Friday and October–May
See listing on page 72

Groveland Hotel at Yosemite National Park | *Groveland, CA*
Valid October 15–April 15
(excluding holidays and special events)
Will offer a room upgrade
See listing on page 73

Hotel Charlotte | *Groveland, CA*
Valid January 1–March 31, 2011 and
October 15–March 31, 2012
(holiday periods excluded)
Will offer a room upgrade
See listing on page 73

Landis Shores Oceanfront Inn | *Half Moon Bay, CA*
Valid Monday–Thursday (excecpt holidays)
See listing on page 75

1859 Historic National Hotel |
Jamestown, CA
Valid Sunday–Thursday (holiday periods
excluded); reservations only 24 hours
in advance
See listing on page 79

Glendeven Inn | *Little River, CA*
Valid January–April
See listing on page 86

Inn at Locke House | *Lockeford, CA*
Valid Sunday–Thursday
(except holiday and special events)
See listing on page 83

Posh Palm Springs | *Palm Springs, CA*
Valid anytime
See listing on page 99

Grandma's Room | *Penn Valley, CA*
Valid anytime
See listing on page 103

Old Yacht Club Inn B&B |
Santa Barbara, CA
Valid anytime
Will offer a room upgrade
See listing on page 113

Casa Tropicana | *San Clemente, CA*
Valid October 1–April 15 (holidays, special
events excluded), may not be combined
See listing on page 106

Jamul Haven | *San Diego, CA*
Valid Monday–Thursday
(not valid with other offers or discounts;
limit one free night per stay)
See listing on page 107

OREGON, USA

Albion Inn | *Ashland, OR*
Valid anytime
Will offer a room upgrade
See listing on page 128

Weasku Inn | *Grants Pass, OR*
May 15–September 15
(excluding weekends and holidays)
Will offer a room upgrade
See listing on page 138

Inn at the Goryo | *Hood River, OR*
Valid November–April
(except holidays and spring break)
See listing on page 138

Inn at Champoeg | *Saint Paul, OR*
Valid anytime
See listing on page 147

WASHINGTON, USA

The Blue Goose Inn | *Coupeville, WA*
Valid anytime
Will offer a room upgrade
See listing on page 153

Miller Tree Inn | *Forks, WA*
Valid October 1–May 15
See listing on page 154

Harrison House | *Friday Harbor, WA*
Valid October–May (except holidays)
See listing on page 154

Guest House Log Cottages |
Greenbank, WA
Valid October 15, 2011–April 30, 2012;
Sunday–Thursday mid-week winter
See listing on page 155

Charles Nelson Guest House |
Ocean Park, WA
Valid September–June 30th
Will offer a room upgrade
See listing on page 161

Reflections B&B | *Port Orchard, WA*
Valid anytime
See listing on page 162

Juan de Fuca Cottages | *Sequim, WA*
Valid September 15–June 15, Sunday–
Thursday (not valid with any other
specials). *Will offer a room upgrade*
See listing on page 169

Bed and Breakfast
GETAWAYS
· · · · · · · · · · · ON THE · · · · · · · · · · · ·
WEST COAST

Other books

BY PAMELA LANIER

*The Complete Guide to Bed and Breakfast Inns
& Guesthouses International*

Bed and Breakfast Getaways in the South

Elegant Small Hotels

All-Suite Hotel Guide

Elegant Hotels–Pacific Rim

Condo Vacations: The Complete Guide

22 Days in Alaska

Cinnamon Mornings & Chocolate Dreams

Cinnamon Mornings & Savory Nights

Bed and Breakfast Guide for Food Lovers

Bed and Breakfast GETAWAYS ON THE WEST COAST

The Ultimate Romantic Escapes

Bed and Breakfast Collection™

BY PAMELA LANIER

LANIER PUBLISHING INTERNATIONAL, LTD.

Petaluma, California

DEDICATION

This book is dedicated to the newest member of our family, Emilia Rose Reimann Valdes, born in the West.

& THANKS

Nicole Day
John Groton
Dennis Hayes
Shannon Holl
Amber Janke
Steve Kelez
Jeanne Kramer
Kelly McRae
Melissa Miranda
Gini Rhoda
John Richards
Geoff Rizzo
Staci van Wyk
George Young

And a special thanks to all those practicing the art of hospitality – especially with travelers. Our world is a happier, more peaceful place because of their efforts and creativity.

This book can be ordered by mail from the publisher. Please include $4.99 for postage and handling for each copy. But try your local bookstore first!

Lanier Publishing International, Ltd.

PO Box 2240
Petaluma, CA 94953
tel. 707.763.0271
fax. 707.763.5762
e-mail lanier@travelguides.com

Find us on the internet at:
www.LanierBB.com
www.TravelGuideS.com

Distributed to the book trade by:
National Book Network
15200 NBN Way, Bldg. B
Blue Ridge Summit, PA 21264-2188
website: nbnbooks.com
tel. 1-800-462-6420

Design by Laura Lamar at MAX DESIGN STUDIO.*net*

Cover photo: view from Albion River Inn on the Mendocino Coast of California by Rita Crane Photography: www.ritacranestudio.com

Introduction

THE IDEA OF GOING WEST has always been
synonymous with adventure, exploration, and
that special charm and lure of the unknown.
The North American West has been drawing
travelers for centuries, with promises of unparalleled landscapes, from the snow capped peaks
of the Yukon to the clear blue surf of Southern
California. Breathtaking cliffs of the Oregon
coast and stunning views of Glacier National
Park have been inspiring wanders since their
creation. Incomparable history dating from the
indigenous tribes of Native Americans, through
the Gold Rush, onto Westward Expansion and
continuing on today has been a characteristic
of the West. A great tradition of innovation and
exploration is seen from the sunny beaches of
San Diego to the Iditarod Trail of Alaska. Whether
travelers are exploring the small, charming town
the West has to offer, or venturing to the big
cities of the coast, each destination will bring a
new set of memories to last you a lifetime.

— PAMELA LANIER

Best West Coast

Our readers and inn guests can vote for the best in our Guests' Greatest Picks program. These properties were voted The Best in their category from inns throughout the United States and Canada. For a complete list of winners go to www.lanierbb.com/awards/bed-and-breakfast-award-winners.html

BEST GIFT SHOP
Spinnakers Brewpub & Guest House,
Victoria, British Columbia, page 36

BEST SUNSET VIEW
Elk Cove Inn & Spa,
Elk, California, page 67

BEST FOR ALL SEASONS
Brewery Gulch Inn,
Mendocino, California, page 84

BEST EDUCATIONAL CLASSES
Stanford Inn by the Sea–Big River Lodge,
Mendocino, California, page 86

BEST RURAL B&B
Bike Lane Inn,
Templeton, California, page 119

BEST FOR FARM ACTIVITIES
North End Crossing Barn & Bed,
Flora, Oregon, page 134

BEST FOR NEARBY MUSEUMS
A Painted Lady Inn,
Portland, Oregon, page 142

BEST FOR NEARBY WINERY
A Touch of Europe,
Yakima, Washington, page 169

Alaska
PAGE 43

British Columbia,
Canada
PAGE 24

Washington
PAGE 150

Oregon
PAGE 126

California
PAGE 54

Baja, Mexico
PAGE 40

West

Coast

Map

How to Use This Guide...

Visit our website at **www.LanierBB.com**...*And please tell your hosts Pamela Lanier sent you!*

ORGANIZATION

This book is organized first, alphabetically by state, and within a state, alphabetically by city. Our web site **www.LanierBB.com** can provide nearby cities and regions.

THREE TYPES OF ACCOMMODATIONS

Inn: Webster's defines an inn as a "house built for the lodging and entertainment of travelers." All the inns in this book fulfill this description. Many also provide meals, at least breakfast, although a few do not. Most of these inns have under 30 guestrooms.

Bed and Breakfast: Can be anything from a home with three or more rooms to, more typically, a large house or mansion with eight or nine guest accommodations where breakfast is served in the morning.

Guest House: Private homes welcoming travelers, some of which may be contacted directly but most of which are reserved through a reservation service organization.

BREAKFASTS

We define a **full breakfast** as one being along English lines, including eggs and/or meat as well as the usual breads, toast, juice, and coffee.

Continental Plus is a breakfast of coffee, juice, and choice of several breads and pastry and possbily more.

Continental means coffee, juice, bread or pastry.

If there is a charge for breakfast, then we note it as (fee).

MEALS

Some inns serve lunch and dinner or have a restaurant on the premises. Be sure to inquire when making your reservation.

CAN WE GET A DRINK?

Those inns without a license will generally chill your bottles and provide you with setups upon request.

PRICES

Price range is for double room, double occupancy in U.S. dollars.

Appearance to the right of the price is a code indicating the type of food services available:
BB: Breakfast included in quoted rate
EP (European Plan): No Meals
MAP (Modified American Plan): Includes breakfasts and dinner
AP (American Plan): Includes all three meals

All prices are subject to change. Please be sure to confirm rates and services when you make your reservations.

PAYMENT METHODS

Not all establishments accept credit cards; however, if they do, it will be noted as **Visa**, **MC**, **AmEx**, **DISC** or **Most CC**. Some inns do accept personal checks. Inquire about the inn's policies.

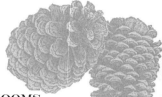

RESERVATIONS

Reservations are essential at most inns, particularly during busy seasons, and are appreciated at other times. When you book, feel free to discuss your requirements and confirm prices, services, and other details. We have found innkeepers to be delightfully helpful. A deposit or advance payment is required at some inns.

SPECIAL CONSIDERATIONS

Children, pets, smoking, and physical handicaps present special considerations for many inns. Be sure to inquire when you book your room. Whether or not they can be accommodated is generally noted as follows:

	Yes	Limited	No
Children	C-yes	C-ltd	
Pets	P-yes	P-ltd	P-no
Smoking	S-yes	S-ltd	S-no
Handicap Equipped	H-yes	H-ltd	H-no

BATHROOMS

We list the number of private baths available directly next to the number of rooms. Bear in mind that those inns with shared baths generally have more than one.

When in accommodations with shared baths, be sure to straighten the bathroom as a courtesy to your fellow guests. If you come in late, please do so on tiptoe, mindful of the other patrons visiting the inn for a little R&R.

MANNERS

Please keep in mind when you go to an inn that innkeeping is a very hard job. It is amazing that innkeepers manage to maintain such a thoroughly cheerful and delightful presence despite long hours. Do feel free to ask your innkeepers for help or suggestions, but please don't expect them to be your personal servant. you may have to carry your own bags.

SAMPLE BED & BREAKFAST LISTING

NAME OF CITY OR TOWN

Name of B&B Inn
Street Address
City or Town, State, Zip Code

Phone numbers | *Name of Innkeepers*
e-mail address | website address

Description given by the innkeeper about the original characteristics of the establishment.

Price and included meals
Number of rooms & private baths
Payments accepted
Special Considerations (Children, Pets, Smoking, Handicap Eq)

Description of breakfast offered; fee
Meals, drinks, amenities, special services, unique features

IF YOU SEE THESE SYMBOLS:

This indicates a Lanier 2011 BEST Award Winner

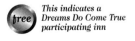
This indicates a Dreams Do Come True participating inn

13

Contents

NEEDLES AND CONES OF THE WESTERN RED CEDAR, OFFICIAL TREE OF BRITISH COLUMBIA

OFFICIAL BIRD SYMBOL OF BRITISH COLUMBIA: STELLER'S JAY

**OFFICIAL BIRD
SYMBOL OF MEXICO:
GOLDEN EAGLE**

*Baja,
Mexico*

Alaska

**ALASKA
STATE BIRD:
WILLOW
PTARMIGAN**

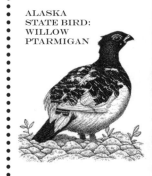

California

CALIFORNIA POPPY; OFFICIAL STATE FLOWER

CONE
AND
NEEDLES
OF THE
CALIFORNIA
REDWOOD
TREE

CALIFORNIA
STATE BIRD:
CALIFORNIA
VALLEY
QUAIL

CALIFORNIA
STATE
FLOWER:
CALIFORNIA
POPPY

California

CALIFORNIA
STATE BIRD:
CALIFORNIA
VALLEY
QUAIL

Oregon

OREGON
STATE TREE:
DOUGLAS FIR
NEEDLES AND
CONES:

OREGON
STATE BIRD:
WESTERN
MEADOWLARK

Oregon

WASHINGTON
STATE BIRD:
GOLDFINCH

Washington

Washington

NEEDLES AND
CONES OF THE
WASHINGTON
STATE TREE:
WESTERN
HEMLOCK

If I have a Sunday

free, I'll go up the

coast and spend some

time on the beach.

PARKER STEVENSON

HAIRY TRITON; OFFICIAL SHELL OF THE STATE OF OREGON

British Columbia

SUNSET IN
BRITISH COLUMBIA

● Vancouver

The Silver Door
1075 Thomson Rd

604-949-1322 | *Reesa Devlin*
rdevlin@thesilverdoor.ca | www.thesilverdoor.ca

A retreat where the mountains touch the stars, where the deer roam and the black bear comes to call. This is our home. The color silver denotes an air of sophistication and excellence and defines the exemplary service and amenities that you will find.

$150–$195
2 rooms, 2 pb
Visa MC   Cash
C-ltd/S-no/P-no/HC-no

BB | Full breakfast
Snacks, fridge for personal items, refreshments, bed snacks, fruit basket, tea, juices coffee
Heated pool, hot tub, steam room, infra red sauna, exercise room, pool table, home theater, library

BRENTWOOD BAY

Benvenuto B&B
1130 Benvenuto Ave.

250-544-1088 | **888-544-1088** | *Carrie & Clint Coleman*
reservations@benvenutobandb.com | www.benvenutobandb.com/

Benvenuto Bed and Breakfast is located "next door to world famous Butchart Gardens". We are a three suite peaceful oasis with nature at your doorstep while being minutes away from downtown Victoria BC and many world class destinations!

$99–$175
3 rooms, 3 pb
Visa MC AmEx   Cash
C-ltd/S-ltd/P-ltd/HC-no

BB |Full breakfast
Coffee, variety of teas, hot chocolate, water, etc.
Private entrances,high quality beds, cable T.V.,free wifi,bathrobes, extra toiletries and much more!

CLINTON

Poolside Paradise B&B
405 Spruce Ave

250-459-7990 | *Lorne & Luan Bernhardt*
poolsideparadisebb@bcwireless.com | www.poolsideparadisebb.com

Themed bedrooms, queen beds, private baths, indoor pool, gardens, solarium, guest dining room, den & bedrooms TV/VCR, 2000 movies, WIFI. Full gourmet breakfast, will accommodate special diet & vegetarians. Romantic, private little paradise in Clinton, BC

$80–$100
3 rooms, 3 pb
Cash Checks
C-yes/S-ltd/P-no/HC-ltd

BB |Full Gourmet breakfast
Also available special diet & vegetarian meals. Beverage bar (coffee, tea, cocoa) & popcorn provided
Indoor pool, guest den & dining room, free WIFI, in-room VCRs/TVs, micro & refrig, library, BBQ

COBBLE HILL

Cobble House B&B
3105 Cameron-
Taggart Rd

250-743-2672 | **866-743-2672** | *Ingrid & Simon Vermegen*
cobblehouse@shaw.ca | www.cobble-house.com

Cobble House is a peaceful haven in the heart of Vancouver Island's growing wine and culinary region in the Cowichan Valley. Centrally located on a forested acreage, we are still only 45 minutes north of Victoria.

$115–$125
3 rooms, 3 pb
Visa MC   Cash
C-yes/S-ltd/P-no/HC-ltd

BB |Full breakfast
Complimentary tea or coffee
Wireless Internet, sitting room, Jacuzzi, cable TV, bar fridge in each room, individual heat control

GABRIOLA

Marina's Hideaway
RR1, Site 14, C64

250-247-8854 | **888-208-9850** | *G. Brunell & R. Hayward*
Georgene@marinashideaway.com | www.marinashideaway.com

We offer all of the amenities of a luxury hotel without the hassles or the pricing! If you are looking for a special treat, whether it's an anniversary, birthday, or just the need to get away, you will love the privacy and luxury of Marina's Hideaway.

$125–$165
3 rooms, 3 pb
Most CC Cash Checks
C-ltd/S-ltd/P-ltd/HC-ltd

BB |Full breakfast

GABRIOLA ISLAND

Bumbleberry Inn
2285 Windecker Dr

250-247-7530 | **866-826-6752** |
reserve@bumbleberryinn.ca | www.bumbleberryinn.ca/

We are situated on Gabriola Island, the island is one of a chain of small islands between Vancouver Island and the mainland of British Columbia. Gabriola Island is just a short distance by ferry from the City of Nanaimo.

$89–$139
4 rooms, 2 pb
C-ltd/S-no/P-no/HC-no

BB | Continental breakfast
WiFi, private decks, country setting

WurHere B&B
3200 Coast Rd
Gabriola Island

250-247-7345 | *Ken & Merrillee Wur*
wurhere@shaw.ca | www.wurherebandbgabriola.com

Share the moments, share the days, share the love! Enjoy a unique bed and breakfast experience on this enchanted acreage. Each cabin is self-contained with a private entrance, kitchen area and an en-suite with heated floors.

$89–$120
2 rooms, 2 pb
Visa MC   Cash
C-ltd/S-yes/P-no/HC-no

BB | Full breakfast
Coffee or tea, juice, breads, bar fridge, microwave
Self-contained rooms, cabins with private entrances, individual en-suites

HALFMOON BAY

Rockwater Secret Cove Resort
Ole's Cove Rd

604-885-7038 | **877-296-4593** | Kevin Toth
reservations@rockwatersecretcoveresort.com
www.rockwatersecretcoveresort.com/

The best kept secret among Sunshine Coast Accommodations is Rock-water Secret Cove Resort. What was once the Lord Jim's Resort Hotel, this magical oasis has been transformed into a private paradise for distinguished guests.

$119–$429
38 rooms, 38 pb
Most CC Cash Checks
C-yes/S-no/P-ltd/HC-yes

EP |
Cocktail bar, restaurant, catering, Sunday Brunch from 11 am to 1 pm
Patio, games room, outdoor heated pool, massage & spa services

KELOWNA

British Columbia, Canada

KELOWNA

A Lakeview Heights B&B
3626 Royal Gala Dr

250-707-1234 | **800-967-1319** | *Anne & Mike Murphy*
info@mountainsideaccommodations.com |
www.mountainsideaccommodations.com/lakeview/

Imagine...a Canada Select 4-star B&B with spectacular lake, mountain & vineyard views, where you can enjoy luxury accommodations with private bathrooms, warm hospitality and gourmet breakfasts at an affordable price... that's A Lakeview Heights B&B.

$105–$155
3 rooms, 3 pb
Visa MC   Cash
C-ltd/S-no/P-no/HC-ltd

BB |Extensive gourmet breakfast
Vegetarian or special diets by advance request,
welcoming beverage on arrival, in-room tea & coffee
Guest living room, view patio with outdoor furniture, local area touring assistance & reservations

A Touch of English
5 Alameda Ct

250 448-6250 | **888 338-1054** | *Clare & Kelly Sucloy*
clare@touchofenglish.com | www.touchofenglish.com/

Welcome to A Touch of English B&B - afternoon tea with home-made scones and fresh fruit, amazing views of the valley & city lights, relax in the large swimming pool, newly renovated rooms with king size beds + self-contained full suite, private entrance.

$125–$155
4 rooms, 4 pb
Visa MC   Cash
C-ltd/S-ltd/P-ltd/HC-no

BB | 4 Course - Gourmet Breakfast
All dietary needs met, gluten free, celiac, vegetarian, afternoon Tea served upon arrival. Enjoy !
Elegant guest living room, patio overlooking swimming pool, English gardens, views of downtown

Aaron's Pool & Spa B&B
2160 Wilkinson St

250-860-6814 | *Rick & Marie Gruenke*
info@kelownabb.com | www.kelownabb.com

We are tucked into a nice, quiet residential area, conveniently located close to the lake, shopping and downtown Kelowna. Enjoy breakfast in the privacy of your own suite or when weather permits, on the patio by the pool.

$95–$150
2 rooms, 2 pb
Visa MC   Cash Checks
C-yes/S-no/P-no/HC-ltd

BB |Continental plus breakfast
In-room coffee & fridge
In-ground swimming pool, spa-suite, TV/DVD movies & cable Internet in rooms, pampering inclusions

MALAHAT

Prancing Horse Retreat
573 Ebedora Ln

250-743-9378 | **877-887-8834** | *Elaine & Allan Dillabaugh*
stay@prancinghorse.com | www.prancinghorse.com

Our Victorian Villa is located just 20 minutes north of Victoria, overlooking the ocean and snow-capped Olympic mountain range. Our luxury suites offer double tubs and fireplaces.

$99–$275
5 rooms, 5 pb
Visa MC   Cash
C-yes/S-no/P-no/HC-ltd

BB |Full breakfast
Restaurant
Tennis, Jacuzzis, pool, suites, fireplace, cable TV, accommodations for business travelers

Getaways on the West Coast   **27**

NANAIMO

Copper Kettle
465 Stewart Ave

250-740-3977 | 877-740-3977 | *Fiona & Maurice*
info@copperkettlebc.com | www.copperkettlebc.com/

We invite you to come for a comfortable and peaceful stay with us where you can enjoy the natural atmosphere where the city meets the sea shore. 5 min walk to downtown.

$100–$125
3 rooms, 3 pb
Visa MC   Cash
C-ltd/S-no/P-no/HC-no

BB | Full breakfast
Tea and Coffee maker in each Room. Discuss special diets or allergies if required.
Clean rooms,ensuite bathrooms/shower,bathrobes, slippers, radio/alarm clock, kettle, coffeemaker.

Flying Cloud B&B
581 Cumberland Pl

250-758-2083 | 888-303-2413 | *Vivian & Neil Reinhart*
info@flyingcloudbedandbreakfast.com |
www.flyingcloudbedandbreakfast.com/
An amazing Nanaimo location with views on Vancouver Island. Come and experience Vancouver Island hospitality with hosts Neil & Vivian Reinhart in their lofty Flying Cloud Bed & Breakfast.

$125–$175
3 rooms, 3 pb
Visa MC   Cash
C-ltd/S-ltd/P-no/HC-no

BB | Full breakfast
West Coast theme lounge, wine & cheese reception on deck 4-6pm, cookies, tea, coffee, popcorn, water
Four fireplaces, billiard room, views of the bay, three decks, hot tub, infared sauna, Internet

Hammond Bay
Oceanside B&B
3804 Hammond Bay Rd

250-751-1409 | 250-618-4300 | *Karen & Bill Stant*
hammondbaybb@Shaw.ca | www.hammondbaybb.com

Two comfortable oceanside rooms with private entrances, bathrooms and kitchen facilities in Nanaimo. Private beach is at your doorstep. Quiet peaceful retreat on the east coast of Vancouver Island.

$100–$125
2 rooms, 2 pb
Visa MC   Cash Checks
C-ltd/S-no/P-no/HC-no

BB | Full breakfast
Private kitchen facilities, picnic area available to guests, morning coffee on our private patio.
Picturesque views of Georgia Strait and the Coastal Mountains, private entrances.

Long Lake
Waterfront B&B
240 Ferntree Place

250-758-5010 | 877-758-5010 | *Gordie & Janice Robinson*
frontdesk@LodgingNanaimo.com | www.lodgingnanaimo.com

Retreat to an old growth forest in the middle of thriving Nanaimo! Long Lake Waterfront B&B features 3 private luxury suites, and guests rave about our exceptional customer service, privacy, lakeside fun, excellent breakfasts and wonderful conversation!

$100–$175
3 rooms, 3 pb
Visa MC   Cash
C-ltd/S-ltd/P-ltd/HC-no

BB | Full breakfast
Fresh fruit, yogurt, refreshments and hot entree varying every day.
Air-conditioning, fridge, ensuite with shower and/or Jacuzzi, WiFi, canoe, kayaks and pedal boat

NORTH SAANICH

The Glenelg B&B
9574 Glenelg Ave

250-656-3629 | *Eric & Hayato*
akabane@telus.net | www.theglenelg.com/

The Glenelg is a beautiful West Coast, contemporary home with separate area for guests including a beautiful private lounge and patio. Surrounded by nature and enjoying clean air and close proximity to the Butchart Gardens and all other amenities.

$110–$135
2 rooms, 2 pb
Visa MC   Cash Checks
C-ltd/S-no/P-no/HC-no

BB | Full breakfast
Complimentary coffee or tea in our Guest Lounge
King or Queen beds, Finnish Sauna Use, fluffy bathrobes, private patio, in-house laundry

NORTH VANCOUVER

Crystal's View
420 Tempe Crescent

604-987-3952 | *Crystal Davis*
Crysview@shaw.ca | www.bc-bedandbreakfast.com

Outstanding panoramic views from every room from this luxurious Bed and Breakfast. Experience modern comforts and fine European hospitality. Centrally located in a quiet neighborhood. Canada Select 4 1/2 Stars!

$135–$295
3 rooms, 3 pb
Visa MC   Cash
C-ltd/S-no/P-no/HC-no

BB | Full home cooked breakfast
Tea, coffee, cookies, refreshments
Panoramic views, double Jacuzzi, sundeck, fireplace,plasma TV/DVD

Lockhaven Waterfront B&B
2136 Lockehaven Rd

604-928-8225 | *Denise and Noulan Bowker*
hosts@lockehaven.ca | www.lockehaven.ca

Right by the ocean with stunning views, Lockehaven offers luxury and privacy with 2 large self-contained suites with exterior hot tubs. Located in idyllic Deep Cove, it is only a 25 minute drive to downtown Vancouver.

$165–$339
2 rooms, 2 pb
Visa MC AmEx   Cash
S-no/P-no/HC-no

BB | Continental Mon-Sat, full Sunday
In-suite kitchenettes
private outdoor jacuzzi hot tubs, shared laundry, in-suite computers, wireless Internet & phones

ThistleDown House
3910 Capilano Rd

604-986-7173 | **888-633-7173** | *Rex Davidson*
info@thistle-down.com | www.thistle-down.com

Internationally acclaimed, ThistleDown is a 1920 Craftsman-style, heritage-listed home, restored with great care & filled with antiques, handcrafted furnishings & works of art from around the world. Breakfast is deliciously gourmet, service is impeccable.

$110–$295
6 rooms, 6 pb
Visa MC   Cash
C-ltd/S-no/P-no/HC-no

BB | Full Gourmet Breakfast
Afternoon tea of homemade pies, cakes or pastries served in the lounge or the garden; sherry & port
Goose down or silk-filled duvets, antiques, fireplaces, library, gardens, WiFi, full concierge

PEMBERTON

Greenwood
Country Inn
1371 Greenwood St

604-894-5607 | *Margit de Haan*
reserve@greenwoodcountryinn.com | www.greenwoodcountryinn.com

Nestled on a bluff high above the village of Pemberton, British Columbia, offering unparalleled views from every direction. Take your breath away beauty!

$120–$175
3 rooms, 3 pb
Visa MC   Cash Checks
C-yes/S-no/P-ltd/HC-ltd

BB | Full breakfast
Home-cooked dinners by request
Kitchenette, small weddings, local art, decks, fireplace, lounge, jacuzzi suite, deck with hot tub

PENDER ISLAND

Oceanside Inn
4230 Armadale Rd

250-629-6691 | **800-601-3284** | *Bill & Maggie Rumford*
oceanside@penderisland.com | www.penderisland.com

Oceanside is nestled on 3 acres of oceanfront, with beach access where our guests can retreat from the rapid pace of city life. Privacy is characteristic of life at Oceanside. Private outdoor hot tubs for all rooms.

$139–$239
3 rooms, 3 pb
Visa MC
S-no/P-no/HC-no

BB | Full breakfast
Complimentary beverages in room
Sitting room, library, private hot tubs/deck, suites, fireplaces, restaurants nearby

PRINCE RUPERT

Eagle Bluff
Lighthouse B&B
201 Cow Bay Rd

250-627-4955 | **800-833-1550** | *Mary Allen & Bryan Cox*
eaglebed@citytel.net | www.citytel.net/eaglebluff

Experience Prince Rupert's waterfront. Fully renovated heritage home in historic Cow Bay with comfortable rooms and extraordinary views!

$80–$125
7 rooms, 5 pb
Visa MC   Cash
C-yes/S-no/P-no/HC-ltd

BB | Full breakfast
Tea, coffee & kitchen facilities, common area
Full decks and sitting room, phone/fax and Internet

Enchanted Rainforest
B&B
706 Ritchie St

250-624-9742 | **888-923-9993** | *Cindy Hardy*
cindyhardy@rain4est.com | www.rain4est.com

We invite you to come stay with us and enjoy our unique blend of prairie and maritime hospitality. Enjoy all the comforts of home while staying at our warm and welcoming B&B.

$59–$119
3 rooms, 1 pb
Cash
C-yes/S-no/P-ltd/HC-no

BB | Continental plus breakfast

Free Satellite TV, wireless Internet, guest kitchenette, laundry service, baby sitting service

Doorknocker B&B
13211 Steveston Hwy

604-277-8714 | 866-877-8714 | *Jeanette & Chris*
thedoorknocker@shaw.ca | www.thedoorknocker.com

The Doorknocker B&B is a Tudor-style Mansion on an estate surrounded by gardens and mountain views. Central to everything in Vancouver, a luxurious quiet getaway in the city. Beautiful rooms, fantastic breakfasts, great rates, the best place to stay.

$89–$139
3 rooms, 3 pb
Visa MC AmEx   Cash
C-ltd/S-no/P-no/HC-no

BB | and special diets
Coffee & assorted teas, filtered water, cookies
Free wireless Internet, free onsite parking, gardens, gazebo, heated indoor pool, sauna, art gallery

SALT SPRING ISLAND

Sky Valley Inn
421 Sky Valley Rd

250-537-9800 | 866-537-1028 | *Richard Slosky*
info@skyvalleyinn.com | www.skyvalleyinn.com

Sky Valley is a Salt Spring Island Bed and Breakfast and the island's only luxury French country retreat, on eleven acres of natural beauty.

$170–$220
3 rooms, 3 pb
Visa MC   Cash Checks
C-ltd/S-no/P-no/HC-ltd

BB |Gourmet breakfast
A complimentary decanter of sipping Sherry
Gardens, pool, fireplace, fresh cut flowers, a complimentary decanter of sipping Sherry, robes

SIDNEY

Beacon Inn at Sidney
9724 Third St

250-655-3288 | 877-420-5499 |
info@beaconinns.com | www.thebeaconinn.com

The Area's only 5-Star property. Near Victoria, Butchart Gardens, ferries & airport. Luxurious guestrooms with spa-like ensuite bathrooms, soaker or jetted tubs, A/C, F/P's, Wi-Fi, CD player/radios. Stroll to local shops, restaurants & the waterfront.

$119–$259
9 rooms, 9 pb
Visa MC AmEx   Cash
C-ltd/S-no/P-no/HC-no

BB | Full gourmet breakfast
Common area guest fridge & coffee/tea/snack station.
Guest lounge w/fireplace, newspapers, free off-street parking, concierge, afternoon Sherry, WiFi.

SOOKE

Cape Cod B&B
5782 Anderson Cove Rd

250-642-3253 | 888-814-7773 | *Gwendolyn Ginman*
capecodbb@shaw.ca | www.capecodbnb.bc.ca/

Cape Cod style home nestled in two wooded acres with spectacular ocean and forest views on the south-west coast of Vancouver Island. Self-contained suite is totally private and peaceful. A scenic forty minute drive from Victoria and the Butchart Gardens.

$130–$155
1 rooms, 1 pb
Visa MC   Cash Checks
C-yes/S-ltd/P-no/HC-ltd

BB | Full breakfast
Snacks, fresh fruit, complimentary sherry
Sitting room, library, kitchen, BBQ, satellite TV/PPV/VCR/DVD, private patio.

SOOKE

Sooke Harbour House
RR #4

250-642-3421 | 800-889-9688 | *Sinclair & Frederique Philip*
info@sookeharbourhouse.com | www.sookeharbourhouse.com

Romantic little inn right on the water, located 45 minutes southwest of Victoria on Vancouver Island, BC. Wonderful attention to detail in every area of the inn.

$259–$659	BB	Full or continental breakfast
28 rooms, 28 pb	Dinner, restaurant
Visa MC Cash	Wet bars, fireplaces, sitting room, piano, steam showers, Jacuzzi, infared sauna,
C-yes/S-no/P-yes/HC-yes	library,bikes,cooking

SPENCES BRIDGE

**The Inn at
Spences Bridge**
3649 Hwy #8

250-458-2311 | 877-354-1997 | *Ray Nigalis*
theinn@spencesbridge.ca | www.spencesbridge.ca

A beautiful country inn and B&B on the scenic Thompson River. Comfortable lodging & fine vegetarian dining in BC's oldest operating hotel, just 3.5 hrs NE of Vancouver through the Fraser Canyon.

$68–$118	BB	Continental breakfast
12 rooms, 5 pb	Restaurant open 11am – 9pm, full menu, vegetarian
Visa MC AmEx	Lounge, riverside dining, gift shop, library, hiking, bicycles
C-yes/S-ltd/P-ltd/HC-yes	

SURREY

Apple Creek B&B
14686 32nd Ave

604-760-7077 | *Beverley Olafson*
info@applecreekbb.com | www.applecreekbb.com

Regarded as one of the premier homes in the Vancouver region, on five landscaped acres. Furnished with a world class collection of Canadian antiques, fireplaces, squash court & indoor pool. Beach & golf nearby. A luxury private or corporate retreat stay.

$100–$175	BB	hearty, home-cooked breakfast
3 rooms, 0 pb	Tea, coffee, beverages & light evening snacks, special diet meal preparation may be
Visa MC Cash	arranged
C-yes/S-no/P-ltd/HC-no	Free wireless Internet, indoor swimming pool, Jacuzzi, TV/DVD/VCR entertainment area

B&B on the Ridge
5741 146th St

604-591-6065 | 888-697-4111 | *Dale & Mary Fennell*
stay@bbridgesurrey.com | www.bbridgesurrey.com

Escape from the city to a delightful, tastefully decorated B&B situated on 1/2 acre, with a quiet country atmosphere. This comfortable escape from the city is conveniently located to everything the Greater Vancouver area has to offer.

$80–$140	BB	Full breakfast
3 rooms, 3 pb	Snacks, refreshments upon arrival, nightly goodies, coffee & tea making facilities
Cash Checks	Cable TV/VCR/DVD,wireless Internet Access, Tourist Info, Free Local Calls, Free Parking,
C-ltd/S-ltd/P-no/HC-no	Sundeck

British Columbia, Canada

A TreeHouse B&B
2490 W 49th Ave

604-266-2962 | **877-266-2960** | *Barb & Bob Selvage*
bb@treehousebb.com | www.treehousebb.com/

"Bauhaus Mood, Zen Spirit": modern metropolitan home featuring contemporary art, warm hospitality, personalized service, and substantial, gourmet breakfasts. A TreeHouse offers refined simplicity in a beautiful, exclusive neighborhood.

$109–$199
4 rooms, 2 pb
Visa MC AmEx   Cash
C-ltd/S-ltd/P-no/HC-no

BB | Full gourmet breakfast
Courtesy beverage for celebrations, chocolates on the pillow, in room tea, coffee, filtered water
Wireless internet, free calls to US&Canada, TV/DVDs, Entertainment Books, parking, concierge service

AAA Catherine's B&B
668 E 29 Ave

604-875-8968 | **800-463-9933** | *Catherine Vong*
bnbvancouver@gmail.com | www.aaabedandbreakfast.com

We offer year round, affordable bed and breakfast accommodations with spectacular views near all major Vancouver tourist attractions, transportation, parks and recreation. Free computer use and unlimited wireless internet. Mini gym for your use.

$59–$169
12 rooms, 10 pb
Visa MC AmEx
C-yes/S-no/P-no/HC-no

BB | Full breakfast

Internet, VCR/cable in guest lounge, discounted local tour rates and car rental

Barclay House
1351 Barclay St

604-605-1351 | **800-971-1351** | *Maria Siy*
info@barclayhouse.com | www.barclayhouse.com

Downtown! AAA 3 Diamonds! Voted best Vancouver B&B by The Independent! *Best Lodging in Vancouver by* The Vancouver Sun! *Recommended by* Los Angeles Times!

$145–$275
6 rooms, 6 pb
Visa MC AmEx   Cash
C-ltd/S-no/P-no/HC-no

BB | Full 3-course gourmet breakfast
Assorted pastries and fruit
Wifi, cable, DVD, alarm, fridge, coffee/tea, robes, hairdryers, safes, free parking & local calls

English Bay Inn
1968 Comox St

604-683-8002 | **866-683-8002** | *Boban Vuckovic*
stay@englishbayinn.com | www.englishbayinn.com

Tucked away between high-rise apartments in a quiet corner of Vancouver's Downtown West End offering an unexpected hideaway in the heart of the city. Walk to Stanley Park, English Bay Beach, and downtown.

$149–$299
6 rooms, 6 pb
Most CC Cash
C-ltd/S-no/P-no/HC-no

BB | Full breakfast
Tea, coffee, port, sherry
Sitting rooms, library, fireplace, laundry, concierge, restaurant reservations etc.

House on Dunbar B&B **604-224-6355** | *Joanne Renwick*
3926 20 Ave West   houseondunbarbandb@gmail.com | http://houseondunbarbandb.com

House On Dunbar is a spacious, contemporary and comfortable B&B that offers guests the warmth and comforts of home and provides an ideal home base to explore all Vancouver has to offer. We provide everything you want and more...Indulge yourself.

$110–$165   BB | Full or Healthy Heart breakfast
3 rooms, 3 pb   Full kitchen for guest use, complimentary tea, coffee, soft drinks and snacks available
Visa MC AmEx   Cash   Computer with high speed and wireless Internet, 50' plasma TV, free laundry,
S-no/P-no/HC-no   luscious yard

Kings Corner B&B   **604-879-7997** | *Anne & Christopher King*
4006 Glen Dr   talkischeap@shaw.ca | www.kingscornerbb.com

You'll always receive a warm welcome at King's Corner 1912 heritage Vancouver bed and breakfast home. With our central location in a quiet residential neighborhood it is the perfect place to stay!

$70–$150   BB | Full breakfast
2 rooms, 2 pb
Cash Checks   Wireless Internet, hot tub, kitchenette, privates entrance
C-yes/S-no/P-ltd/HC-no

Manor Guest House   **604-876-8494** | *Brenda Yablon*
345 West 13th Ave   info@manorguesthouse.com | www.manorguesthouse.com/

An Edwardian mansion on the southeastern edge of downtown Vancouver, in a safe & elegant neighborhood. Spacious rooms, private baths, free parking. Top-floor suite sleeps six. Close to shopping, restaurants & public transit.

$95–$310   BB | Full gourmet vegetarian breakfast
26 rooms, 20 pb   Guest kitchen use, dinner by prior arrangement
Visa MC   Conference facilities for up to 25, parlor & music room, English garden, decks,
C-ltd/S-no/P-no/HC-no   guest lounge

Nelson House B&B   **604-684-9793** | **866-684-9793** | *David Ritchie*
977 Broughton St   info@downtownbedandbreakfast.com | www.downtownbedandbreakfast.com/

Downtown, where you want to be! West End location only steps to the best of Vancouver, near Stanley Park and Robson Street shopping. Character, comfort, convenience for business and vacation.

$88–$198   BB | Full Canadian Breakfast
6 rooms, 4 pb   Mini-refrigerators & filtered water in some rooms, tea & coffee in the Shangri-La Suite
Visa MC   Cash   Off-street parking included, 3 decks, garden, fireplaces, library, WiFi, hairdryers,
C-ltd/S-ltd/P-no/HC-no   ensuite Jacuzzi

VANCOUVER

Stanley Park Inn
1030 Chilco St

604-683-8063 | *Bob Chapin*
info@stanleyparkinn.com | www.stanleyparkinn.com

Experience the elegance of bygone eras and Vancouver's natural appeal. Exquisite 18th and 19th century English and French antiques in a restored 1930s Tudor-style home, 1 block from Stanley Park, English Bay.

$250–$350
3 rooms, 3 pb
Visa MC AmEx   Cash
C-yes/S-no/P-no/HC-ltd

BB | Full breakfast
Sherry & port in the afternoon & evening
Parlour, library, high-speed wireless Internet

VERNON

Lakeside Illahee Inn
15010 Tamarack Dr

250-260-7896 | **888-260-7896** | *Peter & Debbie Dooling*
info@illahee.com | www.illahee.com

A superlative Waterfront Boutique Inn on Lake Kalamalka. Awarded the "6th Best on the Waterfront" for B&B/Country Inns throughout North America. Distinguished as "the Jewel of the Okanagan" for fine accommodations, and amenities by North American Inns.

 Dreams Do Come True participating inn—
Not valid July–August; will offer a free room upgrade

$114–$379
5 rooms, 5 pb
Visa MC   Cash
C-ltd/S-no/P-no/HC-ltd

BB | Full breakfast
Lakeshore sunset dining by reservation May to October of each year.
Corporate boardroom services.
Day lounge, outdoor hot-tub, lakeshore patio, on the water sitting dock, kayaks, firepit, sand beach, WiFi

VICTORIA

Abbeymoore Manor
1470 Rockland Ave

250-370-1470 | **888-801-1811** | *Anne, Ian & Michelle*
innkeeper@abbeymoore.com | www.abbeymoore.com

Choose from 5 gorgeous heritage B&B rooms or for the ultimate in privacy several self-contained suites at ground level. We are a short drive to downtown and a block from Craigdarroch Castle and the 36 acre estate. TripAdvisor's #1 B&B in Victoria since '05

$139–$249
7 rooms, 7 pb
Visa MC   Cash
C-ltd/S-no/P-ltd/HC-no

BB | Gourmet Breakfast
Tea & coffee station, guest refrigerator with complimentary soft drinks, fresh fruit & snacks
High-speed Internet access, library, 2 daily newspapers, Aveda beauty products in every room

OFFICIAL
FLOWER OF
BRITISH
COLUMBIA:
PACIFIC
DOGWOOD

VICTORIA

Abigail's Hotel
906 McClure St

250-388-5363 | **800-561-6565** | *Nick Saklas*
innkeeper@abigailshotel.com | www.abigailshotel.com/

Experience the charm of this unique bed & breakfast boutique hotel, just steps from Victoria's famous attractions, museums and parks! Includes a 3-course gourmet breakfast, evening appetizers, local calls, parking & Internet.

$169–$349
23 rooms, 23 pb
Visa MC AmEx
C-yes/S-no/P-ltd/HC-no

BB | Full gourmet breakfast for two
Complimentary light evening hors d'oeuvres at 5:00 pm, plus coffee and tea 24 hours a day.
Wine, Beer & Champagne Service; Spa services, gift shop; 24 hr concierge, free parking & Internet

**Albion Manor
Bed & Breakfast**
224 Superior St

250-389-0012 | **877-389-0012** | *Don Halton & Fernando Garcia*
info@albionmanor.com | www.albionmanor.com

Our gracious 1892 Heritage Home is located on a peaceful oak-tree lined street in the historic James Bay district, a 5 minute walk from the US ferry terminal, the ocean, shopping and Victoria's major venues. The crowning touch to your Victoria visit.

$99–$199
8 rooms, 8 pb
Visa MC
C-ltd/S-ltd/P-ltd/HC-ltd

BB | Full gourmet breakfast
We are happy to provide for your dietary needs be they vegetarian gluten free, etc.
Gardens, patios, balconies, fireplaces, Jacuzzis, special packages & surprises available

**Ambrosia Historic
B&B**
522 Quadra St.

250-380-7705 | **877-262-7672** | *Bob & Dawna Bailey*
stay@ambrosiavictoria.com | www.ambrosiavictoria.com

The historic Ambrosia B&B offers the ultimate in luxury, romance and relaxation, in the heart of Victoria's Downtown. Our spacious rooms have private en-suite bathroom, renovated in 2004. Gourmet breakfast, our amenities set the tone for a great time.

$135–$285
4 rooms, 4 pb
Visa MC AmEx
S-no/P-no/HC-no

BB | Full breakfast
Jetted tubs for two, rain showers, concierge, Aveda products, Frette linens, in-room spa services

Ashcroft House B&B
670 Battery St

250-385-4632 | **866-385-4632** | *Paulanne & David*
Paulanne@AshcroftHouseBandB.com | www.AshcroftHouseBandB.com

The little touches and attention to details at our Victoria bed and breakfast will leave you wishing you had more time here! At Ashcroft House B&B, we know you will enjoy its unmistakable sense of comfort, peace and all those sunny windows!

$109–$199
5 rooms, 5 pb
Most CC Cash Checks
C-ltd/S-ltd/P-no/HC-no

BB | Full breakfast
Coffee, tea, bottled water, fresh fruit
TV, VCR, electric fireplace, kitchenette, WiFi, guest computer, laundry facilities, bike storage

VICTORIA

Binners'...
A Contemporary Oasis
58 Linden Ave

250-383-5442 | 888-409-5800 | *Binners & Edward Davidson*
hosts@binners.com | www.BinnersVictoria.com

4.5 star boutique-style B&B with elegant, comfortable suites & rooms. Fireplaces, Jacuzzis, gourmet 3-course breakfast. Just 3 minutes from downtown and 1/2 block to stunning ocean & mountain views & walkways. Concierge & spa services available.

$89–$245
3 rooms, 3 pb
Most CC Cash
C-ltd/S-ltd/P-no/HC-ltd

BB | Gourmet multi-course breakfast
In-room microwave, coffeemaker, bar fridge with soft drinks, spring water; in-room coffee & teas
WiFi, guest computer, concierge services, in-room phones, in-room spa services, jetted tubs

Cycle Inn B&B
3158 Anders Rd

250-478-6821 | 877-829-2531 | *Joanne Cowan*
stay@cycleinn.com | www.cycleinn.com

A lovely waterfront residence located on the famous Galloping Goose Trail. Whether you have come to see your child safely into the new school, you are on a golfing holiday, or in business meetings, by evening this is a must stay!

$75–$125
3 rooms, 2 pb
Cash
C-yes/S-ltd/P-ltd/HC-ltd

BB | Delicious breakfast
Drinks on the deck, or English style tea
Rec room fridge, sauna, VCR, library, games, bicycle lock up, maps, swings, BBQ, deck, boats, quiet

Dashwood Manor
Seaside Heritage B&B
1 Cook St

250-385-5517 | 800-667-5517 | *Dave & Sharon Layzell*
info@dashwoodmanor.com | www.dashwoodmanor.com

Best ocean views in Victoria! Dashwood Manor is Victoria's only seaside heritage B&B in walking distance to downtown. Breathtaking views of the ocean and snow-capped mountains of Washington's Olympic Peninsula from each guest room.

$109–$289
11 rooms, 11 pb
Visa MC   Cash
C-ltd/S-no/P-no/HC-no

BB | Full gourmet breakfast

Knowledgeable and experienced owners offer valuable assistance with trip planning and reservations.

Gazebo
Bed & Breakfast
5460 Old W Saanich Rd

250-727-2420 | 877-211-2288 | Linda & Martin Vernon
stay@gazebo-victoria.com | www.gazebo-victoria.com

Relax at a Victorian manor house near the Butchart Gardens in a quiet central location. Stay in a secluded cottage or elegant rooms surrounded by lovely gardens. Massages, packages available. WiFi. Canada Select 5 Stars at 4 star prices.

$155–$220
3 rooms, 3 pb
Visa MC
C-ltd/S-no/P-no/HC-ltd

BB | Full breakfast
Complimentary beverages
Wireless Internet, guest computer & printer, massages, double Jacuzzis, fireplaces, glorious garden

VICTORIA

Humboldt House
B&B Inn
867 Humboldt St

250-383-0152 | **888-383-0327** | *David & Vlasta Booth*
rooms@humboldthouse.com | www.humboldthouse.com

Victoria's most romantic and private B&B. Relax by firelight in your Jacuzzi, and feast on a gourmet breakfast in the privacy of your room. Large windows offer a peaceful view of neighbouring St. Ann's Academy and its apple orchard.

$129–$295
6 rooms, 6 pb
Visa MC AmEx   Cash
C-ltd/S-no/P-no/HC-no

BB | Full Gourmet breakfast
Afternoon tea, complimentary sparkling wine, truffles
Sitting room, library, Jacuzzis, suites, fireplaces, cable TV

Spinnakers Brewpub
& Guest House
308 Catherine St

250-386-2739 | **877-838-2739** | *Paul Hadfield*
fdmanager@spinnakers.com | www.spinnakers.com

From Canada's oldest brewpub, the guesthouses offer heritage and contemporary accommodations in luxurious rooms with queen beds and deluxe bedding, Jacuzzi tubs, wood or gas fireplaces, original art and breakfast.

2011 Lanier Best West Coast Award Winner:
Best Gift Shop

$149–$279
10 rooms, 10 pb
Visa MC AmEx   Cash
C-ltd/S-no/P-ltd/HC-ltd

BB | Gourmet Breakfast Basket
Lunch served from 11am to 4pm, dinner from 4pm to 10:30pm
Restaurant, Bar, Free Wireless Internet Access, Free Parking, Water & Truffles on Arrival

WHISTLER

Cedar Springs
B&B Lodge
8106 Camino Drive

604-938-8007 | **800-727-7547** | *Joern & Jackie Rohde*
info@whistlerinns.com | www.whistlerbb.com

Casual Canadian hospitality and comfort. Sumptuous breakfasts, seasonal afternoon teas and dinners; fireside living and dining room. Comfortable rooms; sauna, hot tub. Canada Select 3 Star Rating.

$99–$279
8 rooms, 6 pb
Visa MC AmEx   Cash
C-yes/S-no/P-no/HC-ltd

BB | Full breakfast
Home baked snacks for afternoon tea, complimentary tea & coffee.
Iced tea in the summer
Guest lounge with TV/DVD/VCR, wet bar, hot tub, decks, gardens, bike rentals;
shuttle;free wireless

British Columbia, Canada

Golden Dreams
6412 Easy St

604-932-2667 | 800-668-7055 | *Ann & Terry Spence*
ann@goldendreamswhistler.com | www.goldendreamswhistler.com

Serving GREAT B&B memories since 1987 with our true west coast hospitality! Be surrounded by mountain beauty, choose one of our unique THEME rooms and awaken to a wholesome breakfast. In hosts words: "Arrive as strangers, leave as friends."

$115–$175
3 rooms, 1 pb
Visa MC   Cash
C-ltd/S-ltd/P-ltd/HC-no

BB | Homecooked nutritious breakfast
Will cater to vegetarian/special diets, complimentary snacks for apres ski,
welcome drink in summer
Free wireless internet. Daily housekeeping. Eco-friendly B&B, recycling, composting,
chemical-free!

Whistler Alpine Chalet
3012 Alpine Crescent

604-935-3003 | 800-736-9967 | *P. Hari*
jhari@whistleralpinechalet.ca | www.whistleralpinechalet.ca

Whistler Alpine Chalet Retreat & Wellness, European boutique hotel/ Chalat, upscale luxury B&B, European Chalet. Ranked 'Best in Canada', 'Best in Western Canada', 'Best in Whistler'. Butler service, yoga, retreat & wellness packages.

$229–$479
8 rooms, 8 pb
Visa MC   Cash
C-ltd/S-no/P-no/HC-yes

BB |Full 3 course Gourmet Breakfast
Chef can accommodate special dietary needs.
FREE Jacuzzi, FREE Steam Room, FREE WiFi, FREE coffee & tea, FREE parking,
FREE smiles.

BRITISH
COLUMBIA
OFFICIAL
MAMMAL:
SPIRIT
BEAR

Baja, Mexico

THE BEACH AT
SAN JOSE DEL CABO

LA PAZ

Casa Tuscany Inn
Calle N Bravo 110

612-128-8103 | *Carol Dyer*
casa@tuscanybaja.com | www.tuscanybaja.com

Charming B&B just one block from the Malecon (waterfront) and close to everything. Reminiscent of a Tuscan Inn in a lovely courtyard setting. All rooms have private entry.

$85–$150
4 rooms, 4 pb
Cash
C-ltd/S-no/P-ltd/HC-no

BB | Full breakfast
Queen size beds, A/C, video and book library, wifi

El Angel Azul
Independencia No 518

+52-612-125-5130 | *Esther Ammann*
hotel@elangelazul.com | www.elangelazul.com

A fascinating place that recaptures the spirit and culture of La Paz. In the heart of the city, the building was formerly the town's courthouse. Completely renovated and redesigned as a B&B inn. A Historic landmark & environmentally friendly.

$105–$195
10 rooms, 10 pb
Visa MC   Cash
C-ltd/S-ltd/P-no/HC-no

BB | Full breakfast
Our Bar is open in the afternoon
Bar&Lounge, WiFi, garden, cable TV for guests in lounge, A/C ,tour planning, afternoon tea & early bird coffee, English Book Store and Art Shop

LORETO

Loreto Playa B&B
109 Oriente Eduardo Estra

+52-613-135-1129 | **775-629-4511** | *Roberto & Paulette Lane*
loretoplaya@gmail.com | www.loretoplaya.com/

Loreto Playa B & B is the most beautiful and romantic hotel in th and historic town of Loreto, Baja California Sur, México. Located right on the beach with private suites that overlook the stunning Sea of Cortez.

$145–$255
4 rooms, 4 pb
Most CC Cash
C-yes/S-no/P-no/HC-ltd

BB | Full breakfast
Many restaurants close by. Refer and micro in room
Wireless Internet, Kayaks, mountain bikes, TV, DVD, terry cloth robes, toiletries, private baths, terraces, courtyard with garden, views, sitting areas and beach.

OAXACA

Hacienda Los Laureles-Spa
Hidalgo 21

+52-951-501-5300 | *Peter Kaiser*
bookings@hotelhaciendalaureles.com | www.hotelhaciendalaureles.com

Hacienda Los Laureles-SPA in a quiet area of Oaxaca is a completely renovated hacienda for guests who want to enjoy a unique locale & a relaxing stay in a 5-star, 4 diamond luxury boutique hotel enhanced by traditional architecture & a personable staff.

$199–$389
23 rooms, 23 pb
Visa MC AmEx Cash
C-yes/S-yes/P-no/HC-yes

BB | Special Oaxacan (Full) Breakfast
18 hrs Full-service restaurant, bar & room service
Welcome cocktail, fruit & flowers on arrival, turn down & laundry service, minifridge, en suite baths, telephones, Internet, spa, heated swimming pool, massage, gardens

OAXACA

Hotel Las Mariposas

619-793-5121 | *Maria Teresa Villarreal*
ventas@lasmariposas.com.mx | www.lasmariposas.com.mx/

A very popular, mid-range hotel with clean and cozy rooms, Las Mariposas is "big on ambiance". Rooms are set around an inviting communal space, perfect for sitting down to read a good book and exchanging stories with other guests!

$35–$50
21 rooms, 21 pb
Visa MC   Cash
C-no/S-ltd/P-no/HC-ltd

BB | Bread cereal, cafe de la olla, tea
Communal kitchen area
TV and sitting-room, DVD's, guidebooks, garden courtyards, sun-loungers,
Free internet, free long-distance phone calls and drinking water

**La Casa de
Mis Recuerdos**
Pino Suarez #508

+52-951-515-8483 | **877-234-4706** | *William & Nora Gutierrez*
misrecue@hotmail.com | www.misrecuerdos.net

Nestled in the emerald hills of Mexico's state of Oaxaca, lies a romantic gem of a city by the same name. This charming colonial town is one of Mexico's national treasures, a showcase of the real Mexico, an authentic Mexican experience.

$65–$120
8 rooms, 6 pb
Visa MC   Cash
C-no/S-no/P-no/HC-no

BB | Two course Oaxaquenian breakfast
Special dietary meals with advance notice
Cool Refreshments on Arrival, Non-smoking, WiFi, daily housekeeping, low-cost
LD calls, purified bottled water, optional cooking classes, private dinner parties

SAN JOSE DEL CABO

Cabo Surf Hotel
Playa Acapulquito, Km. 28

+52-624-142-2666 | **858-964-5117** | *Mauricio Balderrama*
info@cabosurfhotel.com | www.cabosurfhotel.com

Cabo Surf Hotel is located in one of the top surfing beaches in Cabo. Enjoy long rides, ideal for longboarders. Relax with the sound of the ocean waves. Enjoy our infinity pool and Jacuzzi nested within landscaped enhanced lush gardens. Sea Spa now open

$265–$350
22 rooms, 22 pb
Visa MC AmEx
C-yes/S-no/P-no/HC-ltd

EP |
Open for breakfast, lunch and dinner. Fine Dining.
Pool, Rest&Bar, Spa&Salon, Surf School, Weddings, Ocean Front, Marble Floors,
Sat-TV, Terrace, Garden, Jacuzzi, easy Beach access, I-Net, Mini-Fridge, microw,
kitchenette

Villa del Faro
65 Camino Costero,
East Cape

Devora Wise
rental@villadelfaro.net | www.villadelfaro.net

Exquisitely off the grid! An Eco-Hotel, Villa del Faro is a unique oasis nestled on a deserted beach. It was created as a labor of love by artisans and architects. One hour north of the Los Cabos Airport, but a world away in seclusion and serenity.

$140–$425
5 rooms, 6 pb
Most CC
C-yes/S-ltd/P-no/HC-ltd

BB | Full breakfast
Full bar and wine list. Gourmet dinner on request.
Pool, terrace, fountains, custom rugs, private balcony, Sat-TV, private beach, canopy
king bed, kitchen, fireplaces, outdoor shower

Alaska

Anchorage

GLACIER BAY, ALASKA

ANCHORAGE

Anchorage Walkabout Town
1610 E St

907-279-7808 | 866-279-7808 | *Sandra J. Stimson*
reservations@anchoragewalkabout.com | www.anchoragewalkabout.com

Downtown convenience with beautiful park and coastal trail access. Hearty Alaskan breakfast of sourdough waffles and reindeer sausage. Family friendly.

$95–$115
3 rooms, 2 pb
Most CC
C-yes/S-no/P-no/HC-no

BB | Full breakfast
Deck, cable TV, freezer, free laundry, parking, 4 in a room

Big Bear Bed & Breakfast
3401 Richmond Ave

907-277-8189 | *Carol Ross*
bigbearbb@alaska.net | www.alaskabigbearbb.com/

Log home with unique antiques, Alaska Native art & exceptional breakfasts. Enjoy a taste of the real Alaska with food, surroundings, and old fashioned Alaska hospitality hosted by lifelong Alaskan and retired home economics teacher, Carol Ross.

$85–$125
4 rooms, 4 pb
Visa MC Disc Cash Checks
C-yes/S-no/P-no/HC-no

BB | Full breakfast
Variety of complimentary sodas, coffees, hot chocolates & teas
Log home, antiques, Alaska art, Native crafts, private bathrooms, flower garden w/waterfall & pond.

Glacier Bear
4814 Malibu Rd

907-243-8818 | *Cleveland & Belinda Zackery*
gbearak@gci.com | www.glacierbearbb.com

First class accommodations at reasonable rates. Luxurious contemporary home 1.2 miles from the airport & 3 miles to downtown. The rooms of this beautiful inn are decorated with a mix of Oriental and Victorian pieces.

$70–$120
3 rooms, 3 pb
Visa MC
C-ltd/S-ltd/P-no/HC-no

BB | Continental plus breakfast
Complimentary snacks & beverages
Hiking & biking trails, restaurants nearby, sitting room, 8 person spa

BIG LAKE

Sunset View Resort
5322 S Big Lake Rd

907-892-8885 | 877-892-8885 | *Kathy & Newell Glines*
stay@alaskasunsetviewresort.com | http://alaskasunsetviewresort.com/

Come visit our lakefront resort between Anchorage and Denali National Park, and you may wish you could stay forever. Everything you want is right here with your choice of lodging in either vacation homes or our Bed and Breakfast, the ultimate in luxury.

$150–$350
11 rooms, 11 pb
Most CC Cash Checks
C-yes/S-no/P-no/HC-ltd

BB | Full breakfast
Afternoon tea, snacks
Sitting room, Jacuzzis, suites, fireplaces, TV, washer, dryer, iron, computer, gym, weddings

COOPER LANDING

Kenai River
Drifters Lodge
Mile 48.3 Sterling Hwy l

907-595-5555 | **866-595-5959** | *Bob Rima, Frank Williams*
odgemail@arctic.net | www.drifterslodge.com

Located at the Headwaters of the world famous Kenai River, enjoy first class riverfront cabins with incredible views of the Kenai River and Chugach Mountains. Known for the abundance of recreational opportunities, Cooper Landing is a destination for all.

$145–$375
12 rooms, 7 pb
Visa MC Disc   Checks

BB | Continental breakfast, High Season
Fresh baked goods, croissants, fresh fruit, bagels, cereal, juices, brownies, restaurants near by
Awesome views, sauna & nightly campfire at rivers edge, BBQ's, guided fishing, rafting, activities

EAGLE RIVER

Homestays at
Homesteads
1711 South Creek

907-272-8644 | *Sharon Kelly*
aaatours@ptialaska.net | www.lanierbb.com/inns/bb19973.html

Surrounded by wilderness, this secluded valley is 10 miles from Anchorage and 7 miles from the highway. "Heaven Crest" accesses hiking & ski trails back valley to 2 glaciers, a year-round stream, and when visible, perfect views of Denai.

$85–$150
3 rooms, 1 pb
Cash Checks
C-ltd/S-no/P-ltd/HC-no

BB | Full breakfast
Afternoon tea, snacks, kitchen privileges available by request
Take time to enjoy the surroundings—on the porch, in front of the fire or skiing on our trails

FAIRBANKS

2 Kings Country B&B
3714 Mitchell Ave

907-479-2570 | *Sylvia King*
kingscountry@gci.net | www.kingscountrybb.net

Enjoy pioneer Alaskan hospitality. Experience our garden setting, the four quality, cozy and comfortable rooms and a delicious hot breakfast. A full kitchen, TV/DVD/VCR, wireless Internet, laundry facilities and private entrance all for your convenience.

$79–$139
4 rooms, 2 pb
Visa MC Disc Cash Checks
C-yes/S-ltd/P-no/HC-no

BB | Delicious hot breakfast
Business traveler accommodations, WiFi, TV in all rooms

7 Gables Inn & Suites
4312 Birch Ln

907-479-0751 | *Paul & Leicha Welton*
gables7@alaska.net | www.7gablesinn.com

Luxury accommodations at affordable rates. Our rooms and suites have private baths with Jacuzzi tubs, cable TV/VCRs. A full gourmet breakfast is included in the room rates.

$55–$180
30 rooms, 30 pb
Visa MC AmEx Cash
C-yes/S-ltd/P-ltd/HC-yes

BB | Full gourmet breakfast
Complimentary refreshments
Wireless internet throughout; library, cable/DVD, fireplaces, Jacuzzis, canoes

HOMER

Halcyon Heights
1200 Mission Road

907-235-2148 | 877-376-4222 |
info@halcyonheightsbandb.com | www.homerbb.com/

Perched on East Hill in Homer, Alaska, this proud Alaska Bed and Breakfast/Inn will thrill you with its views of the famous Homer Spit, Kachemak Bay, the Grewingk Glacier, the Kenai Mountains, Homer itself, and more!

$95–$195
5 rooms, 5 pb
Most CC Cash Checks
C-ltd/S-no/P-no/HC-no

BB | Full hosted breakfast
Tea, Snacks,
Large decks, BBQ Stove. Wireless Internet. Hottub with glacier & bay view. Piano.
Family Suite.

JUNEAU

A Cozy Log B&B
8668 Dudley St

907-789-2582 | *Judy & Bruce Bowler*
cozylog@alaska.net | www.cozylog.net

A top rated B&B in a civilized wilderness. Imagine yourself in a log home in Alaska, looking out on the forest, with a warm woodstove & local delights like blueberry pancakes and smoked salmon for breakfast.

$125–$155
2 rooms, 0 pb
Visa MC Disc Cash Checks
C-ltd/S-no/P-ltd/HC-ltd

BB | Full breakfast
Complimentary tea, snacks & wine
Guests services include free WiFi, wood stove, cable TV/VCR/DVD, and local information

**A Pearson's Pond
Luxury Inn &
Adventure Spa**
4541 Sawa Circle

907-789-3772 | 888-658-6328 | *Maryann Ray*
pearsonspond@gci.net | www.pearsonspond.com

Casual elegance, exciting activities & magical master-planned gardens. Perfect for adventure, honeymoon, wedding, romance & business travel. Alaska's only AAA 4-Diamond Resort. Complete Alaska Wedding & Trip Planning services. Packages available.

$149–$799
8 rooms, 8 pb
Most CC Cash
C-ltd/S-no/P-no/HC-no

BB | Continental plus breakfast
Afternoon snacks/tea, hospitality hour, packed lunch & dinner catering available for add'l fee.
Hot tubs, sauna, fireplaces, bikes, BBQs, kayaks/boats, WiFi, massage, gym, wedding/tour planning

Alaska's Capital Inn
113 W 5th St

907-586-6507 | 888-588-6507 |
Linda Wendeborn & Mark Thorson
innkeeper@alaskacapitalinn.com | www.alaskacapitalinn.com

Experience turn-of-the-century elegance with contemporary comfort when you spend the night at this award-winning hillside mansion. Located in Juneau's historic district, everything is a short walk away.

$99–$339
7 rooms, 7 pb
Most CC
C-ltd/S-no/P-no/HC-ltd

BB | Full breakfast
Afternoon treats, bottomless cookie jar and refreshments.
Outdoor hot tub. Tour reservations. Wedding Commissioner. Planning and catering.
Champagne/flowers.

KETCHIKAN

Black Bear Inn
5528 N Tongass Hwy

907-225-4343 | *James & Nicole Church*
blackbearalaska@aol.com | www.stayinalaska.com

Ketchikan's Finest Waterfront B&B and Vacation Rentals. We can accommodate our guests with anything from a one-bedroom with private bath rental to an entire house Vacation Rental. Our Elegant Rooms / Fireplaces and Covered Porches Overlooking the Ocean.

$100–$225
6 rooms, 6 pb
Most CC Cash Checks
C-ltd/S-ltd/P-ltd/HC-ltd

BB | Continental plus breakfast
Snacks and drinks are always provided in the Bed and Breakfast.
Fireplaces, TV's with DVD/VCR players, refrigerators, cable TV & wireless Internet,
spa, laundry.

Corner B&B
3870 Evergreen Ave

907-225-2655 | *Carolyn & Win Wilsie*
cjwilsie@KPUNET.net | www.cornerbnb.com

Fully equipped, one bedroom suite. Completely private. No stairs. Private phone and bath. Two TVs, DVD/VCR. Clean and comfortable. One block to bus. Friendly hosts on site.

$100–$145
1 rooms, 1 pb
Cash Checks
C-yes/S-ltd/P-no/HC-ltd

BB | Continental plus breakfast
Breakfast consists of fresh baked muffins or Alaska size biscuits, fresh fruit, yogurt & juice
Kitchen, living room, private bathroom, queen beds, twin roll-away available,
two TV's, DVD/VCR

LOWELL POINT

**Angels Rest on
Resurrection Bay, LLC**
13730 Beach Drive

907-224-7378 | *Lynda & Paul Paquette*
guest.services@angelsrest.com | www.angelsrest.com

This lodging is among the nicest places to stay anywhere! And the cleanest! Experience heavenly relaxation in these charming, modern cabins and view rooms, that sit on the beautiful shores of Resurrection Bay, Seward Alaska. Wildlife & scenery are amazing

$69–$259
7 rooms, 7 pb
Visa MC   Cash
C-yes/S-no/P-ltd/HC-yes

EP |
Kitchenette: sm fridge, toaster, microwave, coffee maker, BBQ grill,
coffee, tea, sugar, 1/2&1/2, ice
FREE hi-speed wi-fi on site, AK reading materials, AK DVDs, binoculars,
free parking, tour bookings.

PALMER

Tara Dells B&B
4504 N Heaton

907-745-0407 | **800-745-0407** (in AK) | *Andy & Donel Dowling*
stay@taradells.com | www.taradells.com

Located in the Hatcher Pass area of the Matanuska-Susitna Valley just one hour from the Anchorage airport. Five wooded acres near Wasilla Creek make the perfect Alaska setting.

$80–$100
5 rooms, 2 pb
Cash Checks
C-yes/S-no/P-yes/HC-yes

BB | Full breakfast
Free Wireless Internet, Sun room, facilities for infants, TV, VCR & telephone, laundry
facilities

SELDOVIA

Seldovia Rowing Club B&B
Bay Street

907-234-7614 | *Susan J. Mumma*
seldrowclub@gmail.com | http://seldoviarowingclub.net/rowingclub.html

Private unit in historic home on Old Sedovia Boardwalk overlooks waterfront, can accommodate a family. Excellent service, cuisine; close to points of interest.

$100–$135
2 rooms, 2 pb
Visa MC   Cash
C-yes/S-no/P-ltd/HC-no

BB | Full breakfast
Lunch, dinner by request
Bicycles, boating, sea kayaks, skiffs

SEWARD

Bear's Den B&B and Lodging
221 Bear Drive

907-224-3788 | **800-232-7099** |
Richard & Shareen Adelmann & Family
innkeeper@bearsdenalaska.com | www.bearsdenalaska.com

Comfort & relaxation await you at Bear's Den B&B and lodging. With three dens to choose from, our goal is to provide the perfect lodging choice for your visit to Seward. Honeymooners, business travelers and families will find what they need at Bear's Den.

$85–$185
3 rooms, 3 pb
Visa MC   Cash Checks
C-yes/S-ltd/P-no/HC-ltd

BB | Hearty continental breakfast
Coffee & tea
Flat screen TV in Den, vcr, dvd, movies, WiFi, gas grill, patio/deck, private entries, extras,

Brass Lantern B&B
331 2nd Ave

907-224-3419 | *Maureen Lemme*
brasslanternbandb@yahoo.com | www.brasslanternbandb.com

Whether you're after holiday adventure or a quiet escape from the world, Brass Lantern B&B is your haven. Rest, relax and retreat.

$95–$150
1 rooms, 1 pb
Visa MC Disc Cash
C-yes/S-no/P-no/HC-ltd

BB | Continental breakfast
Welcome basket, coffee & teas
TV, DVD, CD, radio, coffee pot, microwave, stove, refrigerator, propane grill, deck & patio, WiFi

Harmony B&B
2411 Spruce St

907-224-3661 | *Michael & Karen Vander Vegt*
harmonybnb@arctic.net | www.harmonybedandbreakfast.com

Harmony B&B is peacefully nestled in the Forest Acres neighborhood, located 1 mile north of the harbor. Private rooms tastefully decorated with full baths & cable TV. A generous continental breakfast will get the day started deliciously!

$125–$135
3 rooms, 3 pb
Visa MC Disc Cash Checks
C-yes/S-no/P-no/HC-no

BB | Continental breakfast
Coffee, tea, hot chocolate, at all hours
Cable TV, WI-FI, private baths,   Private entrances & decks

SITKA

**Alaska Ocean View
Bed & Breakfast Inn**
1101 Edgecumbe Drive

907-747-8310 | **888-811-6870** | *Carole & Bill Denkinger*
info@sitka-alaska-lodging.com | www.sitka-alaska-lodging.com

Western red cedar executive home in scenic setting. Walk to beach, wilderness trails, shopping, attractions and historic sites. Wonderful amenities in casual, relaxed setting with king and queen size beds.

$89–$199
3 rooms, 3 pb
Most CC
C-ltd/S-no/P-no/HC-ltd

BB | Full and continental plus available
Snacks, popcorn, cookies, candy, nuts, chocolates, mints, snack mix, herbal, teas, coffee
Concierge, library, robes, hot tub spa, fireplace, WiFi, free-movies, guest computer, Wii/Fit, fax

SOLDOTNA

Longmere Lake Lodge
35955 Ryan Ln

907-262-9799 | *Chuck & Leora Gibbons*
bblodge@ptialaska.net | www.longmerelakelodge.com

Picturesque lake setting, immaculate facilities, and warm service by born and raised Alaskan hosts have given our lodge a strong reputation.

$120–$290
6 rooms, 6 pb
Visa MC   Cash Checks
C-yes/S-no/P-no/HC-no

BB |Hearty breakfast
Sunday continental breakfast
Beautiful lakeside setting, fishing, meetings & groups welcome, WiFi, room with Jacuzzi

TALKEETNA

**Grace & Bill's
Freedom Hills B&B**
22046 S Freedom Drive

907-733-2455 | **888-703-2455** | *Bill & Grace Germain*
gmgermain@att.net | www.gbfreedomhillsbb.com/

Bed and breakfast in Talkeetna, AK with a great view of the Alaska range (Foraker, Hunter and Mt. McKinley). Enjoy accommodations at our B&B with spectacular view of Denali, clean and comfortable lodging, and a hearty full breakfast.

$120–$140
5 rooms, 3 pb
Visa MC   Cash
C-yes/S-no/P-no/HC-no

BB | Full & Continental
Kitchen, sun deck

**Meandering Moose
Lodging**
14677 E Cabin Spike Ave

907-733-1000 | *Kathy Stoltz*
info@meandering-moose-lodging.com | www.talkeetna-alaska-lodging.com

While in Talkeetna Alaska you will find Lodging in our log cabins or B&B suites or rooms to serve as your base camp. Our accommodations will make a great jumping off point for all your memorable Alaska winter or summer vacation adventures.

$60–$150
7 rooms, 5 pb
Visa MC   Cash
C-yes/S-no/P-no/HC-no

BB | Light Continental breakfast
4 private cabins, shuttle service, free WiFi

TALKEETNA

Talkeetna Roadhouse
13550 E Main St

907-733-1351 | *Trisha Costello*
reservations@talkeetnaroadhouse.com | www.talkeetnaroadhouse.com

The Roadhouse, built between 1914-17, is one of the oldest establish-ments in "Beautiful Downtown Talkeetna." Our kitchen is open to the public, we've become famous for breakfast, hearty soups, homestyle baking, genuine frontier hospitality and cozy rooms.

$21–$140
7 rooms, 0 pb
strong coffee
Most CC Cash Checks
C-yes/S-no/P-ltd/HC-ltd

EP |
Breakfast, bakery, soups, beer & wine, pasties, cinnamon rolls, sourdough hotcakes,

Private rooms, bunks and cabins. Coin-op laundry & complimentary WiFi,
coffee, tea & cocoa, library

VALDEZ

Downtown B&B Inn
113 Galena Dr

907-835-2791 | **800-478-2791** | *Glen & Sharron Mills*
1n2rs@gci.net | www.valdezdowntowninn.com/

Downtown B&B Inn offers travelers excellent accommodations year--round. Cozy and clean rooms, private bathrooms, and great continental breakfasts. Perfect location for those interested in fishing, sightseeing, and glacier tours in Prince William Sound.

$55–$110
31 rooms, 21 pb
Visa MC Disc Cash
C-yes/S-no/P-ltd/HC-yes

BB | Continental plus breakfast
Afternoon tea
Sitting room, cable TV, accommodate business travelers, free WiFi

WASILLA

**Alaska's Lake
Lucille B&B**
235 W Lakeview Ave

907-357-0352 | **888-353-0352** | *Carol Smith*
Stay@alaskaslakelucillebnb.com | www.alaskaslakelucillebnb.com

Stay at home with us at Lake Lucille B & B and let us provide you with the perfect romantic getaway. You're at home with country charm and a perfect location for crafting and scrap-booking retreats. We'll do all the work for you.

$89–$189
5 rooms, 5 pb
Visa MC
C-yes/S-no/P-no/HC-no

BB | Choice of Full or Continental
Coffee pot with complimentary coffee, tea & cakes; complimentary popcorn for evening snack
Sitting room, meeting room for 12, lake and mountain views, crafting retreats

**Pioneer Ridge
B&B Inn**
2221 Yukon Dr.

907-376-7472 | **800-478-7472** | *Shannon & Leny Cullip*
info@pioneerridge.com | www.pioneerridge.com

Whether you are looking for a romantic getaway, family vacation, scrap booking retreat or business meeting, Pioneer Ridge provides guests with a home away from home in a setting of casual, Alaskan charm.

$99–$159
6 rooms, 5 pb
Visa MC Disc Cash Checks
C-yes/S-no/P-ltd/HC-ltd

BB | Full breakfast
Self-serve breakfast bar with fruit, cereal, etc.
Great room, 360 degree view room, sauna, WiFi, Internet

WASILLA

Shady Acres B&B
1000 Easy St

907-376-3113 | *Marie Lambing*
lambing@mtaonline.net | www.shadyacresbnb.com

Located in Wasilla near Parks Highway and downtown. Surrounded by quiet, serene forest. Warm, cheerful, homey atmosphere, with indoor and outdoor entertainment space. Completely wheelchair-accessible.

$130–$150
2 rooms, 2 pb
Visa MC AmEx   Cash Checks
C-ltd/S-no/P-no/HC-yes

BB | Hot homestyle breakfast
For breakfast, enjoy fresh eggs from our own chickens, fresh bread, fruit and other side dishes.
Wheelchair accessible, telephones, roll-in showers, cheerful home-style atmosphere, smoke free

WRANGELL-ST. ELIAS NATIONAL PARK

Kennicott Glacier Lodge,
Lot 15,
Millsite Subdivision

907-258-2350 | **800-582-5128** | *Rich & Jody Kirkwood*
info@KennicottLodge.com | www.KennicottLodge.com

Enjoy the awesome beauty of America's largest National Park from the comfort of our first-class wilderness lodge. The Kennicott Glacier Lodge, built in the style of the ghost town, has all the conveniences of a modern hotel, with 35 rooms and restaurant.

$159–$259
35 rooms, 10 pb
Most CC Cash Checks
C-yes/S-no/P-no/HC-yes

BB | Continental plus breakfast
Full service restaurant, breakfast buffet, lunch menu, family-style dinner, beer, wine & snacks
Sitting room, library, panoramic front porch, glacier hikes, flightseeing, rafting, etc.

ALASKA
STATE MAMMAL:
MOOSE

California

Sacramento

SCHOOLHOUSE CREEK
ON CALIFORNIA'S
MENDOCINO COAST

AHWAHNEE

Apple Blossom Inn
44606 Silver Spur Trail

559-642-2001 | **888-687-4281** | *Candy 'Apple' Arthur*
appleblossominn@sti.net | www.appleblossombb.com

The Apple Blossom Inn is located in Gold Country on historic Highway 49, the front yard of Yosemite National Park. Enjoy the serenity of your stay in the midst of our organic apple farm & gardens, while visiting the many recreational spots nearby.

$110–$240
5 rooms, 4 pb
Visa MC AmEx   Cash
C-yes/S-ltd/P-ltd/HC-ltd

BB | Full breakfast
Fruit, snacks & candy apples when the apples are ripe, picnic lunches available on request
Sun deck & spa with gorgeous view of the Sierras, VCR's & video library, organic
apple orchard

Sierra Mountain Lodge
Bed & Breakfast
45046 Fort Nip Trail

559-683-7673 | **800-811-7029** | *John & Brenda Eppler*
innkeepers@sierramountainlodge.com | www.sierramountainlodge.com

Private 1 & 2 bedroom suites nestled in a quiet country oasis near Yosemite's Southern Entrance. Panoramic mountain views, hot continental breakfast, cable TV/DVD collection, and wireless Internet. Children 2 or older are welcome.

$125–$175
7 rooms, 7 pb
Visa MC   Cash
C-ltd/S-ltd/P-no/HC-ltd

BB | Continental plus breakfast
Waffle or pancake bar, sausage (vege too), fresh fruit platter, cold cereal, coffee,
tea, milk, OJ
Private kitchenettes, panoramic mountain views, wireless Internet, DVD & reading
library, cable TV

The Homestead
41110 Rd 600

559-683-0496 | **800-483-0495** | *Cindy Brooks & Larry Ends*
homesteadcottages@sti.net | www.homesteadcottages.com/

Romantic private cottages with fully equipped kitchens on 160 wooded acres close to Yosemite, Gold Country, golf, hiking and restaurants. Equine layover available.

$119–$374
6 rooms, 6 pb
Most CC
C-ltd/S-no/P-no/HC-ltd

BB | Continental breakfast
Free Internet access, toiletries, daily maid service, concierge services,
in room massages available

ALBION

Albion River Inn
3790 Hwy 1 N

707-937-1919 | **800-479-7944** | *Pat Turrigiano*
pat@albionriverinn.com | www.albionriverinn.com

Called "One of the West's Best Small Inns," by Sunset Magazine, our romantic oceanfront Inn and restaurant sits on ten clifftop acres with spectacular ocean views. Enjoy luxury, privacy, comfort, acclaimed cuisine, and our award winning wine list.

$195–$325
22 rooms, 22 pb
list, music.
Most CC
C-ltd/S-no/P-no/HC-yes

BB | Full breakfast
Acclaimed ocean view restaurant serves dinner nightly; full bar, award winning wine
Wine, coffee, teas, robes, fireplaces, decks, spa tubs, cooking classes, wine dinners,
workshops.

ALBION

Fensalden Inn
33810 Navarro Ridge Rd

707-937-4042 | **800-959-3850** | *Lyn Hamby*
inn@fensalden.com | www.fensalden.com

1850s Stagestop on several acres overlooking Pacific. Quiet romantic getaway, w/pampering atmosphere, antique appointed rooms w/fireplaces & private baths, gourmet breakfasts, evening hor d'oeuvres; 2 pigmy goats, 7 ducks, 2 pups & local wildlife & birds.

$139–$253
8 rooms, 8 pb
Visa MC   Cash Checks
C-ltd/S-ltd/P-ltd/HC-ltd

BB | Full three course gourmet breakfast
Wine & hors d'oeuvres at 5pm each evening in our Great Room
Sunporch with board games & jigsaw puzzle; office with fax, wireless Internet, hairdryers in room

APTOS

**Historic Sand
Rock Farm**
6901 Freedom Blvd

831-688-8005 | *Kris Sheehan*
reservations@sandrockfarm.com | www.sandrockfarm.com

Historic, country estate featuring Jacuzzi tubs, arts, antiques, down comforters, private baths, and gracious amenities on 10 wooded acres. Secluded between Santa Cruz and Monterey.

 Dreams Do Come True participating inn—Valid anytime; will offer a room upgrade

$185–$225
5 rooms, 5 pb
Visa MC
C-yes/S-no/P-no/HC-ltd

BB | Chef-prepared gourmet breakfast
Wine reception & special meals by arrangement
Jacuzzis, down comforters, gardens, sitting areas

ARROYO GRANDE

**Casitas of
Arroyo Grande**
2655 Lopez Dr

805-473-1123 | *Pat & Tony Goetz*
tony@casitasag.com | www.casitasag.com

Situated on a 7 acre estate, The Casitas of Arroyo Grande Bed and Breakfast overlook central coast vineyards and hillside; perfectly located half way between Los Angeles and San Francisco. Come for the peace and quiet, leave with your peace of mind.

$179–$399
4 rooms, 4 pb
Most CC Cash
C-ltd/S-no/P-no/HC-no

BB | Full breakfast
In room fireplace, private deck, HDTV, Bose radio with iPod connection, Ralph Lauren bedding, WiFi

ATASCADERO

Oak Hill Manor
12345 Hampton Ct

805-462-9317 | **866-OAK-MANR** | *Maurice & Rise Macare*
macare@oakhillmanorbandb.com | www.oakhillmanorbandb.com

Comfortable elegance on three acres of oak-studded hills, fantastic views and sunsets and gracious hospitality. 3 suites, each styled after a different European country await your visit. Fireplaces and whirlpool tubs surrounded by vineyards.

$179–$239
3 rooms, 3 pb
Most CC Cash
C-yes/S-ltd/P-no/HC-ltd

BB | Full breakfast
Wine, hors d'oeuvres, soft drinks, tea & cookies
Sitting room, library, pool table, Jacuzzi, fireplace, cable TV, views

AVALON

The Avalon Hotel on Catalina Island
124 Whittley Ave

310-510-7070 | *Kathleen Gosselin*
kate@theavalonhotel.com | www.theavalonhotel.com

An environment of understated elegance, where luxurious bedding, unique artwork and hand-crafted hardwoods and tile combine to create an enchanting experience. Most of our rooms have breath-taking views of Avalon harbor.

$195–$545
15 rooms, 15 pb
Visa MC AmEx   Cash
C-ltd/S-ltd/P-no/HC-no

BB | Continental breakfast
In-room complimentary coffee, bottled water and refreshments
Rooftop deck, garden courtyard, koi pond, weddings, fridge, high speed Internet, wet bar, balcony

BALLARD

Ballard Inn & Restaurant
2436 Baseline Ave

805-688-7770 | **800-638-2466** | *Christine Forsyth*
innkeeper@ballardinn.com | www.ballardinn.com

Located in the Santa Ynez Valley, about forty minutes from Santa Barbara, the Ballard Inn offers comfortably elegant accommodations in a peaceful and quiet setting.

$245–$315
15 rooms, 15 pb
Visa MC AmEx   Cash
C-ltd/S-no/P-no/HC-yes

BB | Full breakfast
Afternoon wine & hors d'oeuvres included with stay
Turn down service with homemade cookies

BEN LOMOND

Fairview Manor
245 Fairview Ave

831-336-3355 | *Gael Glasson Abayon & Jack Hazelton*
fairviewbandb@comcast.net | www.fairviewmanor.com

Romantic country-style redwood home, majestic stone fireplace, 2.5 wooded acres in the Santa Cruz Mountains. Total privacy. Walk to town. A whole generation can identify with Santa Cruz, America's beach town.

$149–$159
5 rooms, 5 pb
Visa MC Disc Cash
C-ltd/S-no/P-no/HC-ltd

BB | Full breakfast
Complimentary wine & hors d'oeuvres
Sitting room, bordered by river, weddings & meetings

BERKELEY

Rose Garden Inn
2740 Telegraph Ave

510-549-2145 | **800-992-9005** | *Kevin Allen*
rosegardengm@aol.com | www.rosegardeninn.com

Experience... the charming comfort of our 40 guest rooms surrounded by flowering gardens, some with sweeping views and soothing fountains. Walking distance from UC Berkeley and among the finest of Bay Area highlights.

$109–$399
40 rooms, 40 pb
Most CC
C-yes/S-ltd/P-no/HC-ltd

BB | Full buffet breakfast
Coffee & tea available 24 hr, afternoon cookies
Free parking on a space-available basis, Direct TV, Wi-Fi, fireplaces, housekeeping, newspapers

BERRY CREEK

Lake Oroville
240 Sunday Dr

530-589-0700 | *Cheryl & Ronald Damberger*
cheryl@lakeorovillebedandbreakfast.com | www.lakeorovillebedandbreakfast.com

Lake views, sunsets, stargazing. Secluded country setting, covered porches with private entrances. Enjoy a evening picnic while watching the beautiful sunsets over the lake. A woodburning fireplace in the parlor, or a good book in the sunroom or library.

$135–$175
6 rooms, 6 pb
Most CC Cash Checks
C-yes/S-ltd/P-yes/HC-yes

BB | Full breakfast
Lunch & dinner available, snacks
Sitting room, game room, Jacuzzis, fireplaces, cable TV, accommodate business travelers

BIG BEAR

Alpenhorn B&B
601 Knight Ave

909-866-5700 | **888-829-6600** | *Timothy & Linda Carpenter*
linda@alpenhorn.com | www.alpenhorn.com/welcome.html

This beautiful bed and Breakfast in Big Bear Lake hosts garden weddings, romantic getaways, family reunions and small groups. Near the village, lake and ski resorts. Offering the finest AAA lodging and accommodations in the San Bernardino Mountains.

 Dreams Do Come True participating inn—Valid Monday–Thursday (except holidays)

$185–$275
8 rooms, 8 pb
Most CC Cash
C-ltd/S-ltd/P-no/HC-yes

BB | Full breakfast
Wine with appetizers in the evening, after dinner liqueurs, chocolates
In-room spas for two, fireplaces, TV/VCRs, private balconies, extensive video library, host weddings

Gold Mountain Manor
1117 Anita

909-585-6997 | **800-509-2604** | *Cathy Weil*
info@goldmountainmanor.com | www.goldmountainmanor.com

Historic log cabin B&B, secluded & romantic. Lots of special touches. Park-like setting, woodburning fireplaces, wraparound porch, candlelit breakfast, Jacuzzi tubs, spa treatments.

$149–$299
7 rooms, 7 pb
Visa MC
C-ltd/S-ltd/P-ltd/HC-no

BB | Full Gourmet breakfast
Gooey chocolate chip oatmeal cookies
Billiard table, parlor with woodburning fireplace, wraparound porch, library, concierge service

BIG BEAR LAKE

Eagle's Nest B&B
41675 Big Bear Blvd

909-866-6465 | **888-866-6465** | *Mark & Vicki Tebo*
eaglesnestlodge@earthlink.net | www.eaglesnestlodgebigbear.com

Full log 5 room B&B nestled in Ponderosa pines, mountain lodge decor with antiques and custom furnishings, full hearty breakfast. In 2 additional buildings, 5 cottage spa units, breakfast optional.

$110–$165
10 rooms, 10 pb
Most CC
C-ltd/S-ltd/P-ltd/HC-no

BB | Full breakfast
Snacks
Sitting room, spas, suites, fireplaces, cable TV

Aurora Park Cottages
1807 Foothill Blvd

707-942-6733 | **877-942-7700** | *Joe Hensley*
innkeeper@aurorapark.com | www.aurorapark.com

Free Champagne—Mention Lanier when you make your reservation and we'll have some chilled champagne and chocolates awaiting your arrival. Aurora Park Cottages is your private vacation retreat in Napa Valley wine country.

$199–$269
6 rooms, 6 pb
Visa MC AmEx   Cash Checks
C-yes/S-no/P-no/HC-yes

BB | Continental breakfast
Complimentary bottled water, apples, biscotti, jelly bellies, coffee & tea
Mini-fridge, coffee makers, cable TV, AC, plush towels, comfy robes & private decks

Bear Flag Inn
2653 Foothill Blvd
Hwy 128

707-942-5534 | **800-670-2860** | *McNay Family*
2mcnays@ap.net | www.bearflaginn.com

Featuring charming guest rooms, a full breakfast made with farm-fresh eggs produced here, and wine & appetizers in the afternoon, Bear Flag Inn is your home away from home in Calistoga.

$199–$249
5 rooms, 5 pb
Visa MC Disc
C-ltd/S-ltd/P-ltd/HC-no

BB | Full breakfast
Beverages & snacks
Parlor, pool, hot tub, hammocks, pool table, player piano, garden, treadmill,
cable TV, WiFi

Brannan Cottage Inn
109 Wapoo Ave

707-942-4200 | *Doug & Judy Cook*
brannancottageinn@sbcglobal.net | www.brannancottageinn.com

Charming 1860 cottage-style Victorian, country furnishings, lovely grounds with gardens, lawn & patios. It is walking distance to famous restaurants & spas & 25 wineries are within 3 miles. The inn is available for small meetings and special events.

 Dreams Do Come True participating inn—Valid weekdays only, November 1– March 31; Sunday–Thursday

$155–$280
6 rooms, 6 pb
Visa MC AmEx   Cash Checks
C-yes/S-ltd/P-yes/HC-ltd

BB | Full, multi-course breakfast
Friday evening wine & appetizers with local wineries, homemade chocolate chip cookies every night
A/C, fridge, queen bed, down comforters, ceiling fans, fireplaces in most rooms, WiFi, private entry

Chelsea Garden Inn
1443 2nd St

707-942-0948 | **800-942-1515** | *Dave & Susan DeVries*
innkeeper@chelseagardeninn.com | www.chelseagardeninn.com

This charming Napa Valley B&B is conveniently located near wineries, spas, restaurants & other area activities. Spacious & private romantic suites with fireplaces, robes, cable TV w/DVD. Pool. Afternoon hors d'oeuvres, Free WIFI. AAA 3 diamonds, breakfast

 Dreams Do Come True participating inn—Valid Monday–Wednesday, November 12– April 15 (based on roooms priced $195 or higher); will offer a room upgrade

$165–$275
5 rooms, 5 pb
Most CC Cash Checks
C-yes/S-ltd/P-ltd/HC-ltd

BB | Full breakfast
Afternoon hors d'oeuvres, cheeses, complimentary beverages
Spacious suites, fireplaces, WiFi, TV/DVD, free movies, guest computer, concierge, pool, library

CALISTOGA

Christopher's Inn
1010 Foothill Blvd

707-942-5755 | 866-876-5755 | *Christopher & Adele Layton*
christophersinn@earthlink.net | www.christophersinn.com

Elegant 23-room country inn and gardens. Laura Ashley interiors, cozy wood burning fireplaces, romantic garden courtyards with fountains, in-room Jacuzzis. Christopher's Inn has been honored as a Golden Grape Award Finalist, one of three in the county.

$189–$389
23 rooms, 21 pb
Most CC Cash
C-ltd/S-no/P-no/HC-ltd

BB | Breakfast delivered to your room
Complimentary wine tasting passes, Discounts at restaurants
wireless internet access, a/c, fireplaces, Jacuzzi hot tubs with robes, Cable TV,
Special spa pkg

Hillcrest B&B
3225 Lake Co Hwy

707-942-6334 | *Debbie O'Gorman*
www.hillcrestcountryinn.com

Secluded hilltop home with "million dollar view", furnished with antique silver, china, rugs, artwork, fireplaces, and ensuite Jacuzzis. Swimming, hiking and fishing on 36 secluded acres. Pet friendly.

$69–$165
3 rooms, 3 pb
Most CC Cash Checks
C-yes/S-ltd/P-yes/HC-ltd

BB |Continental breakfast
Sitting room, library, Jacuzzis, movie channel, fireplaces, conference room

**Mount View
Hotel & Spa**
1457 Lincoln Ave

707-942-6877 | 800-816-6877 | *Andrea Hoogendoorn*
relax@mountviewhotel.com | www.mountviewhotel.com/

At the Mount View Hotel & Spa in Calistoga, we celebrate the Art of Relaxation. We provide the blank canvas and the resources for you to experience the perfect wine country getaway.

$169–$439
31 rooms, 31 pb
Most CC
C-ltd/S-ltd/P-no/HC-yes

BB | Continental breakfast
Breakfast delivery, 2 On-site Restaurants (JoLe & Barolo), 2 Full Bars, Located Downtown
Garden Courtyard, Jacuzzi, Heated Swimming Pool, Full Service Day Spa, FREE WIFI,
DVD, IPod docks

Scarlett's Country Inn
3918 Silverado Trail

707-942-6669 | *Derek Dwyer*
scarletts@aol.com | www.scarlettscountryinn.com

A charming 1890 country farmhouse, nestled in a private canyon, with a quiet mood of green lawns and tall pines overlooking the vineyards at the edge of a forest.

$155–$250
3 rooms, 3 pb
Cash Checks
C-yes/S-no/P-ltd/HC-no

EP |
Breakfast avail. upon request. Complimentary wine & cheese, lemonade
Sitting room, A/C, TVs, microwaves & refrigerator, coffeemakers, pool, hot tub,
wireless Internet

CALISTOGA

The Chanric Inn
1805 Foothill Blvd

707-942-4535 | 877-281-3671 | *Ric Pielstick*
ric@thechanric.com | www.thechanric.com

The Chanric Inn is an intimate, boutique inn providing luxurious amenities, a chef prepared gourmet breakfast, pool, spa & full concierge service. It is central to the finest wineries, restaurants & spas Napa Valley & Sonoma have to offer.

$209–$349
6 rooms, 6 pb
Most CC
C-ltd/S-no/P-ltd/HC-no

BB | 3 Course Chef-Prepared Brunch
Select beverages provided throughout your stay, wake-up coffee and tea service
Pool, spa & sauna, full concierge service, property-wide Wi-Fi, bathrobes,
Aveda bath amenities

Trailside Inn
4201 Silverado Trl

707-942-4106 | *Lani Gray*
innkeeper@trailsideinn.com | www.trailsideinn.com

The Trailside Inn is a charming 1930s farmhouse centrally located in the beautiful Napa Valley. Antique furnishings, full private bathrooms, private entrances, heated swimming pool, TV and hi-speed Internet are prized features of our inn. Family friendly!

$165–$185
3 rooms, 3 pb
Most CC
C-yes/S-ltd/P-yes/HC-ltd

BB | Continental plus breakfast
Complimentary wine
Mineral water, fireplace, kitchens, library, A/C, spa, private deck, pool, Internet access, TV

Valley Oak Inn
2273 Grant St

707-942-4720 | *Jeannette*
http://valleyoakinn.com

It is perfect for a romantic getaway—honeymoon, anniversary, or that special occasion. Enjoy relaxation and privacy. Our exclusive cottage or our magnificent suite await your arrival. A continental breakfast is served to you each morning on the patio.

$165–$295
2 rooms, 2 pb
Cash Checks
S-no/P-no/HC-no

BB | Continental breakfast
Use of BBQ and Outdoor Fire Pit
Solar pool, swim towels, wifi access, privacy

Zinfandel House
1253 Summit Drive

707-942-0733 | *Bette & George Starke*
bette@zinfandelhouse.com | www.zinfandelhouse.com

Beautiful home nearby to wineries, situated on wooded hillside, overlooking vineyards and mountains. Lovely full breakfast served on outside deck or in solarium.

$130–$155
2 rooms, 2 pb
Visa MC
C-ltd/S-no/P-no/HC-no

BB | Full breakfast
Complimentary wine
Library, sitting room, hot tub, goose down comforters, music room and deck

CAMBRIA

J. Patrick House
2990 Burton Dr

805-927-3812 | **800-341-5258** | *Ann & John*
jph@jpatrickhouse.com | www.jpatrickhouse.com

Award winning Inn on the California Central Coast. Authentic log home and carriage house nestled in the pines. Irish country comfort in accommodations with rooms uniquely appointed in "traditional" yet comfortable decor. Wood burning fireplaces.

$175–$215
8 rooms, 8 pb
Visa MC
C-ltd/S-no/P-no/HC-no

BB | Full breakfast
Offering evening wine & hors d'oeuveres & killer chocolate chip cookies
Sitting room, library, in-room massage, host weddings/elopements, complimentary concierge services

Olallieberry Inn
2476 Main St

805-927-3222 | **888-927-3222** | *Marjorie Ott*
info@olallieberry.com | www.olallieberry.com

1873 restored Greek Revival home, warm and inviting, nestled in the heart of the enchanting village of Cambria. Walk to antique shops, art galleries, gift shops and fine restaurants.

 Dreams Do Come True participating inn—Valid October 2011–December 20, 2011; Sunday–Thursday nights (excluding holiday periods)

$135–$225
9 rooms, 9 pb
Visa MC AmEx   Cash
C-ltd/S-no/P-no/HC-yes

BB | Full breakfast
Complimentary wine, hors d'oeuvres, cookies
Gathering room, fireplaces, antiques, special diets, massages, wireless Internet connection

Summer Place
1416 Leonard Place

805-927-8145 | **805-684-5745** | *Don Urbano*
www.lanierbb.com/inns/bb15828.html

Charming 2 story Cape Cod home. Lovely gardens, sitting areas, home decor to match. Large stone fireplace is a favorite gathering for guests. Location is very quiet and peaceful. Queen bed private bath in room. Deck ocean view.

$85–$95
1 rooms, 1 pb
Cash Checks
S-no/P-no/HC-no

BB | Great breakfast
Living room with large stone fireplace available to guests for reading, movies, music or relaxing.

The Blue Whale Inn
6736 Moonstone
Beach Dr

805-927-4647 | **800-753-9000** | *Marguerite & Mary*
innkeeper@bluewhaleinn.com | www.bluewhaleinn.com

The Blue Whale Inn Bed and Breakfast is nestled on the green carpeted bluffs of Cambria and overlooks the Pacific Ocean. You will be welcomed with unexpected luxury and gracious hospitality in a setting beside the California Pacific ocean.

$315–$470
7 rooms, 7 pb
Most CC Cash Checks
C-ltd/S-no/P-ltd/HC-yes

BB | Full breakfast
Afternoon tea and baked goods, complimentary wine,hors d'oeuvres & cheese
Sitting room, library, fireplaces, cable TV, romantic mini suites

CAMBRIA

The Squibb House
4063 Burton Dr

805-927-9600 | **866-927-9600** | *Bruce Black*
innkeeper@squibbhouse.net | www.squibbhouse.net

In the heart of Cambria, within steps of galleries, shops & restaurants, there is a place suspended in time. Relax in the main parlor, stroll the garden path or rock on the porch and watch the world go by from this beautifully restored inn.

$125–$195
5 rooms, 5 pb
Visa MC AmEx Cash Checks
C-ltd/S-no/P-no/HC-no

BB | Breakfast delivered to your door
Afternoon cookies & tea, complimentary wine tasting
Gardens, gazebo for small events, weddings, groups, retail store with Amish furniture & antiques

White Water Inn
6790 Moonstone Beach Dr

805-927-1066 | **800-995-1715** | *Cindy Taylor*
innkeeper@whitewaterinn.com | www.whitewaterinn.com

One of the few independently owned inns in Cambria opposite the ocean. A calm, 17 cottage style establishment in the Monterey Marine Wildlife Sanctuary, half way between San Francisco and Los Angeles.

$100–$280
17 rooms, 17 pb
Visa MC Disc
C-yes/S-no/P-ltd/HC-ltd

BB | Continental breakfast
Fireplace, cable TV, hairdryers, iron & board, complimentary videos, sitting room, ocean views

Capitola Hotel
210 Esplanade

831-476-1278 | **877-705-7377** | *Michael & Christine Herberg*
info@CapitolaHotel.com | www.capitolahotel.com/index.html

Steps to the beach, in the center of Capitola Village—clean comfortable upscale rooms, full breakfast, gourmet coffee, biscotti and WiFi. The beach is across the street, live music, great dining, shopping, unique events and year-round outdoor activities

$84–$275
10 rooms, 10 pb
Visa MC Disc Cash
C-ltd/S-no/P-no/HC-yes

BB | Voucher for local restaurant
A complimentary cup of gourmet coffee or tea and a biscotti available in our lobby each morning
Free Wifi, Plasma screen with HBO, free local telephone, private bath, ceiling fan

CARDIFF BY THE SEA

Cardiff by the Sea Lodge
142 Chesterfield

760-944-6474 | *James & Jeanette Statser*
innkeeper@cardifflodge.com | www.cardifflodge.com

Steps away from the blue Pacific Ocean and beach. Minutes from all San Diego has to offer, here is a place where lush gardens bloom year-round.

$140–$385
17 rooms, 17 pb
Most CC Cash
C-yes/S-no/P-no/HC-ltd

BB | Continental plus breakfast
Rooftop Garden, fireplaces, whirlpool tubs, beach chairs, wet bars, free wireless Internet

CARLSBAD

Pelican Cove Inn
320 Walnut Ave

760-434-5995 | 888-PEL-COVE | *Nancy & Kris Nayudu*
PelicanCoveInn@pelican-cove.com | www.pelican-cove.com

Sun, blue skies, endless beaches, glorious sunsets, and the wide Pacific welcome you to Pelican Cove B&B Inn. We strive to make your stay memorable and enjoyable. Only steps from the ocean, fine restaurants and pleasant shops.

$95–$215
10 rooms, 10 pb
Visa MC AmEx
C-yes/S-no/P-no/HC-yes

BB | Full breakfast
Fireplaces, feather beds, business accommodations, TV, private entrances, Internet, beach equipment

CARMEL

Carmel Country Inn
Dolores & 3rd Ave

831-625-3263 | 800-215-6343 | *Amy Johnson*
info@carmelcountryinn.com | www.carmelcountryinn.com

Carmel Country Inn Bed and Breakfast in Carmel, California offers a great blend of convenience, comfort, romance, and surrounding natural beauty near the beaches of beautiful Carmel by the Sea.

$195–$425
12 rooms, 12 pb
Visa MC AmEx
C-ltd/S-no/P-yes/HC-no

BB | Expanded Continental Breakfast
In-room coffeemaker, complimentary cream sherry
Fireplaces, private baths, private entrances, off street parking, wireless Internet, TV/DVD players

Edgemere Cottages
San Antonio between
13th & Santa Lucia St

831-624-4501 | 866-241-4575 | *Gretchen Siegrist-Allen*
info@edgemerecottages.com | www.edgemerecottages.com/

Edgemere features quaint private cottages, continental breakfast, beautiful gardens, and is just a one block walk to Carmel Beach. The perfect setting for a romantic escape to the Monterey Peninsula.

$120–$295
4 rooms, 4 pb
Visa MC Disc Cash
C-yes/S-no/P-yes/HC-ltd

BB | Full, homemade breakfast
Sitting room, fireplaces, cable TV, accommodations for business travelers, WIFI

Happy Landing Inn
Monte Verde bet.
5th & 6th Ave

831-624-7917 | 800-297-6250 | *Diane & Dawn*
info@carmelhappylanding.com | www.carmelhappylanding.com

Hansel & Gretel cottages in the heart of Carmel, like something from a Beatrix Potter book, one of Carmel's most romantic places to stay. All accommodations with private baths, 3 with fireplaces and 3 suites. Enjoy a warm breakfast brought to your room.

$135–$235
7 rooms, 7 pb
Most CC Cash Checks
C-ltd/S-no/P-yes/HC-no

BB | Continental plus breakfast
Hot breakfast served to your room.
Great room, gazebo & gardens, TV, DVD/CD players, WiFi, reading lamps, hairdryers

CARMEL

Lamp Lighter Inn
SE Corner of Ocean Ave
& Camino Real

831-624-7372 | *Bobby Richards*
innkeeper@carmellamplighter.com | www.carmellamplighter.com

Charming inn with two cottages and four guestrooms, just steps to the beach. Couples, families and small groups will find accommodations at the Lamp Lighter Inn, some rooms with fireplaces, all have private baths. An enchanted setting with lush gardens.

$185–$475
11 rooms, 11 pb
Visa MC AmEx   Cash
C-yes/S-no/P-yes/HC-no

BB | Breakfast Basket
Wine & cheese reception Thursday - Sunday from 5 - 7 p.m.
Fireplaces, TVs, phones, private entrances, flat-screen TVs, on-site parking

Monte Verde Inn
& Casa de Carmel
Monte Verde St. at
Ocean Ave.

831-624-6046 | **800-328-7707** | *Randal Gilbert*
reservations@monteverdeinn.com | www.monteverdeinn.com/

Tucked into the famous artisan village of Carmel-by-the-Sea are two classic country-style bed and breakfast inns—Monte Verde Inn and Casa de Carmel. All rooms have a private bath, television, telephone and our signature sherry.

$150–$235
17 rooms, 17 pb
Most CC Cash
C-yes/S-no/P-yes/HC-ltd

BB | Continental plus breakfast
Sherry, coffeemaker, wine & cheese, close by restaurants
TV, phone, refrigerator, hair dryers, gardens & patios

Sandpiper Inn
2408 Bay View Ave

831-624-6433 | **800-590-6433** | *James Hartle*
info@sandpiper-inn.com | www.sandpiper-inn.com/

One-half block to Carmel Beach. European-style 1929 country inn, with some antiques and individual decor. Ocean views, gas-log fireplaces, 3 cottages, patio & garden areas. Mobil 2-star rating, 3 Diamonds AAA rating.

$109–$235
17 rooms, 17 pb
Most CC
S-no/P-no/HC-no

BB | Continental plus breakfast
Afternoon tea & cookies
Library, wireless Internet, fireside lounge, close to tennis, golf, hiking

Sea View Inn
Camino Real
@ 11th & 12th

831-624-8778 | *Marshall & Diane Hydorn*
seaviewinncarmel@gmail.com | www.seaviewinncarmel.com

When you arrive at the Sea View Inn you will be greeted by a friendly and knowledgeable staff, happy to advise you about the restaurants, shops, and the scenic and historic places that make our Village such a special place.

$135–$265
8 rooms, 6 pb
Visa MC AmEx   Cash Checks
C-ltd/S-ltd/P-no/HC-no

BB | Continental plus breakfast
Afternoon tea & coffee
Complimentary evening wine, sitting room, library, garden, free wireless Internet

CARMEL

Tally Ho Inn
Monte Verde at 6th St

831-624-2232 | 800-652-2632 | *John Lloyd*
jlloyd@pine-inn.com | www.tallyho-inn.com/

The Tally Ho features 12 rooms with private decks and ocean views. Rooms have fireplaces, 55" LED TVs, Jacuzzi tubs, Bose Wave radios & refrigerators. Also featuring complimentary wireless Internet and during the week a full American breakfast buffet.

$189–$349
12 rooms, 12 pb
Most CC
C-yes/S-no/P-no/HC-yes

BB | Continental plus breakfast
Afternoon tea, brandy, continental plus breakfast on Sat & Sun, American buffet breakfast Mon-Fri
Floral garden, sun deck, fireplaces, ocean views, close to beach

The Colonial Terrace
San Antonio & 13th

831-624-2741 | 800-345-8220
reservations@thecolonialterrace.com | www.thecolonialterrace.com

Historic boutique hotel, one of Carmel's original hotels. Just steps from Carmel Beach, we offer rooms with fireplaces, ocean views, suites, and whirlpool tubs. Each room offers its own charm and personality.

$119–$599
26 rooms, 26 pb
Most CC
C-ltd/S-no/P-no/HC-ltd

BB | Expanded Continental Breakfast
Afternoon tea reception offering fresh fruit & fresh-baked cookies
All rooms have fireplaces, many with ocean views, Jacuzzi tubs, wet bars, some w/ kitchenettes, WiFi

Tickle Pink Inn
155 Highland Dr

831-624-1244 | 800-635-4774
kparker@ticklepinkinn.com | www.ticklepinkinn.com

Established and operated by the Gurries family, the Tickle Pink Inn at Carmel Highlands has graced this setting since 1956. With 35 rooms and suites, the Inn is intimate and private and offers the discriminating guest a variety of personalized services.

$299–$599
35 rooms, 35 pb
Visa MC AmEx
C-ltd/S-ltd/P-no/HC-yes

BB | Continental plus breakfast
Evening wine and cheese reception, Limited room service and wine list menu.
Limited room service menu, breakfast delivered to your room, daily newspaper, movie library, robes.

Tradewinds Carmel
Mission St & Third Ave

831-624-2776 | 800-624-6665 | *Susan Stilwell*
info@tradewindscarmel.com | www.tradewindscarmel.com

Tradewinds Carmel is the luxury boutique hotel providing an elegant oasis just a short stroll from the Carmel Plaza, galleries and restaurants of Carmel-by-the-Sea. If you are looking for a romantic bed and breakfast, you've found it! Welcome.

$325–$550
28 rooms, 28 pb
Visa MC AmEx   Cash
C-yes/S-no/P-ltd/HC-yes

BB | Continental Breakfast Buffet
Catering upon request, ask our concierge about restaurant reservations and recommendations
Tropical design, exquisite furnishings, romantic atmosphere, fireplaces, Kimono robes, spa slippers

CARMEL

Vagabond's House Inn
4th & Dolores

831-624-7738 | **800-262-1262** | *Julie Campbell*
innkeeper@vagabondshouseinn.com | www.vagabondshouseinn.com

Antique clocks and pictures, quilted bedspreads, fresh flowers, plants, shelves filled with old books. Sherry by the fireplace and breakfast served in your room.

$155–$275
13 rooms, 13 pb
Most CC Cash Checks
C-ltd/S-no/P-yes/HC-no

BB | Continental plus breakfast
Wine, snacks
Sitting room with fireplace, library, courtyard, 2 blocks to downtown

CARMEL VALLEY

Country Garden Inns
102 W. Carmel Valley Rd

831-659-5361 | **800-367-3336** | *Dirk Oldenburg*
concierge@countrygardeninns.com | www.countrygardeninns.com/

#1 Rated B&B in Carmel Valley. Out of the reach of the coastal fog nestled in the Santa Lucia Mountains and close to Carmel-by-the-Sea. Buffet style breakfast with waffle bar included. Walk to village for wine tasting, shopping and dining.

$119–$215
39 rooms, 39 pb
Visa MC AmEx
C-yes/S-no/P-no/HC-no

BB | Buffet with waffle bar
Evening wine & cheese hour

CATALINA ISLAND

Aurora Hotel
137 Marilla Ave.

310-510-7070 | *Kathleen Gosselin*
info@auroracatalina.com | www.Auroracatalina.com

Sleek. Modern. Cool. Welcome to a new era in Catalina Island hospitality. Inspired by the sea, the Aurora Hotel and Spa immerses you in relaxation, inviting you to discover the magic of sensuous waves and the comfort of modern style.

$160–$695
18 rooms, 18 pb
Visa MC AmEx   Cash
C-ltd/S-ltd/P-no/HC-no

BB | Continental breakfast
Free Internet and WiFi, Laptops, Ocean view roof-deck, On-site spa, GPS units, Binoculars and more!

CHESTER

The Bidwell House
One Main St

530-258-3338 | *Eva & Filip Laboda*
reservation@bidwellhouse.com | www.bidwellhouse.com

Historic Inn on the edge of Lassen National Park, beautiful Lake Almanor and next to the Feather River. Gourmet breakfast, a four-season paradise, world class dining, golfing, boating and shopping.

$85–$175
14 rooms, 12 pb
Visa MC   Cash
C-ltd/S-no/P-no/HC-yes

BB | Three course gourmet breakfast
Afternoon sherry served by fireplace, fresh fruit, giant chocolate chip cookies
Sitting room, library, DVD library, Jacuzzi tubs in rooms, fireplaces, wi-fi

CHULA VISTA

El Primero Boutique
B&B Hotel
416 Third Ave

619-425-4486 | *Pie & Sol Roque*
pie@elprimerohotel.com | www.elprimerohotel.com

El Primero is Chula Vista's best-kept hotel secret. An historic, award winning B&B where guests wake up to a sumptuous, gourmet breakfast. Recipient of the city's first Historic Preservation Award and the Mayor's 2005 Beautification Award.

$90–$120
19 rooms, 19 pb
Most CC Cash
C-yes/S-no/P-no/HC-yes

BB | Full breakfast
24 hour guest services, friendly staff, courtyard, kiosk, cable TV, WiFi, off street parking

CORONADO

Cherokee Lodge
964 D Ave

619-437-1967 | **877-743-6213** | *Ed & Mary Melvin*
info@cherokeelodge.com | www.CherokeeLodge.com

The Cherokee Lodge is across the bay from downtown San Diego in the heart of Coronado Island and is located one block from downtown Coronado near numerous charming bistros & restaurants, & just three blocks from the beach & the historic Hotel Del Coronado

$135–$175
13 rooms, 13 pb
Most CC Cash Checks
C-yes/S-no/P-ltd/HC-no

BB | Continental breakfast
Breakfast vouchers for continental breakfast at a local diner, coffee & tea in rooms
WiFi, washer/dryer, satellite TVs, fridge, free phone calls worldwide, AC,
coffee & tea in room

Coronado Village Inn
1017 Park Pl

619-435-9318 | *Jauter & Ana Sainz*
www.coronadovillageinn.com

Located off Coronado's main street, Coronado Village Inn is a historic bed and breakfast decorated in old Spanish style. 1½ blocks to the ocean!

$85–$95
15 rooms, 15 pb
Visa MC AmEx
C-yesHC-yes

BB | Self-serve continental breakfast
Fully-equipped kitchen available to guests 24 hours a day
Laundry, sitting room, cable TV, maid service

CROWLEY LAKE

Rainbow Tarns B&B
At Crowley Lake
505 Rainbow Tarns Rd

760-935-4556 | **888-588-6269** | *Brock & Diane Thoman*
innkeeper@rainbowtarns.com | www.rainbowtarns.com

Relax in the heart of High Sierra Mountains where the soothing sounds of flowing water and gentle breezes in the pines, the crystal clear sky and sparkling starry nights blend into an enchanting and memorable experience. Between Bishop and Mammoth Lakes.

$110–$155
3 rooms, 3 pb
Cash Checks
C-ltd/S-ltd/P-no/HC-yes

BB | Full country breakfast
Afternoon wine, snacks, veggie meals by arrangement
Sitting room, library, 2 rooms with Jacuzzis

DANA POINT

The Blue Lantern Inn
34343 Blue Lantern St

949-611-1304 | 800-950-1236 | *Lin McManon*
bluelanterninn@foursisters.com | www.bluelanterninn.com

Enjoy fabulous views of the Pacific from just about every window of this four diamond bed and breakfast inn—dramatically located on a bluff above the Dana Point Yacht Harbor.

$185–$600
29 rooms, 29 pb
Most CC Cash
C-yes/S-no/P-no/HC-yes

BB | Full breakfast
Afternoon wine, tea & hors d'oeuvres, freshly-baked cookies, drinks available throughout the day
Meeting rooms, bikes, Jacuzzi, evening turndown, WiFi, concierge service, movies, books & games

ELK

Elk Cove Inn & Spa
6300 S. Highway One

707-877-3321 | 800-275-2967 | *Elaine Bryant*
innkeeper@elkcoveinn.com | www.elkcoveinn.com

Situated atop a bluff in peaceful seclusion with breathtaking views this romantic Mendocino coast historic inn offers ocean and garden view rooms in the 1883 mansion, four bluff top cottage units and four luxury oceanfront suites.

2011 Lanier Best West Coast Award Winner: Best Sunset View

$125–$395
15 rooms, 15 pb
Most CC Cash Checks
C-ltd/S-ltd/P-no/HC-ltd

BB | Full gourmet champagne breakfast
Free wine, homemade chocolate chip cookies, champagne, and cocktails.
Direct beach access, European-style day spa, free WiFi, guest lounge with TV, gazebo

Sandpiper House Inn
5520 S Hwy 1

707-877-3587 | 800-894-9016 | *Jaci Schartz*
sandpiperhouseinn@yahoo.com | www.sandpiperhouse.com

Seaside country inn built in 1916. Rich redwood paneling in the living and dining rooms, lush perennial gardens that extend to the ocean bluff, stunning oceanviews, fireplaces in all of the rooms.

$150–$275
5 rooms, 5 pb
Most CC
C-ltd/S-no/P-no/HC-no

BB | Gourmet Breakfast
Wine & hors d'oeuvres in the evening; complimentary wine in your room
Antiques, fresh flowers, gardens, fireplaces, fine linens, down comforters, feather pillows

ENCINITAS

Inn at Moonlight Beach
105 N Vulcan Ave

760 561 1755 | *Ann Dunham & Terry Hunefeld*
www.innatmoonlightbeach.com

Ann Dunham's Inn at Moonlight Beach has been voted San Diego's most romantic Pacific Coast Bed & Breakfast Inn featuring meditative gardens and beautiful sunsets. We overlook Moonlight Beach, the Pacific Ocean and the quaint beach-town of Encinitas.

$129–$169
4 rooms, 4 pb
Visa MC   Cash Checks
S-no/P-no/HC-yes

BB | Continental plus breakfast
Delicious home-made, warm from the oven breads and muffins. See our website for photos and menus.
Our sunny breakfast room with fireplace is yours to use 24/7. WiFi in rooms.

EUREKA

Carter House Inns
& Restaurant 301
301 L St

707-444-8062 | 800-404-1390 | *Mark & Christi Carter*
reserve@carterhouse.com | www.carterhouse.com

Carter House Inns is perched alongside Humboldt Bay in Victorian Eureka with luxurious amenities, superior hospitality, spas, fireplaces, and antique furnishings. Also stop by our Restaurant 301, a Wine Spectator Grand Award winning restaurant.

$155–$385
32 rooms, 32 pb
Most CC Cash Checks
C-yes/S-no/P-yes/HC-yes

BB | Full breakfast
Wine, hors d'oeuvres, cookies, tea, chocolate truffles
Whirlpools, fireplaces, sitting rooms, Jacuzzis, TV/VCR, CD, stereo, gardens, bar on mezzanine level

Cornelius Daly Inn
1125 H St

707-445-3638 | 800-321-9656 | *Donna & Bob Gafford*
innkeeper@dalyinn.com | www.dalyinn.com

A beautifully restored turn-of-the-century mansion, one of Eureka's finest. The Inn is located in the historic section of Eureka a few blocks from the Pacific Ocean and a short drive to the majestic Redwoods State & National Parks.

$130–$225
5 rooms, 4 pb
Most CC
C-yes/S-no/P-no/HC-no

BB | Full breakfast
Wine, hors d'oeuvres
Music room, library, Victorian gardens, game room, TV room, laundry room

The Ship's Inn B&B
821 D St

707-443-7583 | 877-443-7583 | *Genie Wood*
genie@shipsinn.net | www.shipsinn.net

Step back in time to those seafaring days in a cozy, relaxing atmosphere befitting Eureka's Victorian Seaport. Just blocks to charming Old Town and the new boardwalk.

$130–$175
3 rooms, 3 pb
Most CC Cash
C-yes/S-ltd/P-ltd/HC-no

BB | Full breakfast
Cookies & lemonade at check-in, Brandy in the parlor
Internet access, WiFi, TV, VCR, robes, dining room, fireside, common areas, library

FELTON

Felton Crest Inn
780 El Solya Heights Dr

831-335-4011 | 800-474-4011 | *Hanna Peters*
hannapeters@comcast.net | www.feltoncrestinn.com/

A romantic getaway set in the majestic redwoods of the Santa Cruz Mtns. Enjoy all that the beautiful Monterey Bay and California's Central Coast have to offer. Uniquely located between San Francisco, Carmel and Pebble Beach and the Santa Clara Valley.

$199–$375
4 rooms, 4 pb
Visa MC AmEx   Cash Checks
C-ltd/S-ltd/P-no/HC-ltd

BB | Continental breakfast
Champagne & chocolates on arrival
Cable TV, VCR, video library, telephone, private baths

FERNDALE

Victorian Inn
400 Ocean Ave

707-786-4949 | 888-589-1808 | *Lowell Daniels & Jenny Oaks*
innkeeper@victorianvillageinn.com | www.victorianvillageinn.com

The Victorian Inn stands as a monument to luxurious comfort and exquisite craftsmanship. It embodies the elegance and romance of the timber boom era on the North Coast.

$145–$295
13 rooms, 13 pb
Most CC
C-yes/S-no/P-no/HC-ltd

BB | Full breakfast
Lunch & dinner available, snacks, restaurant, bar, afternoon wine & cheese
Sitting room, suites, fireplace, cable TV, wireless & cable Internet access

FISH CAMP

Narrow Gauge Inn
48571 Hwy 41

559-683-7720 | 888-644-9050 | *Martha Vanaman*
ngi@sti.net | www.narrowgaugeinn.com

Celebrating the mountain atmosphere, the Narrow Gauge Inn is just 4 miles from Yosemite. Offering 26 charming rooms with balconies and mountain views, some pet-friendly. Seasonal restaurant. Weddings, reunions and events welcome.

$79–$195
26 rooms, 26 pb
Visa MC Disc
C-yes/S-ltd/P-yes/HC-no

BB | Continental breakfast
Fine dining restaurant (seasonal)
Seasonal pool & hot tub, gift shop, nature trail

FORESTHILL

Christmas Tree Vineyard Lodge
38400 Foresthill Road

916-599-0141 | *Joe, Claudia and Liz*
loglodge1@gmail.com | www.christmastreevineyardlodge.com/index.html

Discover the seasons of the Sierra Nevada back country, minus the crowds! Winter, Spring, Summer or Fall...there are no cozier accommodations anywhere in the high country in the Sierra Nevada Mountains.

$100
6 rooms, 6 pb
Visa MC   Cash
C-yes/S-no/P-no/HC-yes

BB | Full Breakfast
Community Kitchen use is available at a nominal fee per day. TV, DVD player and free WiFi.

FORESTVILLE

Farmhouse Inn and Restaurant
7871 River Rd

707-887-3300 | 800-464-6642 | *Catherine & Joe Bartolomei*
innkeep@farmhouseinn.com | www.farmhouseinn.com

A Northern California Wine Country Inn & Restaurant. One of Travel & Leisure's Top 30 Inns, Michelin star, Zagat Best in Sonoma County, and Chronicle 100 Best Restaurants. Luxury spa on site. Romantic getaway central to Napa & Sonoma wineries.

$295–$695
18 rooms, 18 pb
Most CC Cash
C-ltd/S-no/P-no/HC-yes

BB | Full breakfast
4 star restaurant - Michelin & Zagat reviewed. European style service, superb wine list. Th-Mon
Full concierge services, heated pool, spa services, WiFi, beverage bar, fire pit & s'mores.

FORT BRAGG

Country Inn B&B
632 N Main St

707-964-3737 | 800-831-5327 | *Bruce & Cynthia Knauss*
cntryinn@mcn.org | www.beourguests.com

The Country Inn Bed and Breakfast, located in Fort Bragg surrounded by the splendor of Mendocino, invites you to "be our guest." For 30 years, the Inn has been serving country hospitality along the north coast of California.

 Dreams Do Come True participating inn—Valid anytime; will offer a room upgrade

$55–$145
8 rooms, 8 pb
Most CC Cash Checks
C-yes/S-no/P-no/HC-yes

BB | Full gourmet breakfast
Fireplaces, sun deck, parlor, hot tub, Spa Treatments available, Skunk Train nearby

GEORGETOWN

American River Inn
6600 Orleans St

530-333-4499 | 800-245-6566 | *Will & Maria Collin*
visitus@americanriverinn.com | www.Americanriverinn.com

Historic Queen Anne-style bed & breakfast inn, complete with old fashioned hospitality and turn-of-the-century antique furnishings. Refurbished Summer '07 to exceptional beauty. Fantastic featherbeds. Exotic therapeutic Jacuzzi. Table Service.

 Dreams Do Come True participating inn—Valid Sunday–Friday and October–May

$95–$130
14 rooms, 9 pb
Most CC
C-ltd/S-no/P-ltd/HC-yes

BB | Full breakfast
Complimentary evening wine & hors d'oeuvres in the parlor
Pool, Jacuzzi, Bicycles, Bocce Ball, Table Service

GEYSERVILLE

**Hope-Merrill House/
Hope-Bosworth House**
21253 Geyserville Ave

707-857-3356 | 800-825-4233 | *Cosette & Ron Scheiber*
moreinfo@hope-inns.com | www.hope-inns.com

Facing each other are the Queen Anne Craftsman style Hope-Bosworth House and the strikingly restored Eastlake style Victorian Hope-Merrill House.

$149–$289
12 rooms, 12 pb
Cash Checks
C-yes/S-no/P-ltd/HC-ltd

BB | Full breakfast
Complimentary water, 24-Hour coffee, tea & chocolate machine, other beverages available for purchase
Sitting room, library, Jacuzzis, suites, swimming pool, fireplace, cable TV in some rooms

GROVELAND

**All Seasons
Groveland Inn**
18656 Main St

209-962-0232 | *Ann Schafer*
askdranns@yahoo.com | www.allseasonsgrovelandinn.com

A work of art, located 23 miles from the northwest gate of Yosemite. Five rooms offer beautiful murals and world class amenities: elaborate bathrooms, Jacuzzi tubs, and fireplaces. A Yosemite traveler's primary destination.

$135–$175
5 rooms, 5 pb
Visa MC   Cash
C-yes/S-no/P-no/HC-ltd

BB | Continental plus breakfast
Fresh ground coffee stations; a selection of herbal teas and cocoa
Themed rooms, murals, antiques, Jacuzzis, fireplaces, picnic area by creek (seasonal)

Blackberry Inn B&B
7567 Hamilton
Station Loop

209-962-4663 | 888-867-5001
Steve McCorkle & Alexandra North
innkeepers@blackberry-inn.com | www.blackberry-inn.com

The Blackberry Inn, a Yosemite National Park bed and breakfast, is the quintessential American country farmhouse with a lovely wraparound porch. Hundreds of hummingbirds visit this conveniently located Yosemite lodging facility on Hwy 120 closest to SFO.

$150–$265
5 rooms, 5 pb
Visa MC AmEx   Cash
C-ltd/S-no/P-no/HC-yes

BB | Full breakfast
Chocolate chip cookies, full tea service, lunches available upon request
Wrap-around porch, hummingbirds, loft, snow shoes, chocolate chip cookies, free wireless Internet

Groveland Hotel at
Yosemite National Park
18767 Main St

209-962-4000 | 800-273-3314 | *Peggy & Grover Mosley*
guestservices@groveland.com | www.groveland.com

Comfortable and luxurious rooms, 1849 Gold Rush hotel. 25 minutes to Yosemite. Indoor or courtyard dining, Wine Spectator Award winning wine list. Pet friendly, spa services, hiking, photography, biking. Open all year. Conferences, weddings, retreat

 Dreams Do Come True participating inn—Valid anytime; will offer a room upgrade

$145–$285
17 rooms, 17 pb
Most CC Cash
C-yes/S-no/P-yes/HC-ltd

BB | Full, Hot Innkeeper's Breakfast
Cellar Door Restaurant, Wine Spectator Magazine's "Award of Excellence" wine list, full service bar
Cable TV, free WiFi, balconies, gold rush saloon, weddings, maps & guides, conferences, parties

Hotel Charlotte
18736 Main St

209-962-6455 | 800-961-7799
Victor Niebylski & Lynn Upthagrove
hotelcharlotte@aol.com | www.HotelCharlotte.com

Hotel Charlotte is an historic B&B hotel on the way to Yosemite featuring a full service restaurant & bar. Yosemite National Park & Tuolumne River white water river rafting are popular local activities, as are wine tasting regions & Gold Rush towns.

 Dreams Do Come True participating inn—Valid October 15–April 15 (excluding holidays and special events); will offer a room upgrade

$119–$159
10 rooms, 10 pb
Visa MC AmEx
C-yes/S-no/P-ltd/HC-ltd

BB | Buffet Sausage&Pancakes&Scrambled
Complimentary coffee, tea or iced tea available almost any time, restaurant & bar on site 7 days/wk
Guest salon, Satellite TV, DSL Internet & WiFi, piano, game room, balcony, itinerary planning

GUERNEVILLE

Applewood Inn
13555 Hwy 116

707-869-9093 | **800-555-8509** | *Sylvia & Carlos*
stay@applewoodinn.com | www.applewoodinn.com/

A popular Sonoma County destination for food and wine enthusiasts seeking a getaway to Sonoma County's idyllic Russian River Valley. This historic and casually luxurious B&B is an ideal starting point for excursions.

$195–$345
19 rooms, 19 pb
Most CC Cash
  S-no/P-no/HC-yes

BB | Full breakfast
Our Zagat rated restaurant offers exceptional wine country fare, picnic baskets & cheese boards
Massage and Spa services, Pool with Hot Tub.

**Creekside Inn
& Resort**
16180 Neeley Rd

707-869-3623 | **800-776-6586** | *Lynn & Mark Crescione*
stay@creeksideinn.com | www.creeksideinn.com

A relaxed and friendly atmosphere best describes this bed & breakfast, situated in the redwoods near the Russian River. We have a delightful bed & breakfast, an assortment of charming cottages, sunny decks, a pool, picnic areas, and affordable rates!

$98–$270
28 rooms, 24 pb
Visa MC AmEx Cash
C-yes/S-ltd/P-ltd/HC-yes

BB | Full breakfast
Breakfast not available in cottages, however cottages have full kitchens
Library, sitting room, conference facilities, direct phone, pool, WiFi, HBO, sun decks, picnic area

Fern Grove Cottages
16650 Hwy 116

707-869-8105 | **888-243-2674** | *Mike & Margaret Kennett*
innkeepers@ferngrove.com | www.ferngrove.com

Comfortable cottages in the redwoods - many with living rooms, and fireplaces; some with spa tubs. Relax among beautiful gardens. Enjoy the pool. Easily walk to town, river, or beaches. Expect warm hospitality. Indulge with a great breakfast.

$89–$259
20 rooms, 20 pb
Most CC Cash
C-yes/S-no/P-ltd/HC-yes

BB | Continental plus breakfast
Sitting room, library, spa tubs, suites, pool, cable TV, wine tours, wireless Internet, bbq area

Sonoma Orchid Inn
12850 River Rd

707-869-4466 | **888-877-4466** | *Brian Siewert & Dana Murphy*
innkeeper@sonomaorchidinn.com | www.sonomaorchidinn.com/

Historic Sonoma Orchid Inn is nestled along the Russian River offering comfort & charm, in the heart of Sonoma County's Wine Country. Easy access to wineries, the coast & San Francisco.

$149–$245
10 rooms, 10 pb
Most CC Cash
C-yes/S-ltd/P-yes/HC-ltd

BB | Full gourmet breakfast
Homemade cookies, complimentary water, juice, port & sherry, on-site catering, guest kitchen
Outdoor hot tub, great room w/ fireplace, library, satellite TV/Tivo, cable TV, DVD/VCR, WiFi

Landis Shores
Oceanfront Inn
211 Mirada Rd

650-726-6642 | *Ken & Ellen Landis*
luxury@landisshores.com | www.landisshores.com

Elegant oceanfront accommodations, private balconies, fireplaces, whirlpool tubs, TV/VCRs and more. Enjoy a gourmet breakfast each morning and premium wines and appetizers every afternoon.

 Dreams Do Come True participating inn—Valid Monday–Thursday and November–May (except holidays)

$225–$345
8 rooms, 8 pb
Most CC Cash
C-ltd/S-no/P-ltd/HC-yes

BB | Full breakfast
Appetizers, premium wines
Whirlpool tub, fireplace, TV/DVD, fitness room, private deck, extensive wine list, internet access

Old Thyme Inn
779 Main St

650-726-1616 | **800-720-4277** | *Rick & Kathy Ellis*
innkeeper@oldthymeinn.com | www.oldthymeinn.com

Spend enchanted nights. Herb and flower garden provides tranquil setting in coastal village, 1/2 hour from San Francisco and Silicon Valley. Furnished in antiques and fine art; 7 rooms each with cable TV/VCR, free wi-fi, queen bed, and private bath.

$139–$299
7 rooms, 7 pb
Most CC Cash Checks
C-ltd/S-ltd/P-no/HC-no

BB | Gourmet full breakfast
Complementary afternoon wine & cheese
Library of videos and recent magazines, peaceful herb and flower garden

Pacific Victorian B&B
325 Alameda Ave

650-712-3900 | **888-929-0906** | *Jeff & Lori Matthews*
pacificvictorian@msn.com | www.pacificvictorian.com

Elegantly decorated Victorian style Inn located in beautiful Miramar Beach, Half Moon Bay, California, within easy driving distance of San Francisco. The Inn is nestled in a scenic coastal setting 1.5 blocks from the beach.

$150–$195
4 rooms, 4 pb
Most CC
C-yes/S-ltd/P-no/HC-yes

BB | Full breakfast
Parlor, dining room, down comforters, fine linens, decks, whirlpool tubs, movie library, WiFi

San Benito House
356 Main St

650-726-3425 | *Cristina Carrubba*
inquiries@sanbenitohouse.com | www.sanbenitohouse.com

Located at 356 Main St in Half Moon Bay, the San Benito House is open year round for restful bed and breakfast accommodations. 12 guest rooms, 9 with private bath. Old fashioned saloon, deli-cafe, beautiful gardens. Ideal for weddings and special events.

$90–$150
12 rooms, 9 pb
Most CC Cash Checks
C-yes/S-no/P-yes/HC-ltd

BB | Continental breakfast
delicious sandwiches made on homemade bread, soups, pasta, salsa, salads, muffins, cookies, brownies
Fresh flowers, sauna, redwood deck, garden with croquet lawn and swing, saloon, weddings, deli-cafe

Camellia Inn
211 North St

707-433-8182 | **800-727-8182** | *Lucy Lewand*
info@camelliainn.com | www.camelliainn.com

A charming 1869 Italianate Victorian Inn set in California's Sonoma Wine Country. Surrounded by 50 varieties of its signature camellias, the Inn blends an authentic, vintage environment with modern and luxurious amenities for a memorable romantic getaway.

$139–$329
9 rooms, 9 pb
Most CC Cash Checks
C-yes/S-no/P-ltd/HC-ltd

BB | Full breakfast
Wine & cheese tasting, hot beverages & cookies, on Wednesdays chocolate & more chocolate
Parlor, pool, whirlpool tubs, fireplaces, King beds, WiFi, winery passes, spa discounts, concierge

Haydon Street Inn
321 Haydon St

707-433-5228 | **800-528-3703** | *John Harasty & Keren Colsten*
innkeeper@haydon.com | www.haydon.com

Historic Wine Country Queen Anne home in this friendly Sonoma County town. Walk to historic town plaza with great restaurants, antique stores and wonderful boutiques.

$190–$425
9 rooms, 9 pb
Visa MC Disc Cash Checks
S-no/P-no/HC-no

BB |Full breakfast
Homemade chocolate chip cookies in the afternoon, wine hour in the evening
Comfortable public spaces, all king rooms have fireplaces, jacuzzi and small fridge.

**Healdsburg Inn
on the Plaza**
112 Matheson St

707-433-6991 | **800-431-8663** | *Jennifer Byrom*
healdsburginn@foursisters.com | www.healdsburginn.com

This Four Sisters Inn blends the modern luxuries and sophisticated services of a boutique hotel with the traditional amenities and architecture of a B&B in the best location in town, right on the historic Healdsburg Plaza.

$275–$375
12 rooms, 12 pb
Most CC Cash
C-yes/S-no/P-no/HC-yes

BB | Full breakfast
Afternoon wine, tea & hors d' oeuvres, freshly-baked cookies, drinks available throughout the day
Evening turndown, early newspaper delivery to your room, wireless Internet, movies, books & games

Irish Rose Inn
3232 Dry Creek Rd

707-431-2801 | *Chris & Lanny Matson*
chris@theirishroseinn.com | www.theirishroseinn.com

The Irish Rose is a wonderful Craftsman home built in 1912, and is located in the heart of Dry Creek Valley in Sonoma County, California.

$160–$200
3 rooms, 3 pb
Visa MC
C-ltd/S-no/P-yes/HC-no

BB | Full breakfast

California

HEALDSBURG

Raford Inn
of Healdsburg
10630 Wohler Rd

707-887-9573 | 800-887-9503 | *Dane & Rita*
innkeeper@rafordinn.com | www.rafordinn.com

Victorian farmhouse overlooks vineyards in the heart of the Russian River Valley of Sonoma County. Beautiful country setting is just 1½ hours from San Francisco, a 15 minute drive to Healdsburg Plaza.

$160–$260
6 rooms, 6 pb
Visa MC AmEx   Cash Checks
C-ltd/S-no/P-no/HC-ltd

BB | Full breakfast
Complimentary evening wine & hors oeuvres, tea, coffee & snacks in dining room
Porch, vineyard views, garden, patio, some fireplaces, roses, in-room massage,
WiFi, satellite TV

HOMEWOOD

Rockwood Lodge
5295 West Lake Blvd

530-525-5273 | 800-538-2463 | *Lou Reinkens & Connie Stevens*
lou@rockwoodlodge.com | www.rockwoodlodge.com/

Rockwood Lodge is an "Old Tahoe" estate nestled in a pine forest on the west shore of Lake Tahoe. Many fine appointments, exquisite architecture and beautiful, natural surroundings. Breakfast on the patio in summer.

$100–$225
5 rooms, 5 pb
Visa MC   Cash
C-ltd/S-no/P-ltd/HC-no

BB | Continental breakfast
Complimentary cordials
Sitting room, game room, swimming pool, billiards

HOPE VALLEY

Sorensen's Resort
14255 Hwy 88

530-694-2203 | 800-423-9949 | *John & Patty Brissenden*
info@sorensensresort.com | www.sorensensresort.com

Cozy creekside cabins nestled in the Alps of California. Close to Tahoe and Kirkwood and Hope Valley Outdoor Center. Hope Valley Resort features fly fishing, art and photo classes, and history tours.

$115–$550
35 rooms, 33 pb
Most CC Checks
C-yes/S-no/P-ltd/HC-ltd

BB | Sorensens Country Cafe
Snacks, restaurant, wine & beer service
Library, hot springs nearby, bikes & skis nearby, wood burning stoves

IDYLLWILD

Quiet Creek Inn &
Vacation Rentals
26345 Delano Dr

951-659-6110 | 800-450-6110 | *Jim Newcomb & Mike Ahern*
info@quietcreekinn.com | www.quietcreekinn.com/Quiet-Creek-Inn.html

Quiet Creek Inn offers deluxe, Sunset Magazine recommended, duplex cabins on over 6 acres along Strawberry Creek with fireplaces & private decks. Quiet Creek Vacation Rentals offer individually owned, well-appointed homes & cabins throughout town.

$130–$160
10 rooms, 10 pb
Most CC Cash
C-yes/S-ltd/P-ltd/HC-ltd

EP |
In room gourmet coffee. Water, sodas, Gatorade, hot teas, hot chocolate & popcorn
in the lounge
Iron & board avail., Adventure Pass & Wilderness Trail Map; hiking trail advice.
In room kitchenette

IDYLLWILD

**Strawberry Creek
Bunk House**
25525 Hwy 243

951-659-2201 | 888-400-0071 | *Rodney Williams*
innkeeper@strawberrycreekinn.com | http://strawberrycreekinn.com/index.htm

Seated on a hillside overlooking the San Jacinto State Forest, the Strawberry Creek Bunkhouse is an affordable, eco-friendly lodge tailor-made for hikers, rock-climbers, fisherman, mountain-bikers, or travelers who want a kid or pet friendly vacation.

$89–$189
18 rooms, 18 pb
Most CC Cash
C-yes/S-no/P-yes/HC-ltd

BB | Continental breakfast
All guest rooms have private balconies, a kitchenette, coffee maker, great forest views.

Strawberry Creek Inn
26370 State Hwy 243

951-659-3202 | 800-262-8969 | *Rodney Williams & Ian Scott*
innkeeper@strawberrycreekinn.com | www.strawberrycreekinn.com

Cool, clean mountain air, outdoor decks, hammocks & gardens overlooking Strawberry Creek. A member of the Green Hotels Association. Featured in "Best Places to Kiss" & "Great Towns of Southern CA." Nine inn guestrooms and one private cottage.

$109–$239
10 rooms, 10 pb
Most CC Cash
C-ltd/S-no/P-no/HC-yes

BB | Full breakfast
Sodas, bottled water, coffee, tea, snacks, evening appetizers on Friday & Saturday
Library, fireplaces, refrigerators, hammock, wireless Internet, Aveda amenities, organic ingredients

**The Lodge at
Pine Cove**
24900 Marion Ridge Dr

951-659-4463 | 866-563-4372 | *Geary Boedeker*
innkeeper@thelodgeatpinecove.com | www.thelodgeatpinecove.com

The Lodge at Pine Cove is a 5-room B&B high in the San Jacinto Mountains at 6200 feet, just minutes from the beautiful mountain village of Idyllwild. Romantic packages. Wonderful private getaway.

$85–$105
5 rooms, 5 pb
Visa MC AmEx   Cash
C-ltd/S-no/P-no/HC-no

BB | Full breakfast
Assortment of coffee, teas, hot chocolate
Small refrigerator, decks, VCR & cable TV

INVERNESS

Dancing Coyote Beach

415-669-7200 | 800-210-1692 | *Janet Osborn*
Theparsonage@hotmail.com | www.dancingcoyotebeach.com

You won't forget the time you spend at Dancing Coyote Beach. The graceful curve of the shoreline, the sheltering pines and cedars, and relaxing by a fire crackling in the fireplace will call you back again and again.

$175–$250
3 rooms, 3 pb
Cash Checks
C-ltd/S-ltd/P-ltd/HC-no

BB | Full breakfast
Fully equipped kitchens in our cottages for self-service dining
Fireplaces, views, decks, parking, in-room massages, beachfront, outdoor BBQ, outdoor shower

INVERNESS

Inverness Valley Inn
13275 Sir Francis
Drake Blvd

415-669-7250 | 800-416-0405 | *Alden & Leslie Adkins*
info@Invernessvalleyinn.com | www.invernessvalleyinn.com

*Located on 15 acres of natural beauty, 1½ hours from San Francisco,
our refurbished A-frame cottages each consist of four spacious units with
high ceilings and plenty of light. Some rooms and suites dog-friendly.
Green "eco-friendly" inn.*

$130–$219
20 rooms, 20 pb
Most CC Cash
C-yes/S-no/P-yes/HC-yes

EP |
Kitchenettes stocked with coffee, teas & spices
Cable TV, thermostat-controlled gas fireplace, private patio, clock radio, tennis
courts, pool, WiFi

JAMESTOWN

**1859 Historic National
Hotel & Restaurant**
18183 Main St

209-984-3446 | 800-894-3446 | *Stephen Willey*
info@national-hotel.com | www.national-hotel.com

*Hotel c.1859 in the heart of Gold Rush country. Our rooms are restored
to the elegance of a romantic by-gone era. Enjoy our highly acclaimed
restaurant with full bar on premises. Antique shopping, live theatre, golf,
hiking & wine-tasting. Near Yosemite.*

*Dreams Do Come True participating inn—Valid weekdays only, November 1–
March 31; Sunday–Thursday*

$140–$175
9 rooms, 9 pb
Most CC Cash
C-ltd/S-no/P-yes/HC-no

BB | Breakfast buffet
Dining in our highly-acclaimed restaurant is a gourmet's delight; full-serve saloon
& espresso bar
Historic saloon, concierge services, patio dining, balcony & a fun staff

JENNER

**Jenner Inn Restaurant
& Cottages**
10400 Coast Hwy 1

707-865-2377 | 800-732-2377 | *Richard Murphy*
innkeeper@jennerinn.com | www.jennerinn.com

*A unique country Inn on Sonoma's wine country coast. Panoramic
waterviews from most rooms, suites and cottages. Fine dining, entertainment and many activities. Beautiful sunsets and romance abound.
Whale watching in the winter months.*

$118–$348
21 rooms, 21 pb
Visa MC AmEx   Cash
C-yes/S-no/P-ltd/HC-yes

BB | Meatless breakfast
Tea & coffee, cookies
Sitting room, fireside lounge, sauna, hot tubs & fireplaces

JULIAN

Butterfield B&B
2284 Sunset Dr

760-765-2179 | 800-379-4262 | *Ed & Dawn Glass*
info@butterfieldbandb.com | www.butterfieldbandb.com

*Relax on our three-acre, country garden setting in the quiet hills of Julian.
Five unique rooms from country to formal decor. Famous gourmet breakfast. Just an hour from San Diego.*

$135–$185
5 rooms, 5 pb
Most CC Cash
C-ltd/S-ltd/P-no/HC-ltd

BB | Full breakfast
Complimentary coffees, tea, cider, cocoa, popcorn & dessert in the afternoon; guest
stocked fridge
Sitting room, library, suites, fireplace, cable TV/VCR/DVD/CD,WiFi, piano, guitar, games

JULIAN

Eaglenest B&B
2609 D St

760-765-1252 | **888-345-6378** | *Jim & Julie Degenfelder*
info@eaglenestbnb.com | www.eaglenestbandb.com

Eaglenest offers all the amenities of a four-star resort in the privacy & comfort of a beautiful home in this mountain hamlet in San Diego County. It is a one block walk to local shopping, fine dining, attractions & entertainment in historic Julian.

$165–$185
4 rooms, 4 pb
Most CC
C-yes/S-ltd/P-no/HC-ltd

BB | Full breakfast
Dessert snacks are fresh baked for your stay
Pool, spa, fireplaces, A/C/heat, hot tubs, TV/VCR/CD

Julian Gold Rush Hotel
2032 Main Street

760-765-0201 | **800-734-5854** | *Steve & Gig Ballinger*
bnb@julianhotel.com | www.julianhotel.com

The town's only designated landmark, capturing the charm and character of this 1800's Southern California mining town. In the heart of the Historic District, within walking distance of antique stores, gift shops, restaurants, museums and gold mines.

$135–$210
16 rooms, 16 pb
Visa MC AmEx
C-yes/S-no/P-no/HC-no

BB | Full breakfast
Tea time-Enjoy sharing in our afternoon tea served daily 5pm to 6pm in the historic dining room.
Sitting room, library, wireless internet, parlor games, group meeting space, AC, wake-up calls

Orchard Hill Country Inn
2502 Washington St

760-765-1700 | **800-716-7242** | *Pat & Darrell Straube*
information@orchardhill.com | www.orchardhill.com

Restful and romantic premier bed and breakfast with AAA Four Diamond attention to detail, caring staff and excellent dining. Gracious ambience, sweeping sunset views and seasonal gardens make us an unforgettable destination.

$195–$450
22 rooms, 22 pb
Visa MC AmEx   Cash Checks
C-yes/S-no/P-no/HC-yes

BB | Full breakfast
Complimentary afternoon hors d'oeuvres, a four-course dinner is served on select evenings
Masseuse available, video library, conference facilities, weddings

KENWOOD

Birmingham B&B
8790 Highway 12

707-833-6996 | **800-819-1388** | *Nancy & Jerry Fischman*
info@birminghambb.com | www.birminghambb.com

Sit on the wraparound porch of this historic home and gaze out at the beautiful vineyards and mountains of Sonoma Valley. The Inn is beautifully decorated in the Arts & Craft tradition, featuring Stickley furnishings and original works of art.

$160–$295
5 rooms, 5 pb
Visa MC AmEx   Cash
C-ltd/S-no/P-ltd/HC-ltd

BB | Full breakfast
Upon request afternoon refreshments include tea, coffee, cookies, and other snacks
Parlor, wrap-around porch, vegetable & flower gardens, concierge service, free wine tasting card

KLAMATH

Historic Requa Inn
451 Requa Rd

707-482-1425 | **866-800-8777** | *Janet & Marty Wartman*
reservations@requainn.com | *www.requainn.com*

*The most unique and historical B&B in the Redwood National Park.
Offering spectacular river views and rustic accommodations,
our central location makes the us your ideal basecamp to explore where
the Redwoods meet the Sea.*

$89–$179
12 rooms, 12 pb
Most CC Cash
C-ltd/S-ltd/P-no/HC-ltd

BB | Full breakfast
Dinner/evening meal available. Beverage bar, baked goodies in the afternoon.
Spectacular riverview, fireplace in living room, excellent library

LA JOLLA

**Bed and Breakfast
Inn at La Jolla**
7753 Draper Ave

858-456-2066 | **888-988-8481** | *Margaret Fox*
bedbreakfast@innlajolla.com | www.innlajolla.com

*Whether for business or a relaxing getaway at this historic & elegantly
charming Inn, we have it all. A block from the beach in the heart of
La Jolla by the Sea. So close, yet so far from it all, where romance makes
memories & business becomes a pleasure.*

$179–$479
15 rooms, 15 pb
Most CC Cash Checks
C-ltd/S-no/P-ltd/HC-ltd

BB | Full Gourmet Candlelit Breakfast
Complimentary fresh fruit, wine & cheese, sweets, fine sherry, snacks & tea, bottled water
Library/sitting room—complimentary beach towels, chairs & umbrellas—
tennis rackets/balls—concierge

**Redwood Hollow
Cottages**
256 Prospect St

858-459-8747 | *Martin Lizerbram*
lejolla@aol.com | www.redwoodhollow-lajolla.com

*A registered San Diego Historic Site with cottages and duplex homes in a
garden setting. Cottages are family friendly, 4 with fireplaces, most with
full kitchens. Close to everything La Jolla offers, down the street from
Whispering Sands Beach access.*

$125–$339
8 rooms, 8 pb
Most CC Cash Checks
C-yes/S-no/P-no/HC-ltd

EP |
Kitchens stocked with oatmeal, teas, coffee, popcorn, hot chocolate & goodies on arrival
Free WiFi, private cottages, sleeper sofa, living room, fireplaces, beaches,
maid service (fee)

LA SELVA BEACH

Flora Vista Inn
1258 San Andreas Rd

831-724-8663 | **877-753-5672** | *Deanna & Ed*
info@floravistainn.com | www.floravistainn.com

*Located along the Pacific Coast Bike Route, between Santa Cruz and
Monterey, the historic Flora Vista Inn is nestled among lush flower and
strawberry fields, a short walk from spectacular beaches.*

$195–$240
5 rooms, 5 pb
Most CC Cash
C-ltd/S-no/P-no/HC-ltd

BB | Full breakfast
Complimentary wine (or tea) and cheese in the afternoon, box lunches available
($12 per person)
Clay tennis courts, TV, wireless Internet, private bathrooms, two person spa-tubs,
gas fireplaces

LAGUNA BEACH

**Casa Laguna
Inn & Spa**
2510 S Coast Hwy

949-494-2996 | 800-233-0449 | *Francois Leclair, Kathryn Mace*
innkeeper@casalaguna.com | www.casalaguna.com

*Our mission-style buildings & terraced gardens exude the romantic
ambiance of days gone by. Enjoy our heated pool, sun deck, & spa
services, or picnic at Victoria Beach. Snuggle down in luxurious eco-
friendly linens & dream of our award-winning breakfast.*

$160–$650
22 rooms, 22 pb
Most CC
S-no/P-yes/HC-no

BB | Full gourmet breakfast from menu
Gourmet wine & cheese reception each evening.
A/C, luxurious bedding & robes, DVD & CD players, high speed Internet, flat panel
television

LAKEPORT

Lakeport English Inn
675 N Main St

707-263-4317 | *Karan & Hugh Mackey*
lakeportenglishinn@mchsi.com | www.lakeportenglishinn.com

*Lakeport English Inn is a delightful B&B, and no passports are needed
here. Located in beautiful Lakeport, CA, with the best of Britain: scones
with Devonshire cream and jam, English roses, darts, billiards, shopping and a library.*

$155–$221
10 rooms, 10 pb
Visa MC
C-ltd/S-no/P-no

BB | Full breakfast
High Tea served Saturday & Sunday between 12:00 & 2:30
Evening turndown service, Italian Frette Sheets, plush towels & robes, spa &
concierge service, WiFi

LEMON COVE

Plantation
33038 Sierra Hwy 198

559-597-2555 | *Scott & Marie Munger*
relax@plantationbnb.com | www.theplantation.net

*Nestled in the foothills of the Sierra Nevada Mountains, only 16 miles
from Sequoia National Park. Seven romantic "Gone With The Wind"
themed rooms. Full, gourmet breakfast prepared by Chef Marie.*

$149–$239
7 rooms, 7 pb
Most CC Cash Checks
C-ltd/S-ltd/P-no/HC-no

BB | Gourmet breakfast
Complimentary beverages & snacks
Hot tub, verandas, courtyard, swimming pool, fireplaces, landscaped gardens

LEWISTON

**The Old Lewiston
Inn B&B**
71 Deadwood Rd

530-528-9554 | *J.C. Osborne*
ualfox6314@clearwire.net | www.theoldlewistoninn.com/

*The Inn is located on the Trinity River and all rooms have porches or
balconies over looking the river. There is fly fishing in the back yard and
launching for canoes and kayaks as well.*

$110–$125
7 rooms, 5 pb
Visa MC   Cash Checks
C-yes/S-no/P-yes/HC-yes

BB | Full breakfast
Each lodge room comes equipped with a refrigerator and coffee maker.
Private entrances, private baths, air conditioning, direct T V and decks overlooking
the river.

LITTLE RIVER

Blanchard House B&B
8141 Coast Hwy 1

707-937-1627 | *Melody*
blanchrd@msn.org | www.blanchardhouse.com/

The spacious accommodations, spectacular location and superb hospitality at the Blanchard House will make this your home away from home. With only one room, it is the ultimate romantic hideaway for any couple.

$225
1 room, 1 pb
Visa MC   Cash Checks
C-ltd/S-no/P-no/HC-no

BB | Full breakfast
Coffee pot & bar refrigerator in service alcove
Cable TV with DVD & CD players

Inn at Schoolhouse Creek
7501 N Hwy 1

707-937-5525 | **800-731-5525** | *Steven Musser & Maureen Gilbert*
innkeeper@schoolhousecreek.com | www.schoolhousecreek.com

The Inn at Schoolhouse Creek on the Mendocino Coast provides a unique experience on the Northern California Coast with cottages and rooms spread out over 9 acres of lush gardens, meadows and forested land as well as our cliff side cottages.

$156–$399
19 rooms, 19 pb
Most CC
C-yes/S-ltd/P-yes/HC-yes

BB | Full breakfast
Complimentary wine & hors d'oeuvres
Oceanview hot tub, in-room spa tubs, fireplaces, private beach access, massage & spa services

The Andiron Inn & Cabins
6051 N Hwy One

707-937-1543 | **800-955-6478**
Scott Connolly & Madeline Stanionis
Hello@TheAndiron.com | http://TheAndiron.com

Welcome to The Andiron — Seaside Inn & Cabins, the relaxed vacation rental or overnight room along the Mendocino Coast. Our individual cabins are very private and the large spa in the forest is serene and romantic. See what awaits you.

$119–$279
12 rooms, 12 pb
Most CC Cash Checks
C-yes/S-no/P-yes/HC-no

BB | Full Breakfast
Complimentary wine
Large spa, private cabins or individual rooms, private baths, Internet access available

LOCKEFORD

Inn at Locke House
19960 Elliott Rd

209-727-5715 | *Lani & Richard Eklund*
lockehouse@jps.net | www.theinnatlockehouse.com/

"Experience a treasure, create treasured memories." A destination in itself, The Inn at Locke House is a California Landmark and a National Register of Historic Places site. Located in the heart of the Lodi Wine Appellation.

 Dreams Do Come True participating inn—Valid Sunday–Thursday (except for holiday and special events)

$160–$245
5 rooms, 5 pb
Visa MC   Cash Checks
C-ltd/S-ltd/P-no/HC-no

BB | Full breakfast
Varies: Confection of the day, California cheeses, artisan crackers, local fruit, & special beverage
Private bathrooms, fireplaces,WiFi, phones w/free local calls, I-pod /cd/radios, ceiling fans, AC

LONG BEACH

Dockside Boat & Bed
Dock 5,
Rainbow Harbor

562-436-3111 | 800-436-2574
Kim Harris-Ryskamp & Kent Ryskamp
boatandbed@yahoo.com | www.boatandbed.com/

Spend the night on a Yacht! Guests enjoy their very own private yacht at Rainbow Harbor. Beautiful views and steps away from fine dining, shopping and activities. Convenient to many major Southern California attractions.

$195–$325
6 rooms, 6 pb
Most CC Cash
C-yes/S-no/P-no/HC-ltd

BB | Continental plus breakfast
Complimentary light snacks & water on-board
Complimentary high speed wireless Internet, BBQ grill, DVD library

LOS OSOS

Julia's B&B by the Sea
2735 Nokomis Ct.

805-528-1344 | *Julia Wright*
lmjuliawright@sbcglobal.net | www.lanierbb.com/inns/bb2192.html

B&B by the Sea in the San Luis Obispo area. Charming bed and breakfast overlooking the ocean, perfect for short vacation, weekends, romantic getaways or a retreat. Close to Avila, Cambria, Hearst Castle, Paso Robles and Morro Bay.

$85–$95
1 rooms, 1 pb
Most CC
C-ltd/S-no/P-no/HC-ltd

BB | Continental plus breakfast
Includes small fridge, range top & microwave for guest use
Spectacular view of the ocean and Morro Rock Bay; large deck w/ sitting area & firepit; satellite TV

LOWER LAKE

Spirit Lake B&B
11865 Candy Ln

707-995-9090 | *Elaine Marie*
aquaticmassage@gmail.com | www.spiritlakebnb.com

Our vision as innkeepers was to create a very special place where anyone can come rest, relax and rejuvenate. The profoundly healing modalities of Watsu and Aquatic Massage are celebrated here.

$90–$145
4 rooms, 4 pb
Visa MC
C-ltd/S-no/P-no/HC-no

BB | Breakfast from an extensive menu
Drinks and snacks
98-degree warm pool, private 4 acre lake, canoes, Watsu & massage, lovely trails

CALIFORNIA
STATE FISH:
GOLDEN TROUT

MALIBU CANYON

The Malibu Bella Vista　**818-591-9255** | **818-645-1159** | *Beth & Michael Kin*
25786 Piuma Rd　　　　michael_kin@charter.net | www.malibubellavista.com

Located in Malibu Canyon, 5 miles from the Pacific Ocean. Nestled on the side of the Santa Monica Mountains with gorgeous views, thus the name Bella Vista. Children welcome. There are many amusement parks within a one hour drive.

$125–$165　　　　　　BB | Full breakfast
2 rooms, 2 pb　　　　　Please let us know if you have any special dietary needs
Most CC Cash Checks　　Wood fireplace, A/C, TV/VCR/DVD, spa, private bath, massage, wireless Internet
C-yes/S-ltd/P-ltd/HC-no

MAMMOTH LAKES

Cinnamon Bear Inn　**760-934-2873** | **800-845-2873** | *Russ & Mary Ann Harrison*
113 Center St　　　　　cinnabear1@aol.com | www.cinnamonbearinn.com

"Who needs the Ritz?" We feature friendly folks, full breakfasts, free hors d'oeuvres & fabulous ski packages. Enjoy forest view rooms with private baths.

$89–$198　　　　　　　BB | Full breakfast
22 rooms, 22 pb　　　　Snacks, complimentary wine
Most CC Cash　　　　　Sitting room, Jacuzzis, suites, fireplaces, cable TV, ski packages, WiFi in common areas
C-yes/S-no/P-no/HC-ltd

MARIPOSA

Restful Nest B&B　　**209-742-7127** | **800-664-7127** | *Lois Y. Moroni*
4274 Buckeye Creek Rd　restful@yosemite.net | www.restfulnest.com

We offer relaxation, old California hospitality, and the flavor of Provence in the beautiful foothills of the Sierra Nevada mountains near Yosemite. Private guest cottage.

$125–$150　　　　　　BB | Full gourmet breakfast
3 rooms, 3 pb　　　　　Hot tubs, swimming pool, A/C, spa, DVD & VCR
Visa MC Disc Cash
C-yes/S-ltd/P-ltd/HC-no

MCCLOUD

McCloud River　　　**530-964-2602** | *Kevin & Darlene Mathis*
Mercantile Hotel　　info@mccloudmercantile.com | www.mccloudmercantile.com
241 Main St

Get away from it all and spend your vacation at a McCloud hotel. The McCloud River Mercantile Hotel is in an historic setting surrounded by the beauty of tall pines and the grandeur of Mount Shasta.

$129–$200　　　　　　BB | Full breakfast
10 rooms, 10 pb　　　　Private bathrooms, central heat/air conditioning, spa, massage, yoga, classes,
Most CC Cash　　　　　merchandise store.
C-yes/S-no/P-yes/HC-yes

Alegria Oceanfront Inn & Cottages
44781 Main St

707-937-5150 | 800-780-7905 | *Elaine Wing & Eric Hillesland*
inn@oceanfrontmagic.com | www.oceanfrontmagic.com

Alegria is an ocean front B&B inn located in the village of Mendocino, CA. It features ocean view rooms and cottages, fireplaces, decks, a hot tub and a path to the beach. Interesting shops, galleries, fine restaurants, and the beach is just steps away.

$159–$299
10 rooms, 10 pb
Visa MC   Cash
C-yes/S-no/P-no/HC-ltd

BB | Full breakfast
Complimentary tea, coffee and hot chocolate
Coffeemaker, refrigerator, TV/VCR, microwave, hot tub, fireplace

Brewery Gulch Inn
9401 N Hwy One

707-937-4752 | 800-578-4454 | *Jo Ann Stickle*
manager@brewerygulchinn.com | www.brewerygulchinn.com

Set high on a bluff among natural landscaping overlooking Mendocino's Smuggler's Cove, each of Brewery Gulch Inn's 11 spacious & luxuriously appointed guest rooms are individually designed to capture views of the ocean.

***2011 Lanier Best West Coast Award Winner:
Best for All Seasons***

$210–$495
11 rooms, 11 pb
Most CC Cash Checks
C-ltd/S-no/P-no/HC-yes

MAP | Cooked-to-order gourmet breakfast
Wine hour with light dinner buffet; tea & coffee
Ocean views, televisions w/DVD, Molton Brown bath, fine linens, Wifi, ocean-view decks

Dennen's Victorian Farmhouse
7001 North Hwy 1
Little River

707-937-0697 | 800-264-4723 | *Fred Cox & Jo Bradley*
innkeeper@victorianfarmhouse.com | www.victorianfarmhouse.com

Romantic Victorian home that inspired artist Thomas Kinkade. Private oceanview cottage. Featherbeds, fireplaces, spa tubs, ocean access, breakfast in bed. Free hi speed wireless Internet. AAA Three Diamond. Affordable luxury. Romance without pretense.

$135–$270
11 rooms, 11 pb
Visa MC AmEx   Cash
C-ltd/S-no/P-no/HC-ltd

BB | Full breakfast delivered to room
Complimentary coffee and tea on request during the day and evening.
Spa tubs, wood fireplaces, feather beds, ocean access, in-room massage, free WiFi.
Concierge Services

Glendeven Inn
8205 North Hwy One

707-937-0083 | 800-822-4536 | *John & Mike*
innkeeper@glendeven.com | www.glendeven.com

Vogue Magazine's pick for Mendocino lodging, this 8-acre, luxury farm-stead offers ocean-view suites, fireplaces, private balconies, gardens, pastured llamas, farm-fresh eggs, in-room breakfasts, a wine hour in Glendeven's Wine Bar[n], and free WiFi.

Dreams Do Come True participating inn—Valid January–April

$135–$345
10 rooms, 10 pb
Most CC Cash
S-no/P-no/HC-ltd

BB | Full in-room 3-course hot breakfast
Wine & hors d'oeuvres included, the Wine Bar[n] offers local fine wines, cheeses & charcuterie
Sitting room, suites, wood fireplaces, llamas & chickens, fresh eggs, wine bar, full concierge

MENDOCINO

Headlands Inn B&B
10453 Howard St.

707-937-4431 | **800-354-4431** | *Denise & Mitch*
innkeeper@headlandsinn.com | www.headlandsinn.com/

Relax on a featherbed in a romantic oceanview room, with a crackling fire and an exceptional full breakfast lovingly prepared & delivered to your room! Charming 1868 New England Victorian Salt Box located in the Historic Village of Mendocino.

$99–$249
7 rooms, 7 pb
Most CC Cash Checks
C-ltd/S-no/P-no/HC-ltd

BB | Full breakfast served in rooms
Afternoon tea & cookies, complimentary juices, spring water & sherry always available in the parlor
Robes, hairdryer, CD am/fm clock radio, bath amenities, bedside chocolate, SF newspaper w/breakfast

**MacCallum House
Inn & Restaurant**
45020 Albion St

707-937-0289 | **800-609-0492** | *Herman Seidell, General Manager*
info@maccallumhouse.com | www.maccallumhouse.com

An 1882 vintage Victorian with charming garden cottages, in the heart of Mendocino village. MacCallum House is a collection of the finest properties within the village of Mendocino. Each of our rooms offers a romantic and peaceful environment.

$149–$399
30 rooms, 30 pb
Most CC Cash
C-yes/S-no/P-yes/HC-ltd

BB | Full gourmet breakfast MTO
Fine dining & full bar Lighter fair in Cafe
Gourmet breakfast, bar service, spa tubs, fireplaces, cottages, ocean views, Weddings, Elopements

Sea Gull Inn
44960 Albion St

707-937-5204 | **888-937-5204** | *Jim & Ayla Douglas*
seagull@mcn.org | www.seagullbb.com

Sea Gull Inn is one of Mendocino's first bed and breakfast inns—located in the heart of town, the Sea Gull Inn is best known for its ocean views, garden setting, distinctive guestrooms, and organic breakfast fare.

$75–$198
9 rooms, 8 pb
Visa MC AmEx   Cash
C-ltd/S-no/P-no/HC-ltd

BB | Organic breakfast
Choice of Coffee, tea or hot chocolate
Breakfast delivered to your room, fresh flowers, garden and ocean views, suites, wireless Internet

Seafoam Lodge
6751 N Coast Hwy One

707-937-1827 | **800-606-1827** | *Kathy Smith*
info@seafoamlodge.com | www.seafoamlodge.com/

The Seafoam Lodge is located on a sweeping hillside, overlooking the Pacific Ocean. Panoramic ocean views and breathtaking sunsets await our guests from every room. Our comfortable guest rooms offer an affordable getaway you may wish to visit many times.

$110–$265
24 rooms, 24 pb
Most CC Cash
C-yes/S-no/P-yes/HC-ltd

BB | Continental breakfast
Ocean views, TV, VCR, refrigerators, microwaves, enclosed hot tub, decks

MENDOCINO

**Stanford Inn
by the Sea—
Big River Lodge**
Hwy 1,
Comptche-Ukiah Rd

707-937-5615 | 800-331-8884 | *Joan & Jeff Stanford*
stanford@stanfordinn.com | www.stanfordinn.com

Welcome to Mendocino's most celebrated Resort Lodge—a bed and breakfast hotel on the Mendocino Coast. A truly elegant country inn in a pastoral setting. All accommodations with ocean views, fireplaces, decks, antiques, four posters and TVs.

**2011 Lanier Best West Coast Award Winner:
Best Educational Classes**

$195–$470
41 rooms, 41 pb
Most CC
C-yes/S-yes/P-yes/HC-yes

BB | Full breakfast
Afternoon hors d'oeuvres, wine, organic vegetables, vegetarian cuisine, full bar and dinner service
Indoor pool, hot tub, decks, nurseries, llamas, bicycles, canoe rentals, high speed internet, spa

MIDDLETOWN

Backyard Garden Oasis **707-987-0505 | 888-987-0505** | *Greta Zeit*
24019 Hilderbrand Dr   greta@backyardgardenoasis.com | www.backyardgardenoasis.com

Just 20 minutes from Calistoga, on the quiet side of the wine country, a AAA three Diamonds cottage in the mountains. Hot tub under the stars! King beds! Skylight! Great Breakfasts! Therapeutic Massage! Near Langtry Estate Winery and Harbin Hot Springs.

$95–$184
4 rooms, 4 pb
Most CC Cash
C-ltd/S-ltd/P-no/HC-yes

BB | Full Country Breakfast
Coffee & tea in your own Cottage
Hot tub, king bed, fireplace, A/C, fridge, skylight, wireless Internet, TV/VCR, phone, cottages

MILL CREEK

St. Bernard Lodge
44801 Hwy 36 E

530-258-3382 | *Jim Vondracek & Sharon Roberts*
stbernardlodge@citlink.net | www.stbernardlodge.com

Historical lodge with restaurant and seven rooms upstairs. Each room paneled with rustic knotty pine. Rooms overlook a broad meadow ringed with pine trees. Horse boarding available. Tavern area downstairs with pool table and T.V.

$89–$149
7 rooms, 0 pb
Most CC Cash Checks
C-yes/S-no/P-no/HC-no

BB | Full breakfast
Full restaurant and bar service. Afternoon wine and hors d'oeuvres.
Deck, stocked trout pond, Outdoor Hot Tub, indoor and outdoor games, robes and slippers, ice

MILL VALLEY

Mill Valley Inn
165 Throckmorton Ave

415-389-6608 | **800-595-2100** | *Justin Flake*
millvalleyinn@jdvhospitality.com | www.marinhotels.com/mill.html

This intimate hotel in Mill Valley California is tucked away in a redwood grove at the foot of majestic Mt. Tamalpais, just steps away from the bustling town plaza, where galleries, fine restaurants, boutiques and theaters abound.

$159–$419
25 rooms, 25 pb
Most CC
C-yes/S-no/P-no/HC-yes

BB | Continental breakfast
All day tea service with choice of herbal, green and black teas, evening wine reception
Fireplaces, cable TV, parking, voice mail, CD players, robes, Sun
Terrace Lounge, business services

MONTARA

Goose & Turrets B&B
835 George St

650-728-5451 | *Raymond & Emily Hoche-Mong*
goosenturretsbnb@gmail.com | http://goose.montara.com

A historic, classic B&B focusing on both B's: comfortable beds and four-course breakfasts. A slow-lane haven pampering fast-lane folks. Set in an acre of gardens.

$145–$190
5 rooms, 5 pb
Most CC Cash Checks
C-ltd/S-no/P-no/HC-ltd

BB | Four-Course Delicious Breakfast
Complimentary afternoon tea and treats available
Free WiFi, sitting room with wood stove, books, music; fireplaces, quiet garden

MONTE RIO

Rio Villa Beach Resort
20292 Hwy 116

707-865-1143 | **877-746-8455** | *Ron Moore & Bruce Behrens*
innkeepers@riovilla.com | www.riovilla.com

A cluster of green & white villa suites & studios surrounded by spacious decks, abundant gardens & lush lawns, sheltered by the redwoods. Located on the Russian River.

$110–$199
11 rooms, 11 pb
Most CC
C-yes/S-ltd/P-no/HC-ltd

BB | Continental breakfast
Decks, gardens, river, fireplace

MONTEREY

Jabberwock B&B
598 Laine St

831-372-4777 | **888-428-7253** | *John Hickey & Dawn Perez*
innkeeper@jabberwockinn.com | www.jabberwockinn.com

Once a convent, this charming Arts & Crafts style home sits just 4 blocks above Cannery Row & the Monterey Bay Aquarium. From the sunporch, overlook our gardens and enjoy fine Monterey Bay views. 3 rooms have Jacuzzis for two & 4 have fireplaces.

$169–$299
7 rooms, 7 pb
Visa MC   Cash Checks
C-ltd/S-no/P-no/HC-no

BB | Full breakfast
5:00 hors d'oeuvres, sherry, wine & other beverages, fresh baked cookies
Sitting room, sun porch, 3 rooms with Jacuzzis, suite, massage by arrangement,
bocce ball court

MONTEREY

Old Monterey Inn
500 Martin St

831-375-8284 | 800-350-2344 | *Patti Valletta*
omi@oldmontereyinn.com | www.oldmontereyinn.com

Classic English-style Tudor amid lush gardens. Exceptionally romantic. Service oriented inn with privacy valued. Breakfasts in bed are not to be missed.

$269–$449
10 rooms, 10 pb
Visa MC   Cash Checks
C-ltd/S-no/P-ltd/HC-ltd

BB | Full gourmet breakfast
Tea, evening hors d'oeuvres, wine, breakfast in bed
All rooms have fireplace, 5 whirlpool tubs for 2, robes, hairdryers, weddings, gardens, spa

MOSS BEACH

Seal Cove Inn
221 Cypress Ave

650-728-4114 | 800-995-9987 | *Dana Kelley*
sealcoveinn@foursisters.com | www.sealcoveinn.com

Just 24 miles south of San Francisco, this serene hideaway is spectacularly set amongst a meadow of wildflowers and bordered by towering cypress trees. Enjoy secluded beaches, watch frolicking seals, and the beautiful ocean bluffs of Half Moon Bay.

$215–$350
10 rooms, 10 pb
Most CC Cash
C-yes/S-no/P-no/HC-yes

BB | Full breakfast
Afternoon wine, tea & hors d' oeuvres, freshly-baked cookies, drinks available throughout the day
Executive board room for small meetings up to 14, daily housekeeping, robes, fireplaces

MOSS LANDING

Captain's Inn at
Moss Landing
8122 Moss Landing Rd

831-633-5550 | *Capt. Yohn & Melanie Gideon*
res@captainsinn.com | www.captainsinn.com

Waterfront views with plush top beds, soaking tubs or romance showers, spa bath soaps, fresh flowers & glowing fireplaces. Snuggle & cuddle under comforters & quilts with feather pillows.

$145–$275
10 rooms, 10 pb
Visa MC   Cash
C-ltd/S-no/P-no/HC-yes

BB | Full breakfast
Fresh evening cookies, snacks on Fri and Sat., Early bird brown bag breakfasts for early starters
High speed internet, Fresh flowers, fireplaces, cozy robes, phone w/voice mail, TV, feather pillows

MT. SHASTA

Mount Shasta
Ranch B&B
1008 WA Barr Rd

530-926-3870 | 877-926-3870 | *Mary & Bill Larsen*
mbenton1@snowcrest.net | www.stayinshasta.com

This Northern California, 2-story ranch house offers affordable elegance in a historical setting. Present-day guests can still enjoy the unique atmosphere and mood of those early years which are reflected in the Mt. Shasta Ranch Bed & Breakfast.

$70–$180
12 rooms, 5 pb
Most CC Checks
C-yes/S-no/P-yes/HC-no

BB | Full breakfast
Afternoon tea, wine, snacks
Sitting room, library, ping-pong, pool tables, TV & phone in room

California

Dunbar House, 1880
271 Jones St

209-728-2897 | *Arline & Richard Taborek*
innkeep@dunbarhouse.com | www.dunbarhouse.com

Intimate and authentically historic Italianate style bed & breakfast inn that offers guests a refreshing sense of ease, personal comfort, fine accommodations, hospitality, and unforgettable country cuisine. Walking distance to Main Street.

$210–$290
5 rooms, 5 pb
Most CC
S-no/P-no/HC-no

BB | Full country breakfast
Fresh baked cookies, comp. appetizer plate & local bottle of wine, port, sherry & chocolates
Lovely gardens, sitting rooms, library, gas-burning stoves, clawfoot tubs, TVs, DVD.

The Victoria Inn
402 Main St H

209-728-8933 | *Michael Ninos*
victoria_inn@sbcglobal.net | www.victoriainn-murphys.com/

Charming inn on historic Main Street in Murphys, CA. In the heart of Gold Country, Calaveras County. Fireplaces and wood stoves, clawfoot tubs or spas, eclectic furnishings. 3 large suites, 10 guest rooms and 4 vacation rentals.

$128–$385
17 rooms, 17 pb
Most CC Cash
C-ltd/S-no/P-no/HC-yes

BB | Continental plus breakfast
Fireplaces, woodstoves, clawfoot tubs or spas

NAPA

Beazley House
1910 1st Street

707-257-1649 | **800-559-1649** | *Carol & Jim Beazley*
innkeeper@beazleyhouse.com | www.beazleyhouse.com

Beazley House is a beautifully kept 1902 masterpiece! Elegant guest rooms have private baths and garden views. This Napa Valley Bed and Breakfast includes in-room whirlpool tubs, spa services, free wireless high speed Internet, fireplaces & lush gardens.

$150–$340
11 rooms, 11 pb
Visa MC   Cash
C-ltd/S-ltd/P-yes/HC-ltd

BB | Full gourmet breakfast
Complimentary sherry & fresh baked Chocolate Chip Cookies daily, Daily Wine & Cheese Hour.
HDTVs, fireplaces, garden, in-room whirlpool tubs, wireless internet, Concierge, Dog friendly

Bel Abri
837 California Blvd

707-226-5825 | **877-561-6000** | *Mary Alice Bashford*
info@belabri.net | www.belabri.net

Welcome to the Bel Abri, French for Beautiful Shelter. This 15-room French Country Inn is located just off I-29 and First St in the revitalized town of Napa, nestled in the heart of the famous Napa Valley.

$139–$309
15 rooms, 15 pb
Most CC Cash
C-ltd/S-no/P-no/HC-yes

BB | Full breakfast
For a late night snack, we have a mini refrigerator and honor basket, evening wine & cheese
Egyptian cotton linens, vanities, plush robes, CD/clock radio, cable TV, wine tasting accommodations

NAPA

Blackbird Inn
1755 First St

707-226-2450 | 888-567-9811 | *Emily Deeter*
blackbirdinn@foursisters.com | www.blackbirdinnnapa.com

Blackbird Inn offers the intimacy of a vintage hideaway, yet is an easy walk to many shops and restaurants. With its spacious front porch, huge stone fireplace and liberal use of fine woods, Blackbird Inn creates a warm, welcoming atmosphere.

$160–$285
8 rooms, 8 pb
Most CC Cash
C-yes/S-no/P-ltd/HC-yes

BB |Full breakfast
Afternoon wine, tea & hors d' oeuvres, freshly-baked cookies, drinks available throughout the day
Porch, fireplace, downtown, jet tubs, daily housekeeping, private patio, evening turndown, concierge

Cedar Gables Inn
486 Coombs St

707-224-7969 | 800-309-7969 | *Ken & Susie Pope*
info@cedargablesinn.com | www.cedargablesinn.com/

Built in 1892, this 10,000 square foot Shakespearean mansion contains many intriguing rooms, winding staircases, an Old English Tavern and of course secret passageways. There are full bathrooms in all 9 rooms. Cooking classes are paired with Napa wines.

$199–$359
9 rooms, 9 pb
Most CC Cash
C-ltd/S-ltd/P-no/HC-no

BB | 3 Course Gourmet Breakfast
Chocolate chip cookies, evening wine & cheese in the Tavern, fruits, sodas & teas all day
Jacuzzi tubs, bath bombs, port, chocolates, robes, blow dryer, WiFi, concierge, large screen TV

Churchill Manor
485 Brown St

707-253-7733 | 800-799-7733 | *Joanna Guidotti & Brian Jensen*
Be@churchillmanor.com | www.churchillmanor.com

Magnificent restored 1889 mansion on an acre of beautiful grounds. First home listed on the National Historic Register. Walk to Downtown Napa restaurants. Great staff, great food, great rooms! Complimentary croquet and tandem bicycles to tour Old Town.

$175–$345
10 rooms, 10 pb
Most CC Cash Checks
C-ltd/S-no/P-no/HC-ltd

BB | Full gourmet breakfast
Evening wine reception, tea & coffee service, afternoon sweets
Gardens, veranda, fireplaces, 2-person tubs, 2-person showers, WiFi, croquet, tandem bikes, TV/DVD

Hennessey House B&B
1727 Main St

707-226-3774 | *Kevin & Lorri Walsh*
inn@hennesseyhouse.com | www.hennesseyhouse.com

Napa's 1889 Queen Anne Victorian B&B. "A Great Place to Relax." Walk to restaurants and shops. Share wine and conversation by the garden fountain.

$129–$329
10 rooms, 10 pb
Most CC
C-ltd/S-no/P-no/HC-no

BB | Full scrumptious breakfast
Complimentary wine & cheese, afternoon tea
Patio & garden, parlor with flat panel TV, WiFi, sauna, whirlpool tubs & fireplaces in some rooms

California | Bed and Breakfast

NAPA

Hillview Country Inn
1205 Hillview Ln

707-224-5004 | *Al & Susie Hasenpusch*
info@hillviewinnnapa.com | www.hillviewinnnapa.com

Spectacular 100-year-old estate. Each guest suite is distinctively decorated, with queen size bed, private bath, fruit and wine upon arrival, and a sweeping view of Napa Valley.

$175–$275
4 rooms, 4 pb
Most CC Cash
C-ltd/S-ltd/P-no/HC-no

BB | Full breakfast
Cookies, candy, wine, bottled water, soda, coffee
Living room, deck & lawn area, cable TV

Inn on Randolph
411 Randolph St

707-257-2886 | **800-670-6886** | *Deborah Coffee*
innonrandolph@aol.com | www.innonrandolph.com

Situated on one-half acre of landscaped grounds in historic "Old Town" Napa, you'll enjoy the serenity of a quiet residential neighborhood within walking distance of popular restaurants, tasting salons and entertainment venues.

$149–$349
10 rooms, 10 pb
Most CC
C-ltd/S-ltd/P-no/HC-yes

BB | Full breakfast
Sweet treats, coffee, tea
Parlor, library, game room, grand piano, gardens with patio, sundeck, gazebo, fireplace, spa

McClelland-Priest
B&B Inn
569 Randolph St

707-224-6875 | **800-290-6881** | *Celeste Carducci*
celeste@mcclellandpriest.com | www.mcclellandpriest.com/

Experience the Napa Valley from the stately elegance of the McClelland Priest B&B Inn. Originally built in 1879 with a stained glass entry, ornate ceilings, spacious rooms, European ambience, modern comforts & luxury that sets this B&B apart from others.

$159–$269
6 rooms, 6 pb
Most CC
C-ltd/S-no/P-ltd/HC-no

BB | Gourmet breakfast
Evening hors d'oeuvres, wine receptions
Spa, en-suite Jacuzzis & fireplaces, evening receptions, self-guided winery tours, concierge service

Oak Knoll Inn
2200 E Oak Knoll Ave

707-255-2200 | *Barbara Passino & John Kuhlmann*
oakknollinn@aol.com | www.oakknollinn.com

Romantic, elegant stone country inn surrounded by vineyards and panoramic views in the Napa Valley. Spacious rooms with woodburning fireplaces. Napa's top rated inn has an exceptional concierge service, nearby gym, great rooms, views and food.

$350–$750
4 rooms, 4 pb
Visa MC   Cash Checks
C-ltd/S-ltd/P-no/HC-ltd

BB | Full multi-course breakfast
Substantial evening wine hour & hors d'oeuvres, usually with small winery representative, AM coffee
Complimentary wine, in-room spa services, swimming pool, free use of nearby gym, concierge

NAPA

Stahlecker House
1042 Easum Dr

707-257-1588 | **800-799-1588** | *Ron & Ethel Stahlecker*
stahlbnb@aol.com | www.stahleckerhouse.com

Stahlecker House, a secluded, quiet, charming Bed and Breakfast located on 1.5 acres of lush manicured lawns and flowering gardens. Close to the Napa Valley Wine Train, it is a nostalgic gem of the Napa Valley. Three Course Breakfast. Fireplaces and HDTV.

$112–$349
5 rooms, 5 pb
Most CC Cash
C-yes/S-ltd/P-no/HC-ltd

BB | Full Candlelight Breakfast
Coffee, sodas, lemonade, tea, chocolate chip cookies, brownies, cakes.
Gardens, Creek setting, Sun deck, free WiFi, sitting room, spas in suites, free off street parking

The Inn on First
1938 First St

707-253-1331 | **866-253-1331** | *Jim Gunther & Jamie Cherry*
innkeeper@theinnonfirst.com | www.theinnonfirst.com

The Inn On First is the premier Napa Valley Bed and Breakfast experience for foodies. A unique breakfast awaits you with every visit.

$205–$385
10 rooms, 10 pb
Most CC Cash
S-no/P-ltd/HC-ltd

BB | Full Gourmet Breakfast
Sparkling wine, truffles, specialty refreshments & baked goods are waiting for you upon arrival
Whirlpool tubs, fireplaces in all rooms, private bathrooms, concierge service, free WiFi

NEVADA CITY

Emma Nevada House
528 E Broad St

530-265-4415 | **800-916-EMMA** | *Andrew & Susan Howard*
emmanevada@comcast.net | www.emmanevadahouse.com

This charming home has been carefully restored and sparkles like a jewel from an abundance of antique windows, one of many marvelous architectural details. For the ultimate in gracious living and relaxation plan your next getaway at The Emma Nevada House.

$169–$249
6 rooms, 6 pb
Most CC
C-yes/S-no/P-no/HC-ltd

BB | Full breakfast
Afternoon tea, dessert, non-alcoholic beverage, or a favorite made-to-order espresso drink
A/C, bath robes, fireplace, whirlpool tub, cable TV, business facilities, library, laundry, weddings

Parsonage B&B
427 Broad St.

530-265-9478 | *Patti Woomer*
captcshea@yahoo.com | www.theparsonage.net

The Parsonage Bed & Breakfast, located in Historic downtown Nevada City, is one of the best and most convenient bed and breakfast locations in the area. This B&B is full of history dating back to the mid-1800s.

$90–$195
6 rooms, 6 pb
Visa MC AmEx   Cash Checks
C-ltd/S-no/P-no/HC-ltd

BB | Full Breakfast

NEWPORT BEACH

Little Inn by the Bay
2627 Newport Blvd

949-673-8800 | 800-438-4466 | *Gita, Rahul & Viru*
reservations@littleinnbythebay.com | www.littleinnbythebay.com

Thanks to its abundance of sun, surf, sand and shopping, everything you need for the perfect Newport Beach vacation can be found at the Little Inn By the Bay, one of the best Newport Beach hotels!

$100–$300
18 rooms, 18 pb
Most CC Cash
C-yes/S-no/P-no/HC-ltd

BB | Continental breakfast
Beach equipment, bicycles, chairs, boogie board etc., WiFi, MP3 line-in, HDTV
& luxurious rooms

NIPTON

Hotel Nipton
107355 Nipton Rd

760-856-2335 | *Jerry & Roxanne Freeman*
hotel@nipton.com | www.nipton.com

Hotel Nipton, a romantic adobe inn, was a favorite of 1920s silent film star Clara Bow. Located in Mojave National Preserve.

$78.65
5 rooms, 0 pb
Visa MC Disc Cash
C-yes/S-no/P-no/HC-ltd

BB | Continental breakfast
Restaurant also serves delicious lunch & dinner, catering for groups also available
Outdoor hot tubs, seclusion, mountain biking, parlor

OAKHURST

Hounds Tooth Inn
42071 Hwy 41

559-642-6600 | 888-642-6610 | *Williams - Kiehlmeier*
robray@sti.net | www.houndstoothinn.com

12 room Victorian style inn located 12 miles from Yosemite's Southern entrance in Oakhurst, 6 miles from Bass Lake. One luxury cottage available.

$95–$225
12 rooms, 12 pb
Most CC
C-ltd/S-no/P-no/HC-yes

BB | Full breakfast
Afternoon wine, tea and coffee
Library, Jacuzzis and mini suites available, rooms with fireplaces, cable TV, sitting room

Pine Rose Inn
41703 Rd 222

559-642-2800 | 866-642-2800 | *Anita & Greg Griffin*
pineroseinn@sti.net | www.pineroseinn.com

This quaint 9 room Inn, nestled within the Sierra Mountains, offers the peace and tranquility of the surrounding national forest. We also have vacation houses.

$79–$179
9 rooms, 9 pb
Visa MC   Cash
C-yes/S-ltd/P-yes/HC-no

BB | Hot country breakfast
Complimentary wine, tea, coffee
Rose gardens, weddings, Jacuzzis, in-room spas, kitchens, fireplaces

OCCIDENTAL

Inn at Occidental
3657 Church St

707-874-1047 | 800-522-6324 | *Jerry & Tina Wolsborn*
innkeeper@innatoccidental.com | www.innatoccidental.com

A gem nestled among giant redwoods, near vineyards and wineries, orchards, the Russian River and the ocean. Antiques and comfortable furnishings offer charm and elegance exceeded only by hospitality and a gracious staff.

$199–$339
18 rooms, 18 pb
Visa MC AmEx   Cash
C-ltd/S-no/P-yes/HC-yes

BB | Full breakfast
Coffee, tea, cocoa, sweet treats, wine & cheese
Private bath/spa tub, WiFi, phone, radio/CD player, fireplace, A/C, hairdryer, bathrobe, computer

OJAI

Emerald Iguana Inn
110 Pauline St

805-646-5277 | *Julia Whitman*
innkeeper@iguanainnsofojai.com | www.iguanainnsofojai.com

This property perfectly exemplifies the charm of the Ojai Valley. Exquisitely designed and decorated cottages and rooms in an extraordinarily beautiful and serene setting.

$169–$389
12 rooms, 12 pb
Most CC Cash
S-ltd/P-no/HC-ltd

BB | Continental breakfast
Snacks
Jacuzzis, swimming pool, suites, clawfoot tub, fireplace, cable TV

Lavender Inn
210 E Matilija St

805-646-6635 | 877-646-6635 | *Kathy Hartley*
innkeeper@lavenderinn.com | www.lavenderinn.com

Leave it all behind at Ojai's most sophisticated, boutique hotel The Lavender Inn. A charming 1874 historic inn with private, enchanting gardens located in Ojai Village, with across from shops, galleries and restaurants. The gardens are breathtaking!

$115–$300
8 rooms, 6 pb
Most CC Cash
C-yes/S-no/P-yes/HC-no

BB | Full fresh breakfast
Wine & cheese & hors d'oeuvres, cooking classes
Events & garden weddings, cooking classes, on-site day spa, cancer retreat, romantic, jacuzzi

The Blue Iguana Inn
11794 N Ventura Ave

805-646-5277 | *Julia Whitman*
innkeeper@blueiguanainn.com | www.blueiguanainn.com

Called "Hip & Stylish" by Sunset Magazine, the Blue Iguana is uniquely decorated, with one-of-a-kind furnishings from Mexico & throughout the world & original artwork from local artists.

$119–$299
12 rooms, 12 pb
Most CC
C-yes/S-ltd/P-yes/HC-yes

BB | Continental breakfast
Snacks
Jacuzzis, swimming pool, cable TV, single guestrooms

OJAI

The Ojai Retreat
160 Besant Road

805-646-2536 | *Ulrich, Clare & Teresa*
info@ojairetreat.com | http://ojairetreat.org

With spectacular views from all guest rooms, the Ojai Retreat is a haven of beauty and tranquility. Nestled on a five-acre hilltop with lush gardens and walkways, the Ojai Retreat offers twelve completely renovated guest rooms.

$79–$249
12 rooms, 10 pb
Visa MC   Cash Checks
C-ltd/S-no/P-no/HC-

BB | European Style Buffet
free WIFI, 5 acres of gardens, small library, living & meeting room, yoga classes, massage

PACIFIC GROVE

Gosby House Inn
643 Lighthouse Ave

831-375-1287 | **800-527-8828** | *Sharon Carey*
gosbyhouseinn@foursisters.com | www.gosbyhouseinn.com

Located on the Monterey Peninsula, Gosby House Inn has been welcoming guests for over 100 years. This cheerful yellow and white Victorian mansion, with its carefully tended gardens and central patio, sets the standard for gracious innkeeping.

$120–$225
22 rooms, 22 pb
Most CC Cash
C-yes/S-no/P-no/HC-yes

BB | Full breakfast
Afternoon wine, tea & hors d' oeuvres, freshly-baked cookies, drinks available throughout the day
Morning newspaper delivery, evening turndown, bikes, daily housekeeping, fireplaces, patio

Green Gables Inn
301 Ocean View Blvd

831-375-2095 | **800-722-1774** | *Honey Spence*
greengablesinn@foursisters.com | www.greengablesinnpg.com

Perhaps the most beautiful and famous inn located in California, the Green Gables Inn is a historic gem with panoramic views of the Monterey Bay. Every detail in this exquisite Queen Anne Victorian, built in 1888, has been meticulously restored.

$140–$305
11 rooms, 8 pb
Most CC Cash
C-ltd/S-no/P-ltd/HC-yes

BB | Full breakfast
Afternoon wine, tea & hors d' oeuvres, freshly-baked cookies, drinks available throughout the day
Some with fireplaces, spa tubs; daily housekeeping in all

Inn at 213 Seventeen Mile Drive
213 Seventeen Mile Dr

831-642-9514 | **800-526-5666** | Innkeeper
innkeepers@innat17.com | www.innat17.com

Set between Pebble Beach, Carmel, Monterey and close to the Big Sur coast. The area is renowned for its natural beauty, seasonal Monarch butterflies, grazing deer... along with the finest beaches, world class golf courses and Cannery Row.

$135–$340
16 rooms, 16 pb
Visa MC AmEx Cash
C-yes/S-no/P-yes/HC-yes

BB | Full breakfast
Complimentary hors d'oeuvres, wine; fresh-brewed coffee, light snacks
Garden, sitting & reading rooms, fireplace, spa

Martine Inn
255 Oceanview Blvd

831-373-3388 | 800-852-5588 | *Don Martine*
don@martineinn.com | www.martineinn.com

Steps from the sparkling blue waters of Monterey Bay, this lavish once private home, is now a meticulously restored mansion, where every fixture & furnishing is an authentic antique. Breakfast is served on silver, crystal & lace. WiFi is throughout.

$169–$499
25 rooms, 25 pb
Visa MC Disc
C-yes/S-no/P-no/HC-yes

BB | Gourmet Breakfast
Wine, hors d'oeuvres, water, soda, cookies, coffee, tea, cocoa, fresh fruit
Sitting rooms, Game room, Conference room, display of six Vintage MG autos, library, wifi,courtyard

Old St. Angela Inn
321 Central Ave

831-372-3246 | 800-748-6306 | *Jerry & Dianne McKneely*
dianne@oldstangelainn.com | www.oldstangelainn.com

Intimate Cape Cod elegance overlooking Monterey Bay. Walking distance to ocean and beaches, Monterey Bay Aquarium, Cannery Row, and restaurants. Delicious breakfast.

$139–$285
9 rooms, 9 pb
Visa MC
C-ltd/S-no/P-no/HC-ltd

BB | Full breakfast
Complimentary wine, snacks & cookies
Solarium, garden with waterfall and outdoor firepit, rooms with fireplaces & Jacuzzi tubs

Pacific Grove Inn
581 Pine Ave

831-375-2825 | 800-732-2825 | *Christine Weaver*
info@pacificgroveinn.com | http://pacificgroveinn.com

The Pacific Grove Inn is a boutique hotel in Pacific Grove California that provides charming accommodations with the intimacy of a bed and breakfast.

$115–$259
16 rooms, 16 pb
Most CC Cash
C-ltd/S-no/P-ltd/HC-yes

BB | Gourmet Breakfast served everyday
Hosted Wine reception with hors d'oeuvres with tea & water, freshly baked cookies at night with milk
Fireplaces, TV/VCR, video library, phone, in-room fridge, heated towel racks

Seven Gables Inn
555 Ocean View Blvd

831-372-4341 | *Susan Flatley Wheelwright and Ed Flatley*
reservations@pginns.com | http://thesevengablesinn.com

A truly romantic inn on the very edge of Monterey Bay. All guest rooms have ocean views, private baths and are comfortably furnished with a comfortable collection of fine furnishings. Guest comfort and service is of utmost importance. See you soon!

$199–$729
25 rooms, 25 pb
Visa MC AmEx
C-ltd/S-no/P-no/HC-ltd

BB | Full breakfast
Complimentary Monterey County wines & cheese served 4-6pm, housemade cookies & milk served 8pm.
Complimentary high speed wireless, evening turndown service, concierge services, daily room treats.

PALM DESERT

The Inn at Deep Canyon
74470 Abronia Trl

760-346-8061 | 800-253-0004 | *Linda Carter*
innkeeper@inn-adc.com | www.inn-adc.com

Charming hotel oasis in the desert. Quiet, secluded, heated pool, Jacuzzi and just blocks from El Paseo shopping district.

$111–$261
32 rooms, 32 pb
Most CC
C-yes/S-yes/P-yes/HC-yes

BB | Continental plus breakfast
In room coffee and tea
Jacuzzi, pool, suites, fireplace, cable TV, accommodate business travel, wireless Internet

PALM SPRINGS

Casa Cody Country Inn
175 S Cahuilla Rd

760-320-9346 | 800-231-2639 | *Therese Hayes & Frank Tysen*
casacody@aol.com | www.casacody.com

A historic 1910 adobe two-bedroom house, once owned by Metropolitan Opera star Lawrence Tibbett and frequented by Charlie Chaplin, is now open for our guests to stay in the heart of Palm Springs Village.

$79–$429
27 rooms, 27 pb
Most CC Cash Checks
C-ltd/S-ltd/P-ltd/HC-yes

BB | Continental plus breakfast
Whirlpool spa, 2 swimming pools, cable TV, WiFi

Orbit In
562 W. Arenas Rd.

760-323-3585 | 877-996-7248 | *Kevin Miller*
mail@orbitin.com | www.orbitin.com

Orbit In to the Palm Springs modern vibe, and leave your worries behind as you lounge in luxurious mid-century style. Breathtaking mountain views, poolside breakfast, cocktails, cruiser bikes and spa services —all served up at a small boutique hotel.

$119–$259
9 rooms, 9 pb
Most CC
S-ltd/P-no/HC-yes

BB | Continental breakfast
Complimentary Cocktails, sodas & water + chips & snacks.
Pool chiller, jacuzzi, bikes, in room massage, record players, concierge service, movies & books.

POSH Palm Springs
530 E. Mel Ave.

760-992-5410 | 877-672-6825 | *Susan and Michael Antal*
info@poshpalmsprings.com | http://poshpalmsprings.com/

POSH Palm Springs Inn is Palm Spring's newest luxury boutique Inn, where the true meaning of POSH is exemplified from the moment you arrive. Experience your own POSH vacation right here in the beautiful desert where the sun shines 365 days out of the year

free *Dreams Do Come True participating inn—Valid anytime*

$154–$249
11 rooms, 11 pb
Most CC Cash
S-ltd/P-no/HC-yes

BB | 3 Course Gourmet Breakfast
A complimentary light lunch is available to guests
We provide full Concierge Service for our guests.

PALM SPRINGS

Sakura Japanese
Style B&B Inn
1677 N Via Miraleste

760-327-0705 | *George Cebra*
george@sakurabedandbreakfast.com | www.sakurabedandbreakfast.com

A distinct, quiet, relaxing, authentic Japanese experience, with beautiful Japanese artwork, antique kimonos, handmade futons, shiatsu massage, shoji windows, and a Japanese garden.

$90–$125
3 rooms, 3 pb
Most CC
C-yes/S-ltd/P-no/HC-no

BB | Full breakfast
Breakfast can be served in either American or Japanese fashion, afternoon tea, snacks
Jacuzzis, swimming pool, cable TV, VCR, tennis courts within walking distance,
golf courses

Sea Mountain Inn,
Spa & Resort
9850 Donna Ave

877-928-2827 | **877-928-2827** | *Julie Dewe*
info@seamountaininn.com | www.nudespa.com

An award-winning spa retreat in Southern California. Enjoy 24-hour whirlpool and contemplate the mountains above you. Relax in the sun and swim nude in the fresh pool. The curative mineral waters have been used for centuries. Clothing optional.

$199–$999
18 rooms, 18 pb
Most CC
S-yes/P-no/HC-ltd

BB | Full breakfast
Wine & cheese, coffee, tea, iced tea, gourmet dining, appetizers & sweet-rices,
margaritas, lunch
Pools, sauna, spa services, 24 hr. club, flat-screen plasma & LCD TVs,
wireless Internet access spa

Villa Rosa Inn
1577 S Indian Trail

760-327-5915 | **800-457-7605** | *Jay*
villarosainn@att.net | www.villarosainn.com/

A lovely property in Palm Springs.

$79–$169
6 rooms, 6 pb
C-ltd/S-no/P-no/HC-ltd

EP |

PASO ROBLES

Ann & George's B&B
at Voladores Vineyard
1965 Niderer Road

805-423-2760 | *Ann & George Perham*
ann@voladoresvineyard.com | www.voladoresvineyard.com/bb.htm

Travel down a narrow country road to our secluded property overlooking beautiful westside Paso Robles Wine Country, in Central California. Queen-sized beds in spacious private quarters overlooking Rancho de Voladores Vineyard. Enjoy the incredible views.

$200–$250
2 rooms, 2 pb
Visa MC   Cash Checks
C-yes/S-no/P-no/HC-ltd

BB | Full Ranch Style Breakfast
A bottle of wine, a plate of fruit, cheese & crackers are provided in your room
Coffee maker, fresh flowers in room, hair dryers, robes, wireless Internet, discounts
for local wine

Asuncion Ridge
Vineyards & Inn

805-461-0675 | *Philip Krumal*
asuncionridge@hughes.net | www.asuncionridge.com

Asuncion Ridge Vineyards & Inn rests on 320 private, oak studded acres with unobstructed ocean and forest views. Featuring luxury suites, fine linens, patios and large private baths with soaking tubs. Mouth-watering, Chef prepared gourmet breakfasts.

$249–$349
3 rooms, 3 pb
3 public rooms
Most CC Cash
C-ltd/S-no/P-no/HC-ltd

BB | Full breakfast
Guests are encouraged to enjoy a glass of locally crafted wine and cheese in one of
Elegant suites, patios, private baths with soaking tubs, fine linens, stone fireplace,
private decks

Chanticleer
Vineyard B&B
1250 Paint Horse Place

805-226-0600 | *Carolyn Stewart-Snow*
info@chanticleervineyardbb.com | http://chanticleervineyardbb.com/index.php

A romantic B&B located on 20 acres in Paso Robles. Three rooms with luxury bath, fireplace, private deck and vineyard view. Walking distance to 8 wineries. Enjoy unpretentious comfort, thoughtful attention to detail with a touch of country charm.

$225–$275
3 rooms, 3 pb
Visa MC   Cash Checks
S-no/P-no/HC-yes

BB | Full breakfast
Wine in room on arrival
Full baths, luxury robes, iPod docking stations, fireplaces, morning kitchen,
iron & ironing boards

Creekside B&B
5325 Vineyard Dr

805-227-6585 | *Lynne & Dave Teckman*
LTeckman@percazocellars.com | www.thecreeksidebb.com

Enjoy a relaxing and luxurious get-away in the heart of Paso Robles' Wine Country. Wine tasting, gourmet breakfasts and privacy awaits. Private entrance, baths and kitchenettes. Discover for yourself the best kept secret on the Central Coast.

$199–$250
2 rooms, 2 pb
Most CC Cash
C-yes/S-ltd/P-ltd/HC-no

BB | Gourmet breakfast delivered to you
Complimentary local wine upon arrival
Porch, fireplace, kitchenette

Dunning Ranch
Guest Suites
1945 Niderer Rd

800-893-1847 | *Jim & Angela Dunning*
reservations@dunningranch.com | www.dunningranch.com

Dunning Ranch Guest Suites are located on 40 acres with vineyards and an award-winning winery just steps away... The Inn features very luxurious, private guest suites, a 1 bedroom suite and a 2 bedroom suite. Wine tasting is included.

$210–$350
3 rooms, 2 pb
Visa MC   Cash Checks
C-yes/S-no/P-ltd/HC-no

BB | Continental breakfast
Complimentary wine tasting at neighboring Estate winery, other winery tours
by appointment
Large decks, outdoor BBQ, porches, kitchenettes, wireless Internet, SAT -TV, luxury
bath products

PASO ROBLES

High Ridge Manor
5458 High Ridge Rd

805-226-2002 | *Cynthia Vaughn & James Roberts*
highridgemanor@hotmail.com | www.highridgemanor.net

High Ridge Manor offers magnificent views, tastefully appointed living quarters with oversized whirlpool tubs in every room. Enjoy the best views in Paso Robles from every room! We offer gourmet meals and an elegant dining experience for all guests.

$235–$345
3 rooms, 3 pb
Visa MC   Cash
S-ltd/P-no/HC-no

BB |Gourmet breakfast
Every day at 5:30pm hors d'oeuvres and wine served in the billiard room
Billiard room, wine cellar, fireplaces, large whirlpool tubs in room, private entrance & patios

Orchard Hill Farm
5415 Vineyard Dr

805-239-9680 | *Deborah & Doug Thomsen*
orchardhillfarm@aol.com | www.orchardhillbb.com

Wonderful setting on 36 pristine acres in the Paso Robles Wine Region. Beautiful gardens and views. Fresh flowers, antiques, beautiful interiors, comfy seating areas with fireplaces. Gourmet breakfasts and local wines included.

$230–$285
3 rooms, 3 pb
Visa MC AmEx
C-ltd/S-ltd/P-no/HC-no

BB | Full gourmet breakfast
Assorted beverages, local wines, fresh fruit, homemade baked goods
Fresh flowers, robes, featherbeds, down comforters, fireplaces, private decks, sitting areas

Seven Quails Vineyard
1340 Valley Quail PL

805-237-2598 | *David & Karina Brucker*
info@sevenquails.com | http://sevenquails.com/

Welcome to Seven Quails, an intimate, luxurious two suite Paso Robles, California bed and breakfast for two to six people. Explore the lovely town of Paso Robles. Sample wine with the owner/winemaker. Our home is your home.

$145–$195
2 rooms, 2 pb
C-yes/S-no/P-no/HC-ltd

BB | 3 Course Full Breakfast
Appetizers at dusk, libations, a vineyard tour
Vineyards, Wine tasting, comfortable suite, unmatched amenities and service to our guests

Winemaker's Porch at Frances James Vineyard
4665 Linne Rd

805-237-2168 | *Marlowe & Corinne Evenson*
FJVineyard@aol.com | www.francesjamesvineyard.com/bnb.html

The Winemakers Porch B&B sits on top of a knoll overlooking our Bordeaux vineyards. Our guests are invited to spend time sharing in our vineyard lifestyle. Luxury accommodations, complimentary bottle of wine, wireless Internet and gourmet breakfast.

$190–$265
3 rooms, 3 pb
Most CC Cash Checks
C-ltd/S-no/P-no/HC-ltd

BB | Full breakfast
Complimentary bottle of wine, appetizers & wine tastings in barrel room
Sitting area, soaker tub, fireplaces, wireless Internet, views of the vineyard

PENN VALLEY

Grandma's Room
19365 John Born Rd

530-432-3226 | *Helen Albano*
grandmasroom@gmail.com | www.grandmasroom.info/

Grandma's Room is reminiscent of a time when staying at Grandma's house meant good feelings, warm quilts, hospitality & homebaked cookies. Sit on the porch or beneath the shade trees, swim in the nearby river, watch the wildlife, and enjoy the quiet!

 Dreams Do Come True participating inn—Valid anytime

$75
1 rooms, 1 pb
Most CC Cash Checks
C-ltd/S-no/P-ltd/HC-yes

EP |
Home baked cookies upon arrival. Bottled water/cold/hot drinks/breakfast snacks/fruit—complimentary
Direct TV, DVD player, free WiFi internet, refrigerator, coffee maker, private bathroom, front porch.

PESCADERO

Pescadero Creek Inn
Bed & Breakfast
393 Stage Rd

650-879-1898 | **888-307-1898** | *Ken Donnelly*
ken@pescaderocreekinn.com | www.pescaderocreekinn.com

Offering a romantic escape on the California coast, Pescadero has secluded beaches, miles of hiking trails in redwoods and biking along farm fields. Gourmet organic breakfast and wine & Harley Farm goat cheese included. Walk to Duarte's.

$175–$255
4 rooms, 4 pb
Visa MC   Cash
C-ltd/S-ltd/P-no/HC-no

BB | Full gourmet organic breakfast
Afternoon wine & cheese from nearby Harley Farms Goat Dairy & wine we made ourselves
Free WiFi, snuggly down comforters, feather mattresses, antique claw foot tubs

PLACERVILLE

Albert Shafsky
House B&B
2942 Coloma St

530-642-2776 | **866-385-6466**
Rita Timewell & Stephanie Carlson
stay@shafsky.com | www.shafsky.com

Luxury in the heart of Gold Country. Queen Anne-style Victorian bed & breakfast, built in 1902, is close enough to stroll to town. Stay in Placerville & visit El Dorado wineries, Apple Hill, Coloma. 3 Diamond rated by AAA.

$135–$185
3 rooms, 3 pb
Most CC
C-ltd/S-ltd/P-no/HC-ltd

BB | Full hearty breakfast
Wine & snacks at check-in between 4-7, cookies in the early afternoon, guest refrigerator
Sitting room with library, games & satellite TV/VCR with movies, free high speed wireless Internet

PLACERVILLE

Blair Sugar Pine B&B
2985 Clay St

530-626-9006 | *William & Kay Steffen*
stay@blairsugarpine.com | www.blairsugarpine.com

A unique turreted 1901 Queen Anne Victorian bed and breakfast located in historic downtown Placerville, featuring hillside gardens, original woodwork and a history of romance. Walk to shops, restaurants and more.

$130–$160
3 rooms, 3 pb
Most CC
C-ltd/S-no/P-no/HC-no

BB | Full breakfast
Evening refreshments, tin of chocolates upon arrival
Book & video libraries, WiFi, central A/C, feather beds, private baths, sitting room, chocolates

Eden Vale Inn
1780 Springvale Rd

530-621-0901 | *Mark Hamlin*
innkeeper@edenvaleinn.com | www.edenvaleinn.com

Retreat to Eden Vale Inn, a casually elegant destination in California's Gold Country near Placerville. In this superb Sierra Foothills setting, accommodations are suffused in rich natural colors reflective of the lush gardens and natural beauty.

$149–$349
5 rooms, 5 pb
Most CC Cash Checks
C-yes/S-ltd/P-yes/HC-no

BB | Full breakfast
Beverages available throughout the day
DVD library, delivered newspapers, HDTV & spa tubs in some rooms

POINT REYES STATION

Marsh Cottage

415-669-7168 | *Wendy Schwartz*
wenpaints@gmail.com | www.marshcottage.com

Carefully appointed private cottage along Tomales Bay, near Inverness and Point Reyes National Seashore. Kitchen, fireplace, queen bed, deck overlooking the marsh and "Elephant" Mountain.

$145–$190
1 rooms, 1 pb
Cash Checks
C-yes/S-no/P-no/HC-no

BB | Full and continental plus
Complimentary coffee & tea
Kitchen, library & sitting area, fireplace, porch, sun deck

QUINCY

The Feather Bed
542 Jackson St

530-283-0102 | **800-696-8624** | *Bob Janowski*
info@featherbed-inn.com | www.featherbed-inn.com

Relax on the porch of this country Victorian inn. Enjoy the slower pace of a small mountain town. Savor fresh berry smoothies with a delicious breakfast. Experience the warmth & personal hospitality that are a tradition in Quincy and at The Feather Bed.

$120–$175
7 rooms, 7 pb
Most CC
C-yes/S-no/P-no/HC-yes

BB | Full breakfast
Afternoon tea, cookies & fudge
Sitting room, porch, Victorian garden, bikes, fountain, fireplaces, A/C

QUINCY

The Sporting Inn
505 Main Street

530-283-4300 | **877-710-4300** | *Claudia & Marvin Vickers*
thesportinginn@sbcglobal.net | http://thesportinginn.com

Located in Plumas County at the top of the Feather River Canyon in historic downtown Quincy, California. Walking distance to the museum, theaters, shops, restaurants. Charming old-style hotel atmosphere, with full, country breakfast. Internet access.

$95–$160
8 rooms, 3 pb
Most CC
C-yes/S-no/P-yes/HC-no

BB | Full Country Style Breakfast
Snacks and soft drinks
Wireless Internet access, upstairs facility, guide service available,
boat and trailer parking.

REDDING

Tiffany House B&B
1510 Barbara Rd

530-244-3225 | *Brady Stewart*
tiffanyhse@aol.com | www.tiffanyhousebb.com

Romantic Victorian within minutes of the Sacramento River, beautiful lakes, water sports, championship golf are all near by. Views of the Lassen mountain range. View of Calatrava Sundial Bridge from front yard.

$125–$170
4 rooms, 4 pb
Most CC
C-yes/S-ltd/P-no/HC-ltd

BB | Full breakfast
Complimentary refreshments
Sitting room, 1 room with spa, gazebo, swimming pool, parlor

REDWOOD CITY

Atherton Inn
1201 W Selby Ln

650-474-2777 | **800-603-8105** | *Tricia Young*
athertoninn@gmail.com | www.athertoninn.com

Warmth, luxury & hospitality abound in this newly built French style chateau. Conveniently located in the heart of the San Francisco Peninsula in a quiet residential neighborhood just one block from Atherton. We pamper you.

$139–$249
5 rooms, 5 pb
Visa MC AmEx   Cash Checks
C-ltd/S-ltd/P-no/HC-no

BB | Full breakfast
Cookies, cocoas, selection of teas, freshly squeezed orange juice, large fruit bowl
Free WiFi, TV, DVD, robes, hairdryer, message phone, Euro down pillows, elevator,
fireplaces in room

SACRAMENTO

Amber House B&B
1315 22nd St

916-444-8085 | **800-755-6526** | *Judith Bommer*
info@amberhouse.com | www.amberhouse.com

Just 8 blocks from the State Capitol in Midtown, on a quiet street of historic homes, the Inn offers the perfect blend of elegance, comfort, and hospitality. The Inn is perfectly located, walking distance from downtown, restaurants, shops and galleries.

$169–$279
10 rooms, 10 pb
Most CC
C-ltd/S-no/P-no/HC-no

BB | 2 course gourmet breakfast
Fresh cookies with beverage at turndown, coffee, tea & sodas any time
Jacuzzi tubs, fireplaces, free parking, WiFi, am beverage tray, gourmet breakfast,
in room massages

SAN ANSELMO

San Anselmo Inn
339 San Anselmo Ave

415-455-5366 | 800-598-9771 | *Peter & Julie McNair*
innkeepers@sananselmoinn.com | www.sananselmoinn.com

This European style Inn provides privacy and comfort along with warm hospitality. Our B&B is the perfect base for exploring Marin County, San Francisco, the Napa, Sonoma wine countries, and Pt. Reyes National Seashore. Hosts speak fluent German & French.

$99–$199
15 rooms, 13 pb
Most CC Cash
C-yes/S-no/P-no/HC-yes

BB | Continental plus breakfast
Our Sunflower Cafe offers a full breakfast and lunch menu
Suites, WiFi, cable TV, Irons ironing boards, Hair-dryers

SAN CLEMENTE

**Casa Tropicana
Boutique
Beachfront Inn**
610 Avenida Victoria

949-492-1234 | 800-492-1245 | *Rick & Sue Anderson*
info@casatropicana.com | www.casatropicana.com

Spanish-inspired architecture, ocean views, stylish and comfortable decor, thoughtful amenities and at the pier, beach and sand in San Clemente. Casa Tropicana, not just a San Clemente address, a California state of mind.

 Dreams Do Come True participating inn—Valid October 1–April 15 (holidays, special events excluded), may not be combined

$225–$775
8 rooms, 8 pb
Most CC Cash
C-yes/S-no/P-no/HC-ltd

BB | Extensive Buffet Breakfast
Each room has a mini-fridge stocked with a fun assortment of snacks and goodies—all complimentary!
fireplace, wireless, Jacuzzi tub, flatscreen TV, gated parking, beach bags, super comfy bed, more

SAN DIEGO

Carole's B&B Inn
3227 Grim Ave

619-280-5258 | *C. Dugdale & M. O'Brien*
carolesbnb@hotmail.com | www.carolesbnb.com

Historical house built in 1904, tastefully redecorated with antiques. Centrally located near the San Diego Zoo and Balboa Park. A friendly and congenial atmosphere. New large, saltwater pool.

$119–$259
10 rooms, 5 pb
Most CC
C-ltd/S-ltd/P-no/HC-no

BB | Continental plus breakfast
Cheese
Sitting room, conference for 10, salt water pool, hot tub, player piano, cable TV

CALIFORNIA
STATE ANIMAL:
GRIZZLY BEAR

SAN DIEGO

Jamul Haven
13518 Jamul Drive

619-669-3100 | *William Roetzsheim*
info@jamulhaven.com | www.jamulhaven.com

Fully restored 1890 Victorian mansion in the mountains 25 minutes away from downtown San Diego. The six acre compound features a health spa, game room, gym, pub, disco, spas, pool, waterfalls, and much more.

 Dreams Do Come True participating inn—Valid Monday–Thursday (not valid with other offers or discounts; limit one free night per stay)

$199–$349
4 rooms, 4 pb
Visa MC
C-ltd/S-no/P-ltd/HC-ltd

BB | Full breakfast
Pool, 2 spas, water slide, waterfalls, gym, game room, pub, disco, pool pavilion, business center

SAN FRANCISCO

Annie's Cottage
1255 Vallejo

415-923-9990 | *Annie Bone*
annie@anniescottage.com | http://anniescottage.com

Guestroom with private entrance, private bath, sitting area, deck, refrigerator & microwave. A country hideaway in the middle of San Francisco. Furnished with antiques.

$160–$175
1 rooms, 1 pb
Cash Checks
C-yes/S-no/P-no/HC-no

EP |
Coffee, tea, cereal provided
Near wharf & downtown, phone & answering machine, TV/VCR, queen bed, wireless Internet

Castillo Inn
48 Henry St

415-864-5111 | **800-865-5112** | *Mario*
castilloinn@yahoo.com | www.lanierbb.com/inns/bb25899.html

Gay accommodations mostly, though all are welcome. Clean, quiet and safe. Centrally located close to Castro & Market Streets. Ask about our seasonal discounts (holidays and special events excluded).

$65–$90
4 rooms, 0 pb
Visa MC AmEx   Cash
S-no/P-no/HC-no

BB | Self-serve Continental breakfast
Wireless Internet, phone, voice mail, refrigerator, microwave, parking at $10.00/night

Country Cottage
5 Dolores Ter

415-899-0060 | **800-452-8249** | *Richard & Susan Kreibich*
reservations@bbsf.com | www.lanierbb.com/inns/bb964.html

The Country Cottage B&B is a cozy country-style B&B in the heart of San Francisco. Four guestrooms are comfortably furnished with American country antiques and brass beds. It is a short walk to park, tennis courts, cafes, restaurants & bars. Free WiFi.

$79–$99
4 rooms, 0 pb
Visa MC AmEx
C-ltd/S-ltd/P-no/HC-no

BB | Full breakfast
Two sitting rooms, quiet garden patio, free WiFi Internet in every room, parking available

Inn on Castro
321 Castro St

415-861-0321 | *Jan de Gier*
Innkeeper@innoncastro.com | www.innoncastro.com

An incomparable way to experience San Francisco's charm and hospitality from the heart of the City's gay and lesbian community. The Castro. The Inn on Castro is at Castro and Market on the residential side with views over the city and the Bay.

$125–$195
8 rooms, 7 pb
Most CC
C-yes/S-no/P-no/HC-yes

BB | Full breakfast
Complimentary brandy
Living room, contemporary furnishings, fresh flowers throughout the inn, fireplace, library

Monte Cristo
600 Presidio Ave

415-931-1875 | **888-666-1875** | *Jack & Carl*
jack@montecristosf.com | www.BedandBreakfastSF.com/

The Monte Cristo Inn, a San Francisco bed and breakfast hotel in the city's exclusive and popular Pacific Heights neighborhood, offers the comfort and privacy of an historic inn—European style.

$129–$250
14 rooms, 14 pb
Most CC Cash
C-ltd/S-no/P-no/HC-ltd

BB | Full breakfast
Authentic antiques, Persian rugs, hardwood floors, flat-screen cable TV, complimentary WiFi

Ocean Beach B&B
611 42nd Ave

415-668-0193 | *Joanne*
oceanbeachbb@aol.com | www.oceanbeachbb.com

Distinctive B&B accommodations with views of the Pacific Ocean located in a quiet, residential neighborhood just six blocks from Ocean Beach and three blocks from Golden Gate Park in San Francisco.

$125–$205
2 rooms, 2 pb
Cash
C-ltd/S-no/P-no/HC-no

BB |C ontinental plus breakfast
Homemade cookies always available
Board games, hairdryer, iron, microwave, fridge, library, movies, wireless, Internet

Petite Auberge
863 Bush St

415-928-6000 | **800-365-3004** | *Eric Norman*
petiteauberge@jdvhospitality.com | www.jdvhospitality.com/hotels/hotel/11

With an ideal location, nestled between Nob Hill and Union Square, Petite Auberge is the perfect small hotel for a sightseeing trip to San Francisco or a special romantic getaway.

$139–$269
26 rooms, 26 pb
Most CC
C-yes/S-no/P-no/HC-

BB | Continental plus breakfast
Evening wine & hors d'oeuvres
Parlor, garden patio, fireplaces in most guestrooms

Queen Anne Hotel
1590 Sutter St

415-441-2828 | **800-227-3970** | *Michael Wade*
stay@queenanne.com | www.queenanne.com

*The Queen Anne offers unforgettable accommodations in an unforget-
table city! One-of-a-kind guestrooms & suites with luxurious private
baths. Some with original marble wetbars, fireplaces or Jacuzzi tub.*

$105–$199
48 rooms, 48 pb
Most CC Cash
C-yes/S-no/P-no/HC-yes

BB | Continental plus breakfast
Afternoon tea & sherry with cookies
In-room massage, dry-cleaning, event catering, complimentary limo service

Seal Rock Inn
545 Point Lobos Ave

415-752-8000 | **888-732-5762** | *Rick Landerman*
Reservations@SealRockInn.com | www.sealrockinn.com/

*Located far from the noisy downtown traffic and crowds, yet still in the
city in a resort-like location. We are just two blocks up the hill from
the historic Cliff House and Sutro Bath Ruins and four blocks north of
Golden Gate Park.*

$114–$167
27 rooms, 27 pb
Most CC Cash
C-yes/S-no/P-no/HC-yes

EP |
Restaurant on site
Patio and pool, limited undercover parking, free wi-fi

The Chateau Tivoli
1057 Steiner St

415-776-5462 | **800-228-1647** | *Nico Lizarraga*
mail@chateautivoli.com | www.chateautivoli.com

*Welcome to the Chateau Tivoli! An opulently restored Victorian mansion,
located in San Francisco's historic Alamo Square district, Chateau Tivoli
is one of the city's most charming bed and breakfast inns.*

$100–$290
9 rooms, 7 pb
Visa MC AmEx   Cash
C-yes/S-no/P-no/HC-ltd

BB | Continental plus breakfast
Continental Breakfast M - F; Weekend Champagne Brunch, daily evening wine
& cheese
Wedding facilities, concierge, formal parlors, American Renaissance furniture,
fireplace, suites

The Inn San Francisco
943 South Van Ness Ave

415-641-0188 | **800-359-0913** | *Marty Neely*
innkeeper@innsf.com | www.innsf.com

*Capturing the romantic spirit of the Victorian era, The Inn San Fran-
cisco invites you to be our guest and discover bed and breakfast comfort
and hospitality with a warmth that is distinctly San Franciscan.
Be welcomed as a friend.*

$120–$335
21 rooms, 19 pb
Most CC
C-yes/S-no/P-no/HC-no

BB | Full buffet breakfast
Complimentary fruit, coffee, tea, sherry
Sun deck, English garden, hot tub, phones, TVs, parking, Whirlpool tubs, suites,
complimentary WiFi

The Parsonage
198 Haight St

415-863-3699 | *Joan Hull & John Phillips*
theparsonage@hotmail.com | www.theparsonage.com

An 1883 Historical Landmark, Victorian home (formerly the McMorry-Lagan residence). The Parsonage's large, airy rooms are elegantly furnished with European & American antiques. Convenient to all San Francisco attractions.

$180–$250
5 rooms, 5 pb
Visa MC   Cash Checks
C-ltd/S-no/P-no/HC-ltd

BB | Multi-course breakfast
In the evening guests are welcomed home to a tray of chocolates and brandy!
Marble bathrooms, fireplaces, 2 parlors, library, goose down comforters
& imported linens, wifi

The Studio on Sixth
1387 Sixth Ave

415-504-2142 |
studioonsixth@gmail.com | www.studioonsixth.com

Studio apartment that opens onto an ornamental garden. Private entrance, queen-size bed, fully-equipped kitchen, separate bath and vanity, LCD TV, private phone, and wireless Internet

$65–$115
1 rooms, 1 pb
Most CC Checks
C-yes/S-no/P-no/HC-no

EP |
Coffee houses, cafes & excellent restaurants nearby
Garden, private entrance, fully equipped kitchen, LCD TV, telephone & wireless Internet

**Washington
Square Inn**
1660 Stockton St

415-981-4220 | **800-388-0220** | *Maria & Daniel Levin*
info@wsisf.com | www.wsisf.com

Situated in the very heart of San Francisco, the Washington Square Inn welcomes its guests with all the charm & comfort only a small European hotel can provide. Rooms feature European antiques, cable TV, soft robes and private baths. Apartment available.

$179–$329
15 rooms, 15 pb
Most CC
C-ltd/S-no/P-no/HC-yes

BB | Continental plus breakfast
Wine & hors d'oeuvres in the evening, tea
Self parking, lobby, antiques, fireplace, cable TV, robes, courtyard,
business services in lobby

White Swan Inn
845 Bush St

415-775-1755 | **800-999-9570** | *Eric Norman*
whiteswan@jdvhospitality.com | www.whiteswaninnsf.com

With crackling fireplaces in all 26 guestrooms and suites, the White Swan Inn is a romantic and atmospheric small hotel in the Nob Hill/ Union Square area.

$129–$309
26 rooms, 26 pb
Most CC
C-yes/S-no/P-no/HC-ltd

BB | Continental Gourmet Breakfast
Complimentary wine & hors d'oeuvres, afternoon tea and homemade cookies
Daily laundry & valet service, fitness room, computer station, WiFi,
meeting room w/ deck, concierge

SAN LUIS OBISPO

Bridge Creek Inn B&B **805-544-3003** | *Sally & Gene Kruger*
5300 Righetti Rd   info@bridgecreekinn.com | www.bridgecreekinn.com

Nestled near the vineyards of the Edna Valley, just ten minutes from historic San Luis Obispo, the Bridge Creek Inn offers pastoral views of the Santa Lucia Mountains and a spectacular nightly show of uncountable stars.

$150–$190   BB | Full breakfast
2 rooms, 2 pb   Light, gourmet refreshments, wine to whet your appetite
Most CC Cash   Sauna, outdoor hot tub, close to Historic SLO, secluded, wireless Internet, deck,
C-ltd/S-no/P-no/HC-no TV/DVD

Petit Soleil   **805-549-0321** | **800-676-1588** | *John & Dianne Conner*
1473 Monterey St   reservations@petitsoleilslo.com | www.petitsoleilslo.com

Find a touch of French village life at this delightfully renovated B&B. Individually themed rooms have whimsical art, custom furnishings, and CD players. Rates include wine pairings in the early evening and gourmet breakfasts.

$159–$299   BB | Full homemade breakfast
16 rooms, 16 pb   Complimentary wine & light appetizer in the evening
Most CC Cash Checks Outdoor patio, garden, getaway packages, wine tasting, private baths,
C-yes/S-no/P-yes/HC-ltd wireless Internet, telephones

SAN MIGUEL

Work Family   **805-467-3233** | *George & Elaine Work*
Guest Ranch   elaine@workranch.com | www.workranch.com
75903 Ranchita
Canyon Rd   *Stay on a 5th generation working ranch. Each room has a beautiful view with full breakfast and 3 course dinner included. On the ranch there are walking trails and horseback riding is available. Golf and world class wineries are in the area.*

$225   MAP | Full breakfast
6 rooms, 2 pb   Dinner & complimentary wine included. Lunch optional.
Visa MC   Cash Checks Sitting room, library, tour of farm
C-yes/S-no/P-yes/HC-ltd

SAN RAFAEL

Gerstle Park Inn **415-721-7611** | **800-726-7611** | *Jim Dowling*
34 Grove St   innkeeper@gerstleparkinn.com | www.gerstleparkinn.com

This romantic historic Inn is private and quiet like being in the wine country. It's rural setting in an urban environment offers tranquility yet easy access to all the Bay area. A comfortable, elegant hotel surrounded by rich fabrics and antiques.

$189–$275   BB | Full breakfast cooked to order
12 rooms, 12 pb   Complimentary evening wine & all day sodas & snacks
Most CC Cash   Main parlor with a fireplace, limited open kitchen, 2 1/2 acres of gardens,
C-ltd/S-ltd/P-yes/HC-yes woods & orchard

SAN RAFAEL

Panama Hotel
4 Bayview St

415-457-3993 | 800-899-3993 | *Daniel Miller*
info@panamahotel.com | www.panamahotel.com

A landmark inn and restaurant for 60 years, between San Francisco and the Wine Country. The Panama Hotel is celebrated for its eccentric charm.

$120–$195
10 rooms, 10 pb
Visa MC AmEx   Cash
C-yes/S-no/P-ltd/HC-yes

BB | Continental plus breakfast
Full restaurant
Historic dining room, tropical garden patio, room service

SANTA BARBARA

A White Jasmine Inn
1327 Bath St

805-966-0589 | *Marlies & John*
stay@whitejasmineinnsantabarbara.com | www.whitejasmineinnsantabarbara.com

Charming inn in prime residential downtown area and in the vicinity of beach. Inviting facility. Delightful amenities. Lovely grounds. Cozy parlor. Accommodations range from tastefully playful to romantically elegant.

$154–$309
12 rooms, 12 pb
Most CC Cash Checks
C-ltd/S-ltd/P-no/HC-no

BB | Full, hot, in-room breakfast
Wine & hors d'oeuvres, home made cookies, etc.
Jacuzzis & fireplaces, in-room massages, relaxing gardens, parking,
secure WI-FI throughout & more.

Bath Street Inn
1720 Bath St

805-682-9680 | 800-341-2284
Marie Christensen & Deborah Gentry
innkeepers@bathstreetinn.com | www.bathstreetinn.com

Located close to the heart of old Santa Barbara, the Inn offers the traditional warmth & hospitality of a European Bed & Breakfast.

$136–$295
12 rooms, 12 pb
Visa MC   Cash
C-yes/S-no/P-no/HC-ltd

BB | Complete gourmet breakfast
Afternoon refreshments of home baked cakes & cookies, tea & lemonade,
evening wine & cheese
Complimentary WiFi, video & book library, off street parking, upstairs & downstairs
sitting rooms

Casa Del Mar Inn
18 Bath St

805-963-4418 | 800-433-3097 | *Yun Kim*
yunkim@casadelmar.com | www.casadelmar.com

The Casa Del Mar Bed Breakfast Inn is the perfect accommodation destination of choice for a California beach vacation. A Mediterranean-style villa, quiet, charming and there is a Courtyard Jacuzzi. Several units with fireplaces & kitchens.

$124–$329
21 rooms, 21 pb
Most CC Cash
C-yes/S-no/P-yes/HC-yes

BB | Continental plus breakfast buffet
Evening wine & cheese buffet
Sitting room, hot tub, Internet access, pet accommodations, guest kitchen,
fireplaces, TV

SANTA BARBARA

Cheshire Cat Inn
36 W Valerio St

805-569-1610 | *Christine Dunstan*
cheshire@cheshirecat.com | www.cheshirecat.com

Enjoy the flower-filled gardens amidst the historical ambiance of our two historical Queen Ann houses built in 1894. Our romantic & cozy rooms, suites and cottages feature delightful decor and furnishings, some with in-room jacuzzi, fireplaces & patios.

$159–$425
18 rooms, 18 pb
Most CC Cash
C-ltd/S-no/P-ltd/HC-no

BB | Continental plus breakfast
Wine & hors d'oeuvres every afternoon
Hot tubs, balconies, fireplaces, spa treatments, outdoor Jacuzzi, gardens, WiFi

Old Yacht Club Inn
431 Corona Del Mar Dr

805-962-1277 | **800-676-1676** | *Eilene Bruce & Vince Pettit*
info@oldyachtclubinn.com | www.oldyachtclubinn.com

1 block from famous East Beach! Best location in the area! Complimentary home made breakfast. Free bike rentals, beach chairs and towels. Free wireless Internet & free parking. Complimentary wine & sherry. 1 block to 25 cent electric shuttle.

 Dreams Do Come True participating inn— Valid anytime; will offer a room upgrade

$119–$299
14 rooms, 14 pb
Most CC Cash
C-yes/S-no/P-ltd/HC-ltd

BB | Full breakfast
Afternoon wine & cheese social, sherry in all rooms, candy & chocolate chip cookies throughout day.
Free bike rentals, beach chairs & beach towels, free wireless Internet, whirlpool tubs,free parking

**Secret Garden
Inn & Cottages**
1908 Bath St

805-687-2300 | **800-676-1622** | *Dominique Hannaux*
garden@secretgarden.com | www.secretgarden.com

Guestrooms, suites and private cottages filled with charm, in a delightfully quiet and relaxing country setting. Four rooms with private patio and outdoor hot tubs.

$121–$255
11 rooms, 11 pb
Most CC Cash Checks
C-yes/S-no/P-yes/HC-no

BB | Full gourmet breakfast
Wine & hors d'oeuvres at 5 pm
Sitting room, garden, brick patio, bicycles, massages, weddings, private hot tub in cottage

Simpson House Inn
121 E Arrellaga

805-963-7067 | **800-676-1280** | *Gillean Wilson*
reservations@simpsonhouseinn.com | www.simpsonhouseinn.com

Welcome to North America's only AAA Five-Diamond B&B. This beautiful Inn is located in a prestigious historic neighborhood of downtown Santa Barbara, and secluded in an acre of English gardens.

$255–$615
15 rooms, 15 pb
Most CC Cash
C-ltd/S-ltd/P-no/HC-yes

BB | Gourmet vegetarian breakfast
Wine, Mediterranean hors d'oeuvres buffet, hot/cold beverages, afternoon tea & dessert buffet
Full concierge services, wireless Internet, private patios & decks, in-room massage, morning paper

The Orchid Inn
at Santa Barbara
420 W Montecito St

805-965-2333 | **877-722-3657** | *Riviera California Investments LP*
info@orchidinnatsb.com | www.orchidinnatsb.com

A stylish, contemporary bed and breakfast, two blocks from West Beach in Santa Barbara. The Orchid Inn offers a pleasurable escape to relax and feel at home in the charming ambiance.

$132–$259
8 rooms, 8 pb
Visa MC   Cash
C-ltd/S-no/P-no/HC-ltd

BB | Full hot breakfast
Afternoon wine tasting featuring renown Santa Barbara Winery select wines included in are room rates
Full service spa, Jacuzzi tubs, fireplaces, colorful decor, sitting areas, business accommodation

The Upham Hotel
1404 De La Vina St

805-962-0058 | **800-727-0876** | *Jan Martin Winn*
innkeeper@uphamhotel.com | www.uphamhotel.com

A Victorian treasure in the heart of downtown Santa Barbara. Constructed of redwood with sweeping verandas, the 1871 landmark is surrounded by an acre of gardens and combines the intimacy of a B&B with the convenience of a full-service hotel.

$220–$450
58 rooms, 58 pb
Most CC Cash
C-yes/S-no/P-no/HC-no

BB | Continental plus breakfast
Complimentary wine, coffee, tea, Louie's Restaurant
Garden veranda, garden, valet laundry, phones, WiFi

Villa Rosa
15 Chapala St

805-966-0851 | *Julia Finucan*
villarosainnsb@gmail.com | www.villarosainnsb.com/html/home.html

Let us pamper you in International style. Located just 84 steps from the beach. It exudes a warm, personal and sophisticated atmosphere. A cozy spa and pool are nestled in a walled-in courtyard for your privacy and relaxation.

$129–$339
18 rooms, 18 pb
Most CC Cash
C-yes/S-no/P-no/HC-ltd

BB | Continental plus breakfast
Wine & hors d'oeuvres served from 5 to 7 in the evening, sherry or port served from 9 to 10
Spa, pool, walled-in courtyard, garden, fireplace, conference facilities, dry cleaning, masseuse

SANTA CRUZ

Adobe on Green Street
103 Green St

831-469-9866 | *Brion Sprinsock*
santacruzadobe@gmail.com | www.adobeongreen.com

Peace and quiet just three blocks from downtown. Private bathrooms, fireplaces, jet tubs, the most comfy beds, parking & free WiFi. Midweek rates from $149. Last Minute rates Sun-Thurs: $129.

$149–$219
4 rooms, 4 pb
Visa MC
S-no/P-no/HC-ltd

BB | Continental plus breakfast
Sodas, bottled water, chocolates
Jacuzzi tubs, gas fireplaces, sitting room, courtyards, gardens, DVD library, DVD player in room

Cliff Crest
407 Cliff St

831-427-2609 | **831-252-1057** | *Adriana & Constantin Gehriger*
innkpr@CliffCrestInn.com | www.CliffCrestInn.com

Built in 1887 on Beach Hill above the Santa Cruz Beach Boardwalk, this historic Queen Anne Victorian overlooks the picturesque Santa Cruz Mountains and beaches. The Inn features 6 guest rooms, each with private bath and several with fireplaces.

$95–$265
6 rooms, 6 pb
Most CC
C-yes/S-no/P-no/HC-yes

BB | Full breakfast
Happy to accommodate special dietary needs
Sitting room, large garden, free parking

Pleasure Point Inn
2-3665 E Cliff Dr

831-475-4657 | **877-557-2567** | *Tara & Ivy*
Inquiries@PleasurePointInn.com | www.PleasurePointInn.com

Pleasure Point Inn is an oceanfront B&B at the famous Pleasure Point Beach and offers spectacular views of the Pacific Ocean. The Inn has a large roof-top deck where you can soak in the hot tub.

$225–$295
4 rooms, 4 pb
Visa MC   Cash
C-ltd/S-ltd/P-no/HC-yes

BB | Expanded Continental Breakfast
A welcome basket with goodies
Fireplaces, whirlpool tubs, 4 suites, TV, private phones, private baths, cable TV, iPod dock, WiFi

The Darling House
A B&B Inn by the Sea
314 W Cliff Dr

831-458-1958 | *Darrell & Karen Darling*
ddarling@darlinghouse.com | www.darlinghouse.com

A 1910 oceanside architectural masterpiece designed by William Weeks. Lighted by the rising sun through beveled glass, Tiffany lamps and open hearths, and the grace of genuinely open hearts.

$150–$295
7 rooms, 5 pb
Most CC
C-ltd/S-ltd/P-no/HC-ltd

BB | Continental plus breakfast
Complimentary beverages.   Fresh baked goodies.
Fireplaces, extra large bathtubs, fireplaces in rooms, retreats, weddings, free Wi-Fi,

West Cliff Inn
174 West Cliff Drive

831-457-2200 | **800-979-0910** | *Michael Hoppe*
westcliffinn@foursisters.com | www.westcliffinn.com

This distinctive inn is on a bluff across from Cowell's Beach and the famous Santa Cruz Beach and Boardwalk. The stately, three-story Italianate Victorian with its spacious, wraparound porch was completely renovated and features a breezy, coastal decor.

$185–$400
9 rooms, 9 pb
Most CC Cash
C-yes/S-no/P-no/HC-ltd

BB | Full breakfast
Afternoon wine, tea & hors d'oeuvres, freshly-baked cookies, drinks available throughout the day
Outdoor jetted hot tub, WiFi, evening turndown service featuring delectable Le Belge chocolates

SANTA ROSA

Melitta Station Inn
5850 Melita Rd

707-538-7712 | **800-504-3099** | *Jackie & Tim Thresh*
info@melittastationinn.com | www.melittastationinn.com

English cottage hospitality at its best. The inn is cozily furnished with the owners' European antiques, and lies opposite Annadel State Park for biking. It is central to all Sonoma and Napa wineries.

$159–$219
6 rooms, 6 pb
Most CC Cash
C-ltd/S-ltd/P-no/HC-ltd

BB | Full 3 course gourmet breakfast
English afternoon tea, snacks, tea & coffee, soft drinks all complimentary
Central air, ironing board/iron, free wireless Internet, spa & massage room with 40 jet hot tub

Vintners Inn
4350 Barnes Rd

707-575-7350 | **800-421-2584** | *Percy Brandon*
info@vintnersinn.com | www.vintnersinn.com

A European-styled estate in 92-acre vineyard. All king rooms offer patio/balcony with views of vineyards, gardens or courtyard & fountain. Award-winning John Ash & Co. Restaurant. Luscious grounds and Event Center. AAA Four Diamond rating.

$185–$550
44 rooms, 44 pb
Most CC
C-yes/S-no/P-no/HC-yes

BB |Continental plus breakfast
John Ash & Co. restaurant, Front Room Bar & Lounge, Vintners Inn Event Center, Wedding Pavilion
Wireless Internet, bell service, outdoor hot tub, walking trail, gym, massage room, bocce ball court

SANTA YNEZ

Santa Ynez Inn
3627 Sagunto St

805-688-5588 | **800-643-5774** | *Rick Segovia*
info@santaynezinn.com | www.santaynezinn.com

Discover Victorian grace and hospitality in the heart of Santa Barbara County wine country. Located just 3 miles from Los Olivos and Solvang, the Santa Ynez Inn offers lavish suites with fireplaces, Jacuzzi tubs and many amenities.

$255–$495
20 rooms, 20 pb
Most CC Cash Checks
C-yes/S-no/P-no/HC-yes

BB | Continental plus breakfast
Enjoy wine, hors d'oeuvres, evening desserts, a full gourmet breakfast in the morning
Whirlpool tub, balcony or patios, concierge service, fitness suite with sauna, flat screen HD TV's

SEBASTOPOL

Pearlessence Vineyard Inn
4097 Hessel Rd

707-823-5092 | *Linda and Greg Pearl*
info@pearlessenceinn.com | www.pearlessenceinn.com/

Come enjoy the gardens, tranquil pond, and our scenic vineyard. Private enough for a romantic weekend getaway while only a short drive to the Russian River, Bodega Bay, and area wineries.

$195–$245
1 rooms, 1 pb
Visa MC   Cash
C-yes/S-ltd/P-ltd/HC-ltd

BB | Full breakfast
Complimentary Bottled Water and Soft Drinks, In-Room Gourmet Coffee, Tea, Cocoa, and Hot Cereal, wet bar
New upscale furnishings, heated slate floors, original artwork, cable TV, plush robes

SHAVER LAKE

Elliott House
42062 Tollhouse Rd

559-841-8601 | 888-841-8601 | *Joanne & Greg Elliott*
elliotthouse@psnw.com | www.elliotthousebandb.com

Throughout the B&B, charming collectibles are mixed with stylish furniture, original watercolor paintings by local artists and fresh flowers. The array of warm, vibrant colors and soft lighting complete the design details of the B&B.

$159–$219
7 rooms, 7 pb
Most CC Cash
C-yes/S-no/P-no/HC-yes

BB | Full gourmet breakfast
Evening happy hour with California wines, homemade desserts, breakfast in bed, honor bars
Free Wi-Fi, gardens and decks, weddings, romance packages, honor bars, in-room frig, coffee, Dish

SHELTER COVE

Inn of the Lost Coast
205 Wave Drive

707-986-7521 | 888-570-9676 | *Justin Cordova*
sheltercoveinn@aol.com | www.innofthelostcoast.com/index.html

Freshly remodeled, the 3 diamond AAA rated Inn is perched high on the cliffs overlooking the beautiful Pacific Ocean. Enjoy affordable panoramic views north to Cape Mendocino and south over the rocky shoreline.

18 rooms, 18 pb
Visa MC Cash
C-yes/S-no/P-yes/HC-yes

BB | Continental plus breakfast
Fish Tank Espresso Gallery serving great coffee, espresso and daily treats.
Private balconies, internet Wi-Fi, Direct T.V., fireplaces, common areas, laundry facility, Hot Tubs

SOLEDAD

Inn at the Pinnacles
32025 Stonewall
Canyon Rd

831-678-2400 | *Jon & Jan Brosseau*
info@innatthepinnacles.com | www.innatthepinnacles.com

Mediterranean-style country inn with surrounding vineyard and hillside views. Romantic setting. Four miles to the Pinnacles National Monument (west entrance).

$200–$290
6 rooms, 6 pb
Visa MC Cash Checks
C-ltd/S-no/P-no/HC-yes

BB | Full breakfast
Wine & cheese
Sitting room, suites, gas fireplaces, private patios, air-jet tubs, swimming pool, wireless internet

SONOMA

A Victorian Garden Inn
316 E Napa St

707-996-5339 | 800-543-5339 | *Donna J. Lewis*
info@victoriangardeninn.com | www.victoriangardeninn.com

Let us spoil you at the Victorian Garden Inn. Just a short walk from Sonoma's historic town plaza, breakfast served in the garden, dining room, or in room, free WiFi, pool, and therapeutic hot tub. Everything a quintessential bed and breakfast should be.

$159–$359
4 rooms, 3 pb
Visa MC AmEx Cash Checks
C-ltd/S-ltd/P-no/HC-no

BB | Continental plus breakfast
Breakfast served in the garden, dining room, or in your room, afternoon tea or coffee & snacks
Therapeutic hot tub, swimming pool, lush gardens, on-site massage services, free WiFi, iPod docks

SONOMA

The Inn at Sonoma
630 Broadway

707-939-1340 | **888-568-9818** | *Rachel Retterer*
innatsonoma@foursisters.com | www.innatsonoma.com

Fall in love with the quiet pace, beautiful vistas and fabulous food and wine of the Sonoma Valley. Conveniently located just two blocks from the historic Sonoma Plaza, the Inn at Sonoma is the perfect destination for your Wine Country visit.

$205–$300
19 rooms, 19 pb
Most CC Cash
C-yes/S-no/P-no/HC-yes

BB | Full breakfast
Afternoon wine, tea & hors d' oeuvres, freshly-baked cookies, drinks available throughout the day
Hot tub, bikes, fireplace, wifi access

The Sonoma Hotel
110 W Spain St

707-996-2996 | **800-468-6016** | *Tim Farfan & Craig Miller*
sonomahotel@aol.com | www.sonomahotel.com

A wonderful vintage hotel (circa 1880) on Sonoma's historic plaza. Modern amenities have been added, including private baths, phones, TVs and A/C. Guests can walk to shops, historic sites and wineries.

$110–$248
16 rooms, 16 pb
Most CC
C-yes/S-no/P-no/HC-yes

BB | Continental breakfast
The Girl and The Fig Restaurant on site
A/C, TVs, phone with data port

SOUTH LAKE TAHOE

Black Bear Inn
1202 Ski Run Blvd

530-544-4451 | **877-232-7466** | *Kevin & Jerry*
info@tahoeblackbear.com | www.tahoeblackbear.com

A small luxury lodge with five guestrooms plus three cabins on a wooded acre in South Lake Tahoe. Close to the lake, restaurants, shopping, skiing, hiking, biking and boating.

$210–$315
10 rooms, 8 pb
Visa MC Disc
C-yes/S-no/P-no/HC-yes

BB | Full breakfast
Evening wine & cheese
Hot tub, fireplace, free WiFi, daily maid service, TV/DVD.

SOUTH PASADENA

Arroyo Vista Inn
335 Monterey Rd

323-478-7300 | **888-9ARROYO** | *Pat Wright*
info@arroyovistainn.com | www.arroyovistainn.com

Rooms with a view! This historical and newly restored 1910 Craftsman has 10 elegantly simple suites. Many have views; some have spa tubs; all are luxurious and calming.

$155–$300
9 rooms, 9 pb
Visa MC AmEx
C-ltd/S-ltd/P-yes/HC-ltd

BB | Full Homemade Breakfast
Fresh-baked cookies and gourmet candies, early evening wine, cheese and tea
Events & weddings, bridal showers, catering, wine cellar, parking, wireless Internet, reunions

Bissell House
201 Orange Grove Ave

626-441-3535 | *Janet Hoyman*
info@bissellhouse.com | www.bissellhouse.com/

1887 Victorian mansion beautifully appointed with antiques. 12 minutes and 100 years from downtown LA, we've received many commendations from CABBI. Members PAII, CABBI, CHLA and Pasadena & South Pasadena Chambers of Commerce.

$150–$350
7 rooms, 7 pb
Most CC
C-yes/S-no/P-no/HC-ltd

BB | Full breakfast 7 days a week
24 hour tea service. afternoon dessert.
Library, Premium cable TV/DVD (most rooms), Pool, in room data ports,
wireless Internet access

ST. HELENA

Ambrose Bierce House
1515 Main St

707-963-3003 | *John & Lisa Runnells*
ambrose@napanet.net | www.ambrosebiercehouse.com/

Located on Main street in Historic St. Helena, walk to fine dining and unique shopping. We invite you to experience the romantic charm of our 1872 Victorian bed and breakfast inn,right in the center of the finest wineries of Napa Valley.

$159–$299
4 rooms, 4 pb
Most CC Cash Checks
C-ltd/S-ltd/P-no/HC-no

BB | Full gourmet champagne breakfast
Premium wines & cheeses are served each evening
Hot tub, Jacuzzi tubs, canopy beds, antiques, A/C, satellite TV, wifi, warm hospitality

**Shady Oaks
Country Inn**
399 Zinfandel Ln

707-963-1190 | *John & Lisa Runnells*
shdyoaks@napanet.net | www.shadyoakscountryinn.com/

Romantic and secluded on 2 acres, among finest wineries of Napa Valley on Zinfandel Lane. Walk to wineries. Elegant ambiance, country comforts, antiques, fireplaces, port and fine linens in guestrooms. "Warm and gracious hospitality!"

$189–$269
5 rooms, 5 pb
Most CC Cash Checks
C-ltd/S-ltd/P-no/HC-ltd

BB | Gourmet champagne breakfast
Premium wines & cheeses are served each evening
Fireplaces, Roman pillared patio; innkeepers knowledgeable concierge,
private entrance, TVs, WiFi

The Ink House
1575 S. St Helena Hwy

707-963-3890 | 866-963-3890 | *Kevin Outcalt*
inkhousebb@aol.com | www.inkhouse.com

Treat yourself to Victorian elegance in the Napa Valley's world famous wine growing region. Among the vineyards, and neighbors to some of the finest wineries and restaurants with a fabulous gourmet breakfast, luxurious rooms with flat screen TV & Internet

$135–$260
6 rooms, 6 pb
Visa MC   Cash Checks
C-ltd/S-no/P-no/HC-no

BB | Full gourmet breakfast
Evening wine & appetizers included, sherry & port available
Parlor, VIP Winery pass, game room, bicycles, glass observatory, concierge services,
Internet access

ST. HELENA

The Wine Country
Inn & Gardens
1152 Lodi Ln

707-963-7077 | **888-465-4608** | *Jim Smith*
jim@winecountryinn.com | www.winecountryinn.com

Built to resemble a converted winery, this Inn sits atop a landscaped knoll overlooking the vineyards of Napa Valley. Casual, comfortable, green luxury is the hallmark of this renowned hostelry. Family built, owned and operated for over thirty years!

$215–$660
29 rooms, 29 pb
Visa MC
C-ltd/S-no/P-no/HC-ltd

BB | Full Buffet breakfast
Wine tasting & appetizers at afternoon social; complimentary evening restaurant shuttle service
Heated pool year round, balconies or patios, fireplaces, spa or hot tubs, daily tour to wineries

The Zinfandel Inn
800 Zinfandel Ln

707-963-3512 | *Jerry Payton*
www.zinfandelinn.com

English Tudor that looks like a castle in the vineyard. Located in the heart of Napa Valley. Two acres with a hot tub and beautiful lagoon pool. Acclaimed in Wine Spectator Magazine, Sunset Magazine, Food & Wine, *and* Best Places to Kiss.

$195–$325
3 rooms, 3 pb
Visa MC   Cash Checks
C-ltd/S-no/P-no/HC-no

BB | Full breakfast
Complimentary wine truffles on arrival, world famous cookie jar
Sitting room, whirlpool tubs, suites, fireplaces, cable TV, phones, A/C, YVI lagoon style pool

Wine Country Villa
2000 Howell Mtn Rd

707-963-9073 | **866-963-9073** | *Bill & Diane*
info@winecountryvilla.com | www.winecountryvilla.com

Wine Country Villa is set in a secluded and beautiful area with views of wooded hillsides, mountains and vineyards. Impeccably designed and appointed, it is an ideal retreat in the heart of the Napa Valley.

$125–$300
2 rooms, 2 pb
Visa MC AmEx
C-yes/S-ltd/P-yes/HC-no

EP |
Great room with fireplace, pool, spa, sauna, balconies, gardens. Well equipped kitchen & dining area

SUTTER CREEK

Foxes Inn
of Sutter Creek
77 Main St

209-267-5882 | **800-987-3344** | *Monique & Morgan Graziadei*
innkeeper@foxesinn.com | www.foxesinn.com

Victorian Jewel in historic downtown Sutter Creek. Walking distance to shops, restaurants, wine tasting and theater. Select your gourmet breakfast from the menu, made-to-order and served to each room /the lush gardens. The only AAA 4-Diamond Amador Cty.

$160–$325
7 rooms, 7 pb
Most CC
C-ltd/S-no/P-no/HC-ltd

BB | Choose from numerous entrees
Coffee, tea & homemade cookies
Clawfoot tubs, library, fireplace, TV, VCR, music systems, cathedral ceilings, private entrances

SUTTER CREEK

Sutter Creek Inn
75 Main St

209-267-5606 | *Lindsay Way*
info@suttercreekinn.com | www.suttercreekinn.com

The Inn has been open and serving thousands of guests for over 35 years. Spacious grounds, patios, fireplaces, 17 rooms and cottages, and 4 of Jane Way's famous swinging beds. Eclectic style. Enjoy relaxed hospitality.

$93–$195
17 rooms, 17 pb
Visa MC Disc Cash Checks
C-ltd/S-ltd/P-no/HC-ltd

BB | Full breakfast
Complimentary refreshments
Large living room, piano, library, A/C, gardens, massage, wood-burning fireplaces
& swinging beds!

TAHOE CITY

**Cottage Inn at
Lake Tahoe, Inc.**
1690 W Lake Blvd

530-581-4073 | **800-581-4073** | *Susanne Muhr*
cottage@ltol.com | www.thecottageinn.com

The Cottage Inn, 2 miles south of Tahoe City, features original knotty pine paneling throughout, with unique themes and charming Tahoe appeal.

$158–$340
15 rooms, 15 pb
Visa MC   Checks
C-ltd/S-no/P-no/HC-ltd

BB | Full breakfast
Homemade cookies and coffee bar
Private saunas, fireplaces, TVs/VCRs, fax machine, rock jacuzzi, private beach,
wireless Internet

TAHOMA

**Tahoma Meadows
B&B Cottages**
6821 West Lake Blvd

530-525-1553 | **866-525-1553** | *Dick & Ulli White*
tahomameadows@sbcglobal.net | www.tahomameadows.com

Step back in time at Lake Tahoe and visit our historic and charming little red cottages. This is what Tahoe was 50 years ago. We are located on Lake Tahoe's quiet West Shore. Away from the noise, crowds and casinos of the South and North Shores.

$109–$389
16 rooms, 16 pb
Most CC Cash
C-yes/S-no/P-yes/HC-yes

BB | Full Gourmet Family style breakfast
Afternoon Wine and Cheese Event Catering brunches, BBQ's Weddings and
Special Events
Private entrances and baths, many with claw foot soaking tubs, fireplaces, kitchens.

TEMPLETON

Bike Lane Inn
749 Gough Ave

805-434-0409 | *Scott and Elaine McElmury*
info@bikelaneinn.com | www.bikelaneinn.com/

Comfortable, affordable and fun! Located in the heart of Templeton, a perfect starting point for bike- and motor-touring thru the rolling vineyards of Templeton and Paso Robles. Close to dozens of wineries, great restaurants, spas and salons.

**2011 Lanier Best West Coast Award Winner:
Best Rural B&B**

$89–$99
2 rooms, 2 pb
Most CC Cash
C-ltd/S-ltd/P-no/HC-no

BB | Full breakfast
Wi-fi, patio, TV with DVD, CD player, toiletries and robes for use during stay

TEMPLETON

Carriage Vineyards B&B
4337 S El Pomar

805-227-6807 | 800-617-7911 | *Leigh Anne Farley*
Stay@CarriageVineyards.com | www.carriagevineyards.com/bbhome.html

100-acre ranch with 28 acres of wine grapes & 850 olive trees. Lovely rooms, great hospitality & delightful breakfasts. Peaceful & quiet.

$140–$260
4 rooms, 4 pb
Visa MC Disc Cash Checks
C-ltd/S-no/P-no/HC-ltd

BB | Full breakfast
Snacks, complimentary soft drinks, estate olive oil tasting
Sitting room, carriage house with 18 carriages, vineyards and olives, carriage rides, vineyard tours

The Hidden Hills B&B
4490 S El Pomar

805-239-3115 | *Kris Jardine*
info@hiddenhillsbb.com | www.hiddenhillsbb.com/

A scenic vineyard drive leads you through glorious countryside to the serenity of Hidden Hills Bed & Breakfast. This wine country getaway is nestled amongst rolling hills and majestic oaks.

$155–$325
4 rooms, 4 pb
Visa MC Disc Cash
C-ltd/S-ltd/P-no/HC-ltd

BB | Continental breakfast
Morning coffee, afternoon tea or a glass of regional wine at sundown
Light refreshments, en suite bathrooms, king size beds, superior linens, luxurious comfort

The Santa Rita Inn
1215 Santa Rita Rd

805-434-1634 | 805-748-6134 | *Charlotte*
santaritainn@yahoo.com | http://santaritainn.com/

Begin your journey to the Paso Robles Wine Country with a relaxing afternoon on our wrap-around porch. Sip our estate bottled wine. Stroll through our lush vineyards and enjoy the quiet beauty of the Santa Rita hills.

$125–$175
4 rooms, 4 pb
Visa MC   Cash
C-ltd/S-ltd/P-yes/HC-yes

BB | Full breakfast
Fresh baked goodies
Garden, barbecue area, picnic area, pool, parlor, cottages include kitchenette & complimentary wine

TIBURON

Waters Edge Hotel
25 Main St

415-789-5999 | 877-789-5999 | *Catherine Nelson*
watersedgehostl@jdvhospitality.com | www.marinhotels.com/waters.html

Located on a historic dock along Tiburon's Main St, Waters Edge brings an added ambience of global sophistication to this unique part of Northern California. 23 guestrooms, including two Grand Suites with views of San Francisco and Angel Island.

$169–$499
23 rooms, 23 pb
Most CC
C-yes/S-no/P-no/HC-yes

BB | Continental breakfast
Complimentary wine & cheese hour, fresh green apples
Fireplaces, cable TV, VCR, CD player, spa robes, A/C, viewing deck, complimentary in room WiFi

TWAIN HARTE

McCaffrey House
23251 Hwy 108

209-586-0757 | 888-586-0757 | *Michael & Stephanie McCaffrey*
stephanie@mccaffreyhouse.com | www.mccaffreyhouse.com

Four Diamond AAA - Pure Elegance In a Wilderness Setting. An exquisite experience of comfort blended with fresh adventure, culinary excellence, and personal guest services.

$139–$169
8 rooms, 8 pb
Visa MC AmEx
C-yes/S-no/P-yes/HC-no

BB | Full breakfast
Complimentary wine & sparkling cider in the early evening; tea & cookies in the afternoon
Spa, concierge, business facilities, black iron fire stoves, individual thermostats, private patios

UKIAH

Vichy Hot Springs Resort
2605 Vichy Springs Rd

707-462-9515 | *Gilbert & Marjorie Ashoff*
vichy@vichysprings.com | www.vichysprings.com

The best of two worlds—a hot springs resort and country inn. Rates include a full buffet breakfast, use of the naturally carbonated warm mineral baths and hot soaking pool, Olympic size pool in season and 700 private acres for walking and hiking.

$195–$390
26 rooms, 26 pb
Most CC Cash Checks
C-yes/S-ltd/P-no/HC-yes

BB | Full buffet breakfast
Warm carbonated Vichy mineral baths, hot pool, Olympic size pool, hot stone massage, facials

VENTURA

Bella Maggiore Inn
67 S California St

805-652-0277 | 800-523-8479 | *Thomas J. Wood*
bminn@pacbell.net | www.lanierbb.com/inns/bb1860.html

The Bella Maggiore is an intimate Italian-style small hotel in the heart of downtown Ventura. Nona's Courtyard Cafe is on site. Complimentary evening appetizers and beverages and a full breakfast are included.

$75–$180
28 rooms, 28 pb
Most CC
S-no/P-no/HC-yes

BB | Full breakfast
Appetizers & beverages served between 5pm - 6pm daily
Free parking, TV, Internet, private baths, some rooms with decks, A/C, spas, fireplaces

Victorian Rose B&B
896 E Main St

Nora & Richard Bogatch
victrose@pacbell.net | www.victorianroseventura.com

The Victorian Rose is a one-of-a-kind Victorian Gothic church turned Bed & Breakfast. Appreciate 26-foot high carved beam ceilings graced by an abundance of elaborately-designed stained glass windows.

$99–$169
5 rooms, 5 pb
Most CC Cash
C-ltd/S-no/P-no/HC-no

BB | includes hot entree

WEAVERVILLE

Weaverville Hotel
481 Main St

530-623-2222 | **800-750-8853** | *Jeanne & Brian Muir*
stay@weavervillehotel.com | www.weavervillehotel.com

Located in the midst of the Trinity Alps, in the historic downtown district of the old Gold Rush town of Weaverville, California. There is not a single stoplight in the entire county. This is truly God's country!

$99–$260
7 rooms, 7 pb
Visa MC   Cash Checks
C-ltd/S-no/P-no/HC-ltd

EP |
Daily $10 Hotel Credits for each room, good at several nearby restaurants.
Lounge, parlor/library, porch, on-site gift store, wifi, use of gym across the street.

WESTPORT

Howard Creek Ranch
40501 N Hwy 1

707-964-6725 | *Charles & Sally Grigg*
howardcreekranch@mcn.org | www.howardcreekranch.com

Historic, rural farmhouse on 60 acres filled with collectibles, antiques & memorabilia. Unique health spa with privacy & dramatic views adjoining a wide beach. Refurbished historic carriage barn from virgin redwood milled by Inn owner. Onsite trails.

$75–$198
12 rooms, 12 pb
Most CC
C-ltd/S-ltd/P-yes/HC-ltd

BB | Full Ranch Breakfast
Complimentary coffee, hot cocoa & tea (garden fresh mint tea), kitchenettes & barbecues
Piano, hot tubs, sauna, gardens, library, solarium, swinging bridge, massage, WiFi, hiking, beach

YORKVILLE

LindaVista Bed and Breakfast
33430 Hwy 128

707-894-2591 | *Bob & Linda Klein*
reservations@lindavista.com | www.lindavista.com/

Visit beautiful Yorkville in Mendocino County, only eight miles from Cloverdale. Enjoy intimate lodging in large bedroom suites with queen sized beds, private baths with whirlpool bathtubs and separate showers. All rooms are suites.

$165
2 rooms, 2 pb
Cash Checks
C-yes/S-no/P-no/HC-no

BB | Full Breakfast
Pool, courtyard, whirlpool tubs, suites, sitting room

YOUNTVILLE

Bordeaux House
6600 Washington St

707-944-2855 ext. 19 | **800-677-6370** | *Jean*
bordeauxhouse@gmail.com | www.bordeauxhouse.com/

The Bordeaux House, nestled in the midst of lush landscaped grounds, features a formal red brick structure with classic English and French influences. We offer everything you need for a comfortable, well appointed Napa Valley vacation.

$115–$247
8 rooms, 8 pb
Visa MC   Cash Checks
S-no/P-no/HC-ltd

BB |Full buffet breakfast
Guests may relax with a late afternoon beverage (or a glass of port, sherry, or brandy). Contemporary decor & French antiques, gas/wood fireplaces, outdoor whirlpool, patios or decks.

YOUNTVILLE

Lavender
2020 Webber Ave

707-944-1388 | 800-522-4140 | *Gina Massolo*
lavender@foursisters.com | www.lavendernapa.com

Intimate and luxuriously cozy, Lavender combines the warm colors of Provence with contemporary design elements to create a vibrant setting that blends old and new. A lovely heritage home is the centerpiece of the inn's four buildings.

$225–$300
8 rooms, 8 pb
Most CC Cash
C-yes/S-no/P-no/HC-yes

BB | Full breakfast
Afternoon wine, tea & hors d'oeuvres, freshly-baked cookies, drinks available throughout the day
Porch, veranda, daily housekeeping, patios, fireplaces

Maison Fleurie
6529 Yount St

707-944-2056 | 800-788-0369 | *Gina Massolo*
maisonfleurie@foursisters.com | www.maisonfleurienapa.com

Napa Valley's Maison Fleurie, the "flowering house," is situated on half an acre of beautifully landscaped gardens — welcoming visitors to a Napa Valley inn reminiscent of southern France.

$130–$300
13 rooms, 13 pb
Most CC Cash
C-yes/S-no/P-no/HC-yes

BB | Full breakfast
Afternoon wine, tea & hors d' oeuvres, freshly-baked cookies, drinks available throughout the day
Concierge services, daily housekeeping, private patio, fireplace, robes, hot tub, pool

YUBA CITY

The Harkey House
212 C St

530-674-1942 | *Bob & Lee Jones*
lee@harkeyhouse.com | www.harkeyhouse.com

An elegant and historic inn with intricacies not to be quickly unraveled. This B&B will charm newcomers with its beauty, while still engrossing those who know it well. Voted 'The Best Inn Yuba-Sutter Area 2009'. Walking distance to restaurants & parks.

$125–$225
4 rooms, 4 pb
Visa MC AmEx   Cash Checks
C-yes/S-ltd/P-yes/HC-ltd

BB | Fresh ground coffee, scones, breads
In room coffee & teas, afternoon tea, cookies, hot chocolate
Concierge services, phones, wireless Internet, TV/CD/DVD, pool, spa, library, horse shoes, weddings

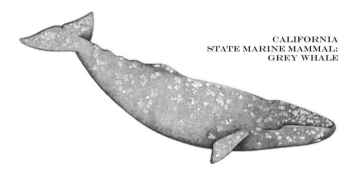

CALIFORNIA
STATE MARINE MAMMAL:
GREY WHALE

Oregon

Salem

THE ROGUE RIVER NEAR
GRANTS PASS, OREGON

ALBANY

Edelweiss Manor
1708 Springhill Dr.

541-928-0747 | **800-531-4306** | *Linda & Larry*
info@edelweissmanor.com | www.edelweissmanor.com

Edelweiss Manor is an historic landmark located on several acres of landscaped gardens, lawns, water features and gazebos. Separate buildings house a day spa and gift boutique featuring local artisans work, studio and art class room, near Country Club.

$150–$250
1 rooms, 1 pb
Visa MC   Cash
S-no/P-no/HC-ltd

BB | Full breakfast
Guest room offers a mini fridge with assorted beverages
Queen size bed, closet, and a private bath with shower, sink, and dressing area.
Access to sauna.

ARCH CAPE

Arch Cape Inn
31970 E Ocean Lane

503-436-2800 | **800-436-2848** | *Cynthia & Stephen Malkowski*
innkeeper@archcapeinn.com | www.archcapeinn.com

The setting of Arch Cape is between a forest and the sea, creating a feeling of tranquility and peacefulness. The beach is a 2 minute walk from the inn, and six of the rooms have an ocean view.

$149–$399
10 rooms, 10 pb
Most CC Cash Checks
C-ltd/S-no/P-ltd/HC-yes

BB | Gourmet Breakfast
Gardens, Jacuzzi, oceanview deck, WiFi, 2 min walk to beach, spa/sauna room,
fine dining

**At Ocean's Edge
B & B**
80199 Pacific Rd.

503-791-2499 | *Lucy and Daryl Eigen*
eigencst@gmail.com | http://atoceansedge.com/

At Ocean's Edge is a new luxury boutique bed and breakfast located in the Cannon Beach area. Enjoy the calm and serenity this well-appointed B&B offers you: excellence in accommodations, epicurean delights, and expansive ocean vistas.

$145–$365
3 rooms, 3 pb
Visa MC   Cash Checks

BB | Full organic breakfast
Private bath, IPod docking station, complimentary WiFi, TV/DVD/cable,
and iron and ironing boards.

ASHLAND

**A Midsummer's
Dream**
496 Beach St

541-552-0605 | **877-376-8800** | *Lisa Beach*
info@amidsummer.com | www.amidsummer.com

Housed in a completely restored 1901 Victorian, all five rooms boast a king-size bed, fireplace,and a large private bathroom with a two person jetted tub and glass block shower. Within walking distance of town and the university in a quiet neighborhood.

$150–$230
5 rooms, 5 pb
Most CC Cash Checks
C-ltd/S-no/P-no/HC-yes

BB | Full breakfast
All suites have fireplaces & spa tubs; finest linens, towels & robes, gardens

ASHLAND

Albion Inn
34 Union St

541-488-3905 | 888-246-8310 | *Cyd and Gary Ropp*
info@albion-inn.com | www.albion-inn.com/

Historic 1905 farmhouse offers peaceful serenity in quiet residential neighborhood only one block from Ashland's restaurants, galleries, and shops. Guests enjoy delicious, organic breakfasts out on the patio or indoors overlooking the rose garden.

 Dreams Do Come True participating inn—Valid anytime; will offer a room upgrade

$124–$164
5 rooms, 5 pb
Visa MC Disc Cash
C-ltd/S-ltd/P-yes/HC-yes

BB | Full breakfast
Coffee is available at 7 AM; tea anytime. Afternoon cookies. Most of our food is fresh and organic.
Spacious, comfortable rooms, inviting common areas filled with fine art, privacy of our gardens.

Arden Forest Inn
261 W Hersey St

541-488-1496 | 800-460-3912 | *William Faiia*
info@afinn.com | www.afinn.com

Providing a sanctuary for theatre lovers, our unique Ashland bed & breakfast is situated on an acre of lush, park-like gardens & offers over 20 years of hospitality excellence. Breathtaking grounds offer a casual and relaxed atmosphere unlike any other.

$149–$245
5 rooms, 5 pb
Visa MC   Cash Checks
S-no

BB | 2 course family-style breakfast
Complimentary coffee, tea, iced refreshments
Library, art, guest kitchen, high-speed Internet, garden, fountains, gazebo, heated pool, sundeck

Chanticleer Inn
120 Gresham St

541-482-1919 | 800-898-1950 | *Ellen Campbell*
comfy@ashlandbnb.com | www.ashland-bed-breakfast.com

Elegant 1920 Craftsman in Ashland's historic neighborhood a short stroll to the Oregon Shakespeare Festival, restaurants, galleries, and Lithia Park. The Chanticleer offers mountain views, comfortable quiet rooms, full gourmet breakfasts, AC & more

$165–$199
6 rooms, 6 pb
Visa MC   Cash Checks
C-ltd/S-no/P-ltd/HC-ltd

BB | Full breakfast
Cookies, sherry and port
Living room with fire place, NY Times, AC & TV-DVD in each room, WiFi, gardens, koi pond & hammock

Country Willows B&B Inn
1313 Clay St

541-488-1590 | 800-945-5697 | *Kara & Dan Burian*
innkeeper@countrywillowsinn.com | www.countrywillowsinn.com

The ultimate resort-style Oregon B&B inn, snuggled against a rolling hillside on a lush 5 acres of farmland. Surrounded by magnificent southern Oregon Siskiyou and Cascade Mountain ranges. Nine unique rooms and suites furnished with antiques. Pool & spa.

$120–$275
9 rooms, 9 pb
Most CC Cash
C-ltd/S-no/P-no/HC-yes

BB | Full breakfast
Complimentary cookies, quick breads and scones; selection of local whole-leaf organic teas.
Porches, heated pool, Jacuzzi, wireless, lawns & gardens, barn-style suites, fireplaces, hiking

Hersey House
& Bungalow
451 N Main St

541-482-4563 | 888-343-7739 | *Lorraine Peterson*
innkeeper@herseyhouse.com | www.herseyhouse.com

A beautifully preserved Craftsman home surrounded by lush gardens within walking distance of downtown theaters. Five guestrooms with king/queen beds & private baths or a fully equipped cottage. A delightful gourmet breakfast is served each morning.

$99–$275
6 rooms, 6 pb
Visa MC Disc Cash Checks
C-ltd/S-no/P-ltd/HC-no

BB | Full Gourmet Breakfast
Cookies, afternoon beverage & truffles each evening
WiFi, deck, gardens

McCall House
153 Oak St

541-482-9296 | 800-808-9749 | *Nola O'Hara*
mccall@mccallhouse.com | www.mccallhouse.com

Just one block from the acclaimed Oregon Shakespeare Festival, our lovingly restored Italianate mansion offers luxurious accommodations in Victorian-inspired suites and guest rooms.

$105–$250
10 rooms, 10 pb
Most CC Cash
C-ltd/S-no/P-no/HC-ltd

BB | Full sumptuous breakfast
Afternoon treats
High-speed Internet access, guest phones, off-street parking, fireplaces

Oak Street Cottages
171 Oak St

541-488-3778 | *Constance Dean*
osc@mind.net | www.oakstreetcottages.com

Gather your family and friends for your very own "Ashland Experience". Our four cottages sleep 6, 8 or 11, and children are welcome. Let Oak Street Cottages be your family's "home away from home." Stay 6 nights, 7th night is free! We specialize in groups.

$184–$295
4 rooms, 4 pb
Visa MC AmEx Cash Checks
C-yes/S-no/P-yes/HC-yes

BB | Full breakfast
Each cottage has a full-sized and fully equipped kitchen, dining room and living room. All cottages have HVC and A/C, fireplace,free wireless, phones, TV, DVD, patio, BBQ, private parking

Pelton House B&B
228 B Street

541-488-7003 | 866-488-7003
info@peltonhouse.com | www.peltonhouse.com

In Ashland's Railroad District near the Shakespeare theater, the historic Pelton House Bed & Breakfast has all the amenities. AAA rated, wireless Internet, a scrumptious breakfast, exquisite bathrooms, turn-down service and wonderful hospitality.

$95–$185
5 rooms, 5 pb
Visa MC   Cash Checks
C-ltd/S-no/P-no

BB | Full breakfast
Afternoon tea, dessert, non-alcoholic beverages included; optional lunch and dinner available

ASHLAND

The Iris Inn
59 Manzanita St

541-488-2286 | **800-460-7650** | *Vicki & Greg Capp*
innkeeper@irisinnbb.com | www.irisinnbb.com

Our tradition of 29 years of excellence continues! On a quiet street near theaters & town, relax in the garden or enjoy a winter escape. View rooms & delectable breakfasts! Awarded 3 Diamonds by AAA. WiFi.

$100–$185
5 rooms, 5 pb
Visa MC
C-ltd/S-no/P-no/HC-ltd

BB |E legant full breakfasts
Lemonade & sun tea for hot summer days, wine at 5 p.m.; sherry, port & chocolates after theater
Mountain views, cottage garden, WiFi, custom amenities, robes, nightly turndown, great reading light

**The Winchester Inn,
Restaurant
& Wine Bar**
35 South Second St

541-488-1113 | **800-972-4991** | *Michael & Laurie Gibbs*
innkeeper@thewinchesterinn.com | www.winchesterinn.com

Victorian hideaway complete with lush gardens & fine dining. This enchanting Inn is within walking distance of the Oregon Shakespeare Festival, Lithia Park, restaurants & shopping.

$140–$325
19 rooms, 19 pb
Most CC Cash Checks
C-yes/S-no/P-no/HC-ltd

BB | Two course gourmet breakfast
Full service restaurant & wine bar
Garden, gazebo, jetted tubs, fireplaces, balcony, antiques, afternoon treats delivered to room

ASTORIA

Astoria Inn
3391 Irving Ave

503-325-8153 | **800-718-8153** | *Mickey Cox*
www.astoriainnbb.com

Often mentioned as the best location in Astoria, the inn's new make-you-smile colors on the outside make you feel welcome and relaxed inside. A happy place with good food for happy times.

$85–$100
4 rooms, 4 pb
Visa MC
S-ltd/P-no/HC-no

BB | Hearty breakfasts
Fresh baked cookies
Veranda overlooks the Columbia River, sitting room, cable TV

Grandview B&B
1574 Grand Ave

503-325-5555 | **800-488-3250** | *Charleen Maxwell*
grandviewbedandbreakfast@usa.net | www.pacifier.com/~grndview

Light, airy, cheerful Victorian close to superb Maritime Museum, Lightship, churches, golf, clam-digging, fishing, beaches and rivers.

$66–$188
9 rooms, 7 pb
Most CC
C-ltd/P-no

BB | Full breakfast
Snacks
Sitting room, canopy beds, books, games, binoculars, liquor not permitted

ASTORIA

Rose River Inn B&B
1510 Franklin Ave

503-325-7175 | 888-876-0028 | *David & Pam Armstrong*
roseriverinn@charter.net | www.roseriverinn.com

Historic bed and breakfast in Astoria, Oregon on the Columbia River. The Rose River Inn is a beautiful 1912 Craftsman style home in a National Historic district of Astoria, Oregon, the oldest American city west of the Rockies.

$85–$150
5 rooms, 5 pb
Visa MC   Cash
C-ltd/S-no/P-no/HC-no

BB | Full breakfast
Breakfast is served at 8:30 a.m.
Sitting room, suites, fireplaces, cable TV, DVD, wireless Internet, bicycle storage

AURORA

Anna Becke House B&B
14892 Bobs Ave

503-678-6979 | 866-383-2662 | Terri Roberts
info@annabeckehouse.com | www.annabeckehouse.com

Spend a night in a classic craftsman bungalow that could be right out of the pages of your favorite decorating magazine! And just a short stroll from its quiet historic neighborhood to the heart of Oregon's Antiques Capital.

$130–$130
2 rooms, 2 pb
Visa MC Disc Cash
C-ltd/S-ltd/P-no/HC-no

BB | Full gourmet breakfast
"Serve yourself" afternoon & evening refreshment guest lounge
Cable TV, DVDs, wireless Internet & guest robes

BEAVERTON

Cornerstone B & B
17290 SW Alvord Ln.

503-747-2345 | *Harold & Margaret Meyering*
info@cornerstonebedandbreakfast.com | www.cornerstonebedandbreakfast.com

Cornerstone Bed and Breakfast welcomes you to the fresh and relaxing atmosphere at the base of Cooper Mountain in Washington County, Oregon. The Cornerstone B&B is a warm and friendly place with the happiness and comfort of guests in mind.

$95
3 rooms, 3 pb
Most CC Cash Checks
C-ltd/S-no/P-no/HC-yes

BB | Buffet
Buffet offers main entree and other, refrigerator available on request for guest use.
Flat Panel Televisions, Private Baths, Private Entrances, Queen beds or twins, heat and A/C

BEND

Cabin Creek B&B
22035 Hwy 20 East

541-318-4798 | 888-572-5856 | *Dave & Melody Spicer*
innkeeper@cabincreekbandb.com | http://cabincreekbedandbreakfast.com/

This custom log home B&B was built in 2007 and is surrounded by more than 13 acres of woods and pasture land. It was designed with your comfort and privacy in mind. The moment you step into the grand entrance of this log home, you will not want to leave.

$99–$165
3 rooms, 3 pb
Most CC Cash
C-ltd/S-no/P-no/HC-no

BB | Full breakfast
Fresh baked cookies at 8:30 p.m. Beverages and snacks available 24/7
The 14 acres offers plenty of room to park boats, snowmobiles, and safe out of the weather storage.

BEND

Lara House Lodge B&B
640 NW Congress St

541-388-4064 | 800-766-4064 | *Lynda and Peter Clark*
info@larahouse.com | www.larahouse.com

Lara House Lodge is a magnificent 1910 Craftsman Style Historic Home conveniently located in downtown Bend's historic district, across the street from beautiful Mirror Pond & Park. Enjoy our luxurious furnishings, exquisite bedding, and gourmet breakfast

$149–$329
6 rooms, 6 pb
Most CC Cash Checks
S-no/P-no/HC-no

BB | Multi-course gourmet breakfast
Pacific Northwest wines and hors d' ouevres are served daily from 4:30-5:30
Sun room, fireplace, outdoor sunny deck and shady front porch, historic neighborhood near park

BORING

Fagan's Haven B & B

503-658-2010 | *Jane McClain*
info@FagansHavenBnb.com | http://faganshavenbnb.com/

Fagan's Haven has been described at the best kept B&B secret in Oregon. A wonderful place to indulge your creative passion, spend time with friends, work on that secret Christmas present, or find a temporary respite.

$65–$85
3 rooms, 1 pb
Cash Checks
C-ltd/S-no/P-ltd/HC-ltd

BB | Full breakfast

TV/VCR, extensive library of craft and quilt books, craft room, skylights, microwave, and fridge.

BRIGHTWOOD

Brightwood Guesthouse
64725 E Barlow Trail Rd

503-622-5783 | *Bonnie Rames*
brightwoodbnb@hotmail.com | www.Mounthoodbnb.com

Peaceful, private, romantic cabin of your own in the river valley forest of Mt Hood. Huge hot soaking tubs outdoors; pretty territorial views from each window, fantastic breakfasts. Everything provided for your comfort and convenience.

$145–$175
1 rooms, 1 pb
Cash Checks
C-ltd/S-ltd/P-no/HC-ltd

BB | Full 5-course breakfast
Snacks, beverages; complimentary wine or bubbly when notified of special occasion
Living room, library, washer & dryer, TV/VCR, games, flowers, art supplies

BROOKINGS

A Beachfront B&B by Lowden's
14626 Wollam Rd

541-469-7045 | 800-453-4768 | *Gary & Barbara Lowden*
glowden@charter.net | www.beachfrontbb.com

Ocean and river frontage with easy beach access. Near a redwood forest. Lovely ocean front suites with fireplace, private entry and private bath. Located where the Winchuck River meets the Pacific Ocean.

$109–$139
2 rooms, 2 pb
Visa MC   Cash Checks
C-yes/S-no/P-no/HC-no

BB | Continental breakfast
Coffee, tea, popcorn, milk, hot chocolate, orange juice, water, jams & peanut butter
Ambiance fireplace with remote control, free WiFi, 2 night & 5 night discounts

BROOKINGS

**A Country Retreat
B&B**
16980 Coho Dr

541-661-3773 | **800-856-8604** | *Bill & Evelyn*
info@countryretreatbnb.com | www.countryretreatbnb.com

*Two private, large luxury guest rooms with high window views, private
baths and entrances, robes Jacuzzi, wireless Internet, a Billiard Room,
grand piano and fireplaces. Private park for reunions and weddings,
lots of amenities and close to the beach.*

$100–$147
2 rooms, 2 pb
Visa MC   Cash
C-ltd/S-no/P-no/HC-ltd

BB | Full Country Breakfast
Afternoon Tea, coffee & cookies
Cable TV/DVD/VCR, free wireless Internet, Billiard Room, Grand Piano, Fireplace

Holmes Sea Cove B&B
17350 Holmes Dr

541-469-3025 | **888-290-0312** | *Lorene Holmes*
http://personal.kitusa.com/holmes/

*Overlooking the beautiful Oregon coast with a scenic trail to a semi-
private beach. Holmes Sea Cove B&B is a place of peace and privacy.
Cottage and 2 room suite available. 3 night minimum stay on the Pacific
Suite.*

$150
2 rooms, 2 pb
Visa MC   Cash
C-yes/S-no/P-no/HC-ltd

BB | Continental plus breakfast
Hot tub/spa with ocean view, gazebo, scenic trail, semi-private beach

CARLTON

**Lobenhaus B&B
and Vineyard**
6975 NE Abbey Rd

503-864-9173 | *Joe & Shari Lobenstein*
innkeeper@lobenhaus.com | www.lobenhaus.com

*Nestled in a peaceful wooded setting on 27 acres, our unique tri-level
lodge has 6 beautifully appointed guestrooms, each with a private
bathroom. View the woods and spring fed creek from your window or
open your door to step onto the expansive deck.*

$160–$190
6 rooms, 6 pb
Visa MC Disc Cash Checks
C-ltd/S-no/P-no/HC-ltd

BB | Full Oregon Bounty Breakfast
Refreshments & snacks provided at check-in, wine for purchase, guest refrigerator
in dining area
Wireless Internet, fireplace, satellite big screen HD TV DVD, large common areas,
grounds, vineyard

R.R. Thompson House
517 N. Kutch St.

503-852-6236 | *Roselyn and Mike*
innkeeper@rrthompsonhouse.com | www.rrthompsonhouse.com/index.htm

*Stroll from the Thompson House to over 30 tasting rooms/wineries in
Carlton, offering the finest of Oregon wines. Return to the warmth of an
historic inn, renovated with private marble-tile baths for all
suites/rooms. Hearty gourmet breakfast served.*

$150–$245
5 rooms, 5 pb
Most CC Cash
C-ltd/S-no/P-no/HC-no

BB | Full breakfast
The guest refrigerator holds a selection of sodas and water for your enjoyment anytime.
Wireless Internet, HDTV, AC, Whirlpool Tubs, Parking, Gardens, Living Room and
Board Games

CAVE JUNCTION

Vertical Horizons
Treehouse Paradise
3305 Dick George Rd.

541-592-4751 | *Phillip & Jodie Moskios*
verticalhorizons@frontiernet.net | http://treehouseparadise.com/

Sleep in state of the art luxury tree houses! Each unique in design. Disc golf, fishing, technical tree climbing and more on site. Serving local organic whenever possible.

$200–$225
3 rooms, 1 pb
Most CC Cash Checks
C-yes/S-ltd/P-no/HC-ltd

BB | Continental plus breakfast
BBQ/gas grill, disk golf course, volleyball, horse shoes, fishing, rafting, technical tree climbing+

CENTRAL POINT

The Willows
3347 Old Stage Rd

541-665-3020 | **866-664-1425** | *Joe & Sandra Dowling*
scu73@aol.com | http://thewillowsbedandbreakfast.com

Experience the modern yet historic accommodations at this authentic Rogue Valley Orchard Mansion. The upscale bed and breakfast resort is listed in the National Register and has a wonderful history. Each room is appointed with elegant furnishings and art.

$150–$225
5 rooms, 5 pb
Visa MC AmEx   Cash Checks
C-ltd/S-no/P-ltd/HC-no

BB | Full breakfast
Afternoon tea/snacks during summer season
In-room TV and DVD/VCR, telephone/data port, WiFi, A/C, in-ground pool, tennis, croquet,classes

COOS BAY

Old Tower House
B&B
476 Newmark Ave

541-888-6058 | *Thomas & Stephanie Kramer*
oldtowerhouse@yahoo.com | www.oldtowerhouse.com

Historic home in Coos Bay filled with history, antiques, and ambiance. Gourmet breakfasts served in the main house. The Old Tower House is listed on the National Register of Historic Places, and is set a few yards from the Bay.

$75–$165
4 rooms, 4 pb
Visa MC   Cash Checks
C-ltd/S-no/P-no/HC-no

BB | Continental & Gourmet
Tea & coffee available upon request
TV/DVD, video library, antiques, sun porch

CORVALLIS

Harrison House
2310 NW Harrison Blvd

541-752-6248 | **800-233-6248** | *Hilarie Phelps & Allen Goodman*
stay@corvallis-lodging.com | www.corvallis-lodging.com

Gracious hospitality & comfort in a beautifully furnished, historic Dutch Colonial home. 4 rooms with private baths & a lovely detached Cottage Suite. Walk to OSU, restaurants, and shopping. Seasonal breakfasts, local wines, & all business amenities.

$129–$149
5 rooms, 5 pb
Most CC Cash Checks
C-yes/S-no/P-no/HC-no

BB | Full breakfast
Willamette Valley wines, afternoon tea, cold sodas, spring water & snacks
Sunroom/library, in-room WiFi, phones, TV with DVD, local truffles, hazelnuts & spring water

CORVALLIS

**The Hanson
Country Inn**
795 SW Hanson St

541-752-2919 | *Patricia Covey*
hcibb@aol.com | www.hcinn.com

*Charming country home with splendid architectural details. Brimming
with cozy warmth, unique charm and elegant ambience. A truly wonderful experience that you will want to enjoy again and again!*

$125–$175
4 rooms, 4 pb
Most CC
C-ltd/S-no/P-ltd/HC-ltd

BB | Full breakfast
Sitting rooms, private decks, garden area, library, Internet access

DAYTON

Wine Country Farm
6855 Breyman
Orchards Rd

503-864-3446 | **800-261-3446** | *Joan Davenport*
jld@winecountryfarm.com | www.winecountryfarm.com

*Surrounded by vineyards and magnificent views, we provide warm
gracias hospitality and comfortable accommodations in the heart
of Oregon's famous Dundee Hills wine country. You can find us in "1000
Places To See Before You Die" by Patricia Schultz.*

$150–$225
12 rooms, 12 pb
Visa MC Disc Cash Checks
C-ltd/S-no/P-no/HC-yes

BB | Full country breakfast
Home baked cookies, complimentary tasting wine.
Indoor & outdoor sitting areas, Jacuzzi, sauna,fireplaces, massage services, horse-
back riding, wine.

DEPOE BAY

**An Ocean Paradise
Whales Rendezvous
B&B**
147 NW Hwy 101

541-765-3455 | *Joe and Dian Forbis*
info@WhalesRendezvous.com | www.whalesrendezvous.com/

*A unique, one of a kind find right on the ocean with nothing to block
your amazing view. Two elegant suites each with private entrances, and
private outdoor areas with firepits. Each has an elegant private bathroom.*

$295–$385
2 rooms, 2 pb
Most CC Cash
S-no/P-no/HC-no

BB | Full hot gourmet breakfast
We provide coffee, tea, hot chocolate, water, soda, popcorn, and other treats, all
complimentary.
Each suite has a private large outdoor area with a fire pit to enjoy while watching
the ocean waves.

EUGENE

C'est La Vie Inn
1006 Taylor St

541-302-3014 | **866-302-3014** | *Anne-Marie Lizet*
contact@cestlavieinn.com | www.cestlavieinn.com

*All of the guest offerings, from the cozy Gauguin room to the opulent
Casablanca, are uniquely decorated, and all have private en-suite baths
and fireplaces. Elegant features include individual cooling/heating
controls, robes, cable TV/DVD, and free WI-FI*

$125–$250
4 rooms, 4 pb
Visa MC AmEx
C-ltd/S-ltd/P-ltd/HC-no

BB | Full breakfast
Coffee, tea, cold beverages & beer, cookies in the butler's pantry, wine available to
purchase
Flat screen TV with CD player & DVD, free WiFi, computer, library, fireplaces, robes,
hair-dryers

EUGENE

Lorane Valley B&B
86621 Lorane Hwy

541-686-0241 | *Esther & George Ralph*
LoraneValleyBandB@att.net | www.loranevalleyBandB.com

Three and a half miles from the hustle and bustle of Eugene is a haven of tranquility. Our corner of the world is a beautiful, two level cedar home set on 15 acres overlooking the Lorane Valley.

$125–$145
1 rooms, 1 pb
Visa MC AmEx
C-yes/S-ltd/P-no

BB | Full breakfast
Fresh cut flowers, book loans, PBS documentaries, Jacuzzis

River Walk Inn
250 N Adams St

541-344-6506 | **800-621-2904** | *Richard & Donna Cribbs*
innkeeper@ariverwalkinn.com | www.ariverwalkinn.com

River Walk Inn Bed and Breakfast is located in a quiet residential neighborhood on the edge of downtown Eugene. We consider it the perfect location for out-of-town guests.

$100–$120
3 rooms, 3 pb
Visa MC   Cash Checks
C-ltd/S-no/P-no/HC-no

BB | Full breakfast
Tea & snacks are available in the dining room at all times, evening port in the library
Wireless Internet with a laptop available for guest use, bicycles

FLORA

North End Crossing
Barn and Bed
80903 College Lane

541-828-7010 | **888-897-8020** | *Dan & Vanessa*
northendcrossing@tds.net | www.northendcrossing.com/

Early risers may help milk the cows or gather eggs, slop the hogs and feed the drafts. Or sleep in covered with old time quilts. But be sure to wake in time for a hearty country breakfast cooked on a wood cookstove.

2011 Lanier Best West Caost Award Winner:
Best for Farm Activities

$85–$85
2 rooms, 0 pb
Cash Checks
C-yes/S-ltd/P-yes/HC-ltd

BB | Full country breakfast
Refreshments offered throughout the day, coffee, tea, hot chocolate, scones, fruit & more
Learn the old ways and pioneer skills, sitting room, library, antiques,
hiking & walking... more

FOSSIL

Wilson Ranches
Retreat B&B
16555 Butte Creek Rd

541-763-2227 | **866-763-2227** | *Phil & Nancy Wilson*
info@wilsonranchesretreat.com | www.wilsonranchesretreat.com

Welcome to the Wilson Ranches Retreat Bed and Breakfast in North Central Oregon. A 9,000 acre working cattle ranch takes you off the beaten track to our rustic hideout.

$79–$109
6 rooms, 2 pb
Visa MC AmEx
C-yes/S-ltd/P-no/HC-ltd

BB | Full 'cowboy' breakfast
Fully equipped kitchen
Satellite television, business traveler accommodations

GOLD BEACH
Tu Tu' Tun Lodge
96550 N Bank Rogue

541-247-6664 | **800-864-6357** | *Kyle Ringer*
tututunlodge@charter.net | www.tututun.com

Secluded lodge nestled on banks of the Rogue River, with country inn hospitality, gourmet meals, white water excursions and guided fishing. Two houses, two suites, and sixteen rooms available.

$125–$595
20 rooms, 20 pb
Visa MC
C-ltd/S-ltd/P-no/HC-ltd

EP |
Meal plans: breakfast only, $18, b'fast & dinner, $57.50, lunch $15, outside guests by reservation
Library, sitting room, swimming pool, games, 2 outdoor hot tubs

GOLD HILL
Rogue River
Guest House
41 Rogue River Hwy

541-855-4485 | **877-764-8322** | *Joan Ogilvie & Doug Rowley*
www.rogueriverguesthouse.com

A completely refurbished 1890's farmhouse along the Rogue River in Southern Oregon, halfway between Medford and Grants Pass. Comfortable surroundings with all the amenities.

$65–$170
2 rooms, 2 pb
Cash Checks
C-yes/S-no/P-ltd/HC-no

BB | Full breakfast
Lunch & dinner by request; complimentary wine
Jacuzzi suite with oceanview, business services, family friendly, kids welcome,
pet friendly

GRANTS PASS
Flery Manor B&B
2000 Jumpoff Joe
Creek Rd

541-476-3591 | *Marla & John Vidrinskas*
flery@flerymanor.com | www.flerymanor.com

*"Get away from the hurried world…" Elegant, Romantic, Secluded."
7 mountain view acres near the famous Rogue River. Suites, king bed, fireplace, jacuzzi, private balcony. Library, parlor w/piano, huge balcony/extraordinary views. Ponds, waterfall, streams*

$120–$220
5 rooms, 4 pb
Visa MC   Cash Checks
C-ltd/S-no/P-no/HC-no

BB | Full 3 course gourmet breakfast
Afternoon tea, coffee, snacks, wine
Library, Suites/fireplace, jacuzzi, robes, fresh flower, piano, gazebo, waterfalls, pond,
trails, rafting

The Lodge at Riverside
955 S.E. 7th St

541-955-0600 | **877-955-0600** | *Tamara Bushnell*
tamara@thelodgeatriverside.com | www.thelodgeatriverside.com

Let the scenic Rogue River become your backyard as you catch your breath in richly decorated, oversized rooms. Experience the best of Grants Pass, Oregon for quiet pleasures, whirlwind vacations or corporate meetings.

$125–$325
32 rooms, 32 pb
Most CC
C-yes/S-no/P-no/HC-yes

BB | Continental breakfast
Evening wine & cheese reception, bedtime milk & cookies
Outdoor pool & spa, fireplaces, Jacuzzis, meeting rooms, restaurant, catering
& special events

GRANTS PASS

Weasku Inn
5560 Rogue River Hwy

541-471-8000 | **800-4-WEASKU** | *Kirt Davis*
kirt@countryhouseinns.com | www.weasku.com

A cozy riverfront inn built around a colorful, historic fishing lodge. Decorated with locally hand-crafted furniture, one of a kind lamps, pillow top beds with feather duvets, chairs & fishing memorabilia.

 Dreams Do Come True participating inn—Valid May 15–September 15 (excluding weekends and holidays); will offer a room upgrade

$199–$329
17 rooms, 17 pb
Most CC Cash
C-yes/S-ltd/P-no/HC-yes

BB | Continental plus breakfast
Wine & cheese reception each afternoon, fresh baked cookies each night
Sitting room, fireplaces, cable TV, wireless Internet, conference facility & outdoor deck

HOOD RIVER

Hood River BnB
918 Oak St

541-387-2997 | *Jane & Jim Nichols*
jane@hoodriverbnb.com | www.hoodriverbnb.com

Just 3 blocks from downtown Hood River, OR, our B&B is ideal for those who want a comfortable place to relax & call home during your stay in the Gorge or at Mount Hood. Large, comfortable rooms with local fruit and good breakfasts.

$85–$135
4 rooms, 2 pb
Visa MC Disc Cash Checks
C-ltd/S-no/P-ltd/HC-yes

BB | Full breakfast
Tea, snacks & cookies, all in a great home
Sitting rooms, guest-use computer with Internet access, library, deck, hammock, grill, picnic table

Inn At The Gorge
1113 Eugene St.

541-386-4429 | **877-852-2385** | *Frank & Michele Bouche*
stay@innatthegorge.com | www.innatthegorge.com

Built in 1908, this Queen Anne style home has operated as a Bed and Breakfast since 1987. We are located within walking distance to downtown shops and restaurants.

 Dreams Do Come True participating inn—Valid November–April (except holidays/spring break)

$119–$159
5 rooms, 5 pb
Visa MC   Cash Checks
C-ltd/S-no/P-no/HC-ltd

BB | Full breakfast
Wraparound porch, backyard terrace, free wireless Internet service, DVDs, off-street parking

IDEYLD PARK

Steamboat Inn
42705 N Umpqua Hwy

541-498-2230 | **800-840-8825** | *Sharon & Jim Van Loan*
patricialee@hughes.net | www.thesteamboatinn.com

Commanding a breathtaking view of the North Umpqua River, the Steamboat Inn is nestled among the towering firs of the Umpqua National Forest. We are about two hours by car from airports at Eugene and Medford.

$170–$300
19 rooms, 19 pb
Visa MC   Cash Checks
C-yes/S-no/P-ltd/HC-yes

EP |
Evening dinner available, aperitif and hors d'oeuvres
Library, fireplaces, decks, A/C, fly-fishing guides,

Country House Inns
Jacksonville
240 E California St

541-899-2050 | 800-367-1942 | *Lydia Gibson*
innkeeper@countryhouseinnsjacksonville.com | countryhouseinnsjacksonville.com

Combining five unique properties, Country House Inns Jacksonville has an accommodation for every taste or budget. Stay at the historic McCully House, the budget friendly Stage Lodge, the one of a kind Wine or Pine Cottages or the B&B-style Reames House.

$99–$295
40 rooms, 40 pb
Most CC
C-yes/S-no/P-yes/HC-yes

BB | Danish/Juice or Other as Below
Stage Lodge guests receive a danish & juice breakfast. Others receive a cert to a local restaurant.
Fax, copy, Premium bath products, coffee makers, microwaves, mini-fridges

Elan Guest Suites
& Gallery
245 West Main St.

541-899-8000 | 877-789-1952 | *Duane Sturm and Cherie Reneau*
contact@elanguestsuites.com | www.elanguestsuites.com/

Elan's executive lodging is a jewel box of comfort, technology and pure panache. In the Wild West backdrop of historic Jacksonville, Elan exceeds the expectations of our most distinguished guests. Luxurious suites, complimentary Wi-Fi and private garage.

$160–$250
3 rooms, 3 pb
Most CC Cash
C-ltd/S-ltd/P-no/HC-no

BB | Gift card to local coffee shop
Coffee,teas,chocolate and bottled water are complimentary. Local wines offered for sale in rooms.

Jacksonville Inn
175 E California St

541-899-1900 | 800-321-9344 | *Jerry & Linda Evans*
jvinn@mind.net | www.jacksonvilleinn.com

The Inn offers its guests elegance in a historic setting, with gourmet dining, a connoisseur's wine cellar, luxurious hotel accommodations, and 4 honeymoon cottages that are "suites extraordinaire."

$159–$465
12 rooms, 12 pb
Most CC Cash
C-yes/S-no/P-ltd/HC-yes

BB | Full breakfast
Restaurant, lounge, wine tasting, lunch & dinner additional, gourmet catering on and off premises
Luxurious cottages with many amenities available; a connoisseur's wine shop with over 2,000 wines

Jacksonville's
Magnolia Inn
245 N 5th St

541-899-0255 | 866-899-0255 | *Robert & Susan Roos*
maginn@charter.net | www.magnolia-inn.com

Featured in Sunset Magazine and AAA's Via magazine. Located across from the museum, just two short blocks to town. Park your car and walk to award winning restaurants. Comfortable elegance in the heart of Jacksonville, voted 1 of 10 coolest US small towns

$99–$169
9 rooms, 9 pb
Most CC
C-ltd/S-no/P-yes/HC-yes

BB | Continental breakfast from bakeries
Gourmet coffees, teas, European pastries, homemade baked goods, yogurt, waffles, oatmeal, fruit
TV/VCR/extended cable, high-speed wireless Internet, guest kitchen, outdoor veranda

JACKSONVILLE

TouVelle House B&B
455 N Oregon St

541-899-8938 | 800-846-8422 | *Gary Renninger Balfour*
info@touvellehouse.com | www.touvellehouse.com

TouVelle House Bed & Breakfast is ready to welcome you with a gentle, serene environment where you can relax knowing that all of your needs have already been anticipated.

$139–$189
6 rooms, 6 pb
Visa MC Disc Cash Checks
C-ltd/S-no/P-no/HC-no

BB | Full breakfast/continental
Tea & hot beverages
Beautiful gardens, swimming pool, sauna, spacious verandas, high speed
wireless Internet, fridge, AC

LAFAYETTE

Kelty Estate B&B
675 3rd St

503-560-1512 | 800-867-3740 | *Nicci Stokes*
info@keltyestate.com | www.keltyestatebb.com/

The Kelty Estate is a historic B&B in the heart of Oregon's wine country, one hour from Portland and the coast. As a guest of the Kelty, you are welcome to book our limousine to chauffeur you around the lush landscape or your own private wine tour.

$129–$179
5 rooms, 5 pb
Most CC Cash Checks
C-ltd/S-ltd/P-ltd/HC-ltd

BB | 3-Course Gourmet Breakfast
Complimentary wine & cheese
Concierge services, corporate retreats, weddings, wireless Internet

LINCOLN CITY

Coast Inn B&B
4507 SW Coast Ave

541-994-7932 | 888-994-7932 | *Rosie Huntemann*
coastinn@oregoncoastinn.com | www.oregoncoastinn.com

Welcome to Coast Inn Bed & Breakfast! We're only 2–2½ hours from Portland International Airport. Located in the historic Taft Heights district of Lincoln City. A short walk from Siletz Bay and beach access. Our pristine, level beach beckons you.

$109–$198
4 rooms, 4 pb
Visa MC AmEx   Cash
C-ltd/S-ltd/P-ltd/HC-no

BB | Full breakfast
Smoked salmon, wine & cheese, lemonade & Fresh Lemon English Shortbread
Library, WiFi

MANZANITA

Zen Garden B&B
8910 Glenesslin Lane

503-368-6697 | *Mrs. Smigel*
csmigel@nehalemtel.net | www.neahkahnie.net/zengarden

Zen Garden B&B provides deluxe accommodations only a few feet from level access to the legendary Manzanita seven mile beach. This lovely beach is only a short walk from your room.

$100–$165
2 rooms, 2 pb
Cash Checks
S-no/P-no/HC-no

BB | Full breakfast
Vegetarian, macrobiotic & vegan as well as eggs and bacon etc. selection of teas,
coffee all day
Zen Bath, robes, patio, private living room, refrigerator, big screen TV, VCR, DVD,

MCMINNVILLE

A'Tuscan Estate
809 NE Evans

503-434-9016 | 800-441-2214 | *Jacques & Liz Rolland*
innkeeper@a-tuscanestate.com | www.a-tuscanestate.com

1928 historic estate, 5 blocks from historic downtown. Close to Linfield College, Delphian School, antique shopping & wineries. 45 minutes to coast, 50 minutes to Mt. Hood ski resorts.

$140–$250
5 rooms, 5 pb
Most CC Cash Checks
C-ltd/S-no/P-no/HC-no

BB | Full breakfast
Afternoon coffee, tea & fresh baked cookies, private dinners
Sitting parlor, morning coffee room, fireplace

Baker Street B&B Inn
129 SE Baker St

503-472-5575 | 800-870-5575 | *Cheryl Hockaday*
cheryl@bakerstreetinn.com | www.bakerstreetinn.com

In the heart of Wine Country, Baker Street Inn is a downtown B&B with 3 guestrooms and 2 private cottages, near Linfield College and historic downtown. Three breakfast options. Midway between the Coast and Portland. Ask about La Nouveau Chateau!

$99–$159
5 rooms, 5 pb
Most CC
C-ltd/S-ltd/P-ltd/HC-no

BB | Light healthy breakfast
Restaurants nearby
One block from city park, jetted tub, clawfoot tubs with showers, cottages

Joseph Mattey House
10221 NE Mattey Ln

503-434-5058 | 877-434-5058 | *Jack & Denise Seed*
mattey@matteyhouse.com | www.josephmatteyhouse.com

An 1892 Queen Anne Victorian surrounded by stately cedars and overlooking the vineyard, the Joseph Mattey House offers a secluded setting in the heart of the Oregon wine country. Centrally located for all wineries, restaurants and local attractions.

$150–$225
4 rooms, 4 pb
Visa MC AmEx Cash Checks
C-ltd/S-no/P-no/HC-no

BB | Full breakfast
Refreshments & cookies in the afternoon, local wines available by the glass
Sitting room, parlor, porch swing, vineyard, orchard, indoor & outdoor games

Steiger Haus
360 SE Wilson St

503-472-0821 | *Dale & Susan DuRette*
reservations@steigerhaus.com | www.steigerhaus.com

In the heart of Oregon Wine Country. Unique architecture in a park-like town setting. Walking distance to gourmet restaurants. Charm and hospitality plus!

$95–$150
5 rooms, 5 pb
Visa MC Disc
C-ltd/S-no/P-no/HC-ltd

BB | Full seasonal breakfast
Early continental breakfast baskets, cheese & fruit plates, seasonal picnics, honor bar
Sitting room, movies & games, English garden, WiFi, regional wine list, wine tours

MCMINNVILLE

Youngberg Hill Vineyards & Inn
10660 SW Youngberg Hill Rd

503-472-2727 | 888-657-8668 | *Nicolette Bailey*
info@youngberghill.com | www.youngberghill.com/

Oregon's premier wine country inn and one of Wine Spectator's favorite locations; set on a 50 acre hilltop surrounded by organic vineyards. We will take your breath away with the most beautiful views, warm luxurious Inn, and exceptional estate wines.

$200–$350
8 rooms, 8 pb
Visa MC   Cash
C-ltd/S-no/P-no/HC-ltd

BB | Full breakfast
Full Wine Tasting included with each stay.
Library, lounging salon, dining rooms, & wine tastings.

MEDFORD

Under the Greenwood Tree
3045 Bellinger Ln

541-776-0000 | *Joseph & Barbara Lilley*
utgtree@qwest.net | www.greenwoodtree.com

This Country B&B Inn is set on 10 quiet and peaceful acres of idyllic grounds. It is surrounded by gracious Oregon gardens and interesting antique farm buildings dating to the Civil War Era.

$120
4 rooms, 4 pb
Most CC
C-ltd/S-no/P-yes/HC-no

BB | Full breakfast
Complimentary tea & treats
Pond, gazebo, garden, llamas, weddings, hammocks, massage services

MT. HOOD

Mt. Hood Hamlet B&B
6741 Hwy 35

541-352-3574 | 800-407-0570 | *Paul & Diane Romans*
info@mthoodhamlet.com | www.mthoodhamlet.com

Reach out & touch Mt. Hood from our 18th century New England Colonial style home with modern conveniences & amenities. 13 miles mountain top to rooftop, and a world apart from your daily cares. WiFi hotspot & DSL for those who must!

$145–$165
4 rooms, 4 pb
Visa MC Disc Cash Checks
C-ltd/S-no/P-ltd/HC-ltd

BB | Full breakfast
Complimentary juice, soft drinks, coffee & tea. House red or white wine may be purchased
Private baths, 4 rms with fireplaces, 2 with Jacuzzis, outdoor spa, library, WiF

NEWBERG

University House of Newberg B&B
401 N. Meridian St

503-538-8438 | 866-538-8438 | *Leigh Wellikoff*
hostess@universityhousenewberg.com | www.universityhousenewberg.com

University House provides the quintessential Oregon wine country experience. We offer the intimate charm of a beautifully restored 1906 home furnished with the warmth of stunning family antiques. There are no other guests in the house during your stay.

$175–$275
3 rooms, 2 pb
Visa MC   Cash Checks
C-ltd/S-no/P-no/HC-no

BB | Continental breakfast
Tea, popcorn, chocolate, crackers, juice, other snacks.
Hot tub, massage therapy available, full business center with wi-fi, concierge service, etc.

NEWPORT

Oregon

**Ocean House, An
Oceanfront Inn**
4920 NW Woody Way

541-265-3888 | 866-495-3888 | *Charmaine & Lex*
oceanhouse@gmail.com | www.oceanhouse.com

*Unforgettable in any season, Ocean House offers gracious lodging for
adult travelers. Spectacular views of the ocean and the incomparable
Oregon coastline can be seen from every room as well as the Great
Room, dining area and the spacious decks.*

$135–$250
8 rooms, 8 pb
Most CC Cash Checks
C-ltd/S-no/P-no/HC-yes

BB | Full breakfast
Complimentary beverages including wine, sodas, teas, bottled water, popcorn &
homemade cookies too
All rooms with ocean views & fireplaces, 4 rooms with whirlpool, oceanfront
gardens, WiFi

**The Lightkeeper's
Inn B&B**
811 SW 12th St.

541-265-5642 | *Cheryl Lalack*
innkeeper@thelightkeepersinnbb.com | www.thelightkeepersinnbb.com

*Spectacular bay views from all rooms in the house. Close to attractions,
events, shopping, beach, and more. Enjoy one of innkeeper Cheryl's
fantastic breakfasts in our dining room, or enjoy a quiet breakfast in
your private suite.*

$195–$248
2 rooms, 2 pb
Visa MC AmEx
C-ltd/S-no/P-ltd/HC-no

BB | Full breakfast
Hor d'ovres and wine in your suite
Laundry room, soda, bottled water, microwaveable popcorn, hot tea, and coffee

**Tyee Lodge
Oceanfront B&B**
4925 NW Woody Way

541-265-8953 | 888-553-8933 | *Charmaine & Lex*
reservations@tyeelodge.com | www.tyeelodge.com

*Come and enjoy our natural setting along the bluffs of peaceful Agate
Beach in Newport. Our park-like setting is unequaled on the Oregon
Coast. Sit by your window or by the fire and watch the waves. All 6
rooms have gas fireplaces.*

$99–$210
6 rooms, 6 pb
Most CC
C-ltd/S-no/P-no/HC-ltd

BB | Full Course Breakfast
Complimentary hot & cold beverages, wines, fresh baked cookies, popcorn;
special diets accommodated
Private trail to beach, outdoor fire pit, sitting room, WiFi, TV on request

OTIS

Lake House B&B
2165 NE East Devils
Lake Rd

541-996-8938 | 888-996-8938 | *Mary Sell*
lakehousebnb@charter.net | www.lakehousebb.com

*Cedar home and guest cabin located on a 680-acre freshwater lake, only
two miles from the Pacific coastline & downtown Lincoln City. Very quiet
area, large rooms, private entrance.*

$95–$220
3 rooms, 3 pb
Visa MC Disc Cash Checks
C-yes/S-ltd/P-no/HC-no

BB |Full breakfast
Fireplace, sitting room, private hot tub, rowboat or canoe, dock, fishing

PACIFIC CITY

**The Craftsman
Bed & Breakfast**
35255 4th St

503-965-4574 | *Michael Rech*
innkeeper@craftsmanbb.com | www.craftsmanbb.com/

The Craftsman B&B welcomes you to experience the beautiful Oregon Coast in style, grace and comfort. Everything in town is within walking distance. Park your car, relax and unplug. No lace, no doilies!

$110–$170
4 rooms, 4 pb
Most CC Cash
C-ltd/S-ltd/P-no/HC-no

BB | Full breakfast
Baked goodies upon arrival and throughout the day. Miele Nespresso coffee machine. Wine list.
Game table, hot tub, sun deck, DVD library, fireplace, reading inglenook, wi-fi, fisherman's sink

PORT ORFORD

**WildSpring
Guest Habitat**
92978 Cemetery Loop

541-332-0977 | **866-333-9453** | *Michelle & Dean Duarte*
info@wildspring.com | www.wildspring.com

WildSpring Guest Habitat is a small, ecofriendly resort in Port Orford overlooking the spectacular south Oregon coast. On 5 secluded acres, it offers luxury accommodations in a peaceful, naturally beautiful environment.

$198–$306
5 rooms, 5 pb
Most CC Cash
C-ltd/S-no/P-no/HC-yes

BB | Healthy Buffet
Coffee, teas, hot chocolate, juices, fruit, popcorn, chocolates
LCD TV/DVD, CD/iPod stereo, refrig, 500 DVDs, massage table, wine glasses, candles, spa robes

PORTLAND

A Painted Lady Inn
1927 N.E. 16th Ave.

503-335-0070 | *Jody Runge*
jrunge15@comcast.net | www.apaintedladyinn.com/

Located in vibrant, hip Northeast Portland, A Painted Lady Bed and Breakfast Inn offers a calm oasis in the heart of the city. Just steps from wonderful shops and fine restaurants, A Painted Lady will be your Portland home-away-from-home.

***2011 Lanier Best West Coast Award Winner:
Best for Nearby Museums***

$109–$179
5 rooms, 3 pb
Visa MC Disc Cash
C-yes/S-no/P-no/HC-ltd

BB | Full breakfast
Delightful garden patio & covered front porch with swing, Central City Location!

Bellaterra B&B
3935 SW Corbett Avenue

503-332-8125 | *Ellen*
bellaterrainfo@gmail.com | http://bellaterrabnb.com/

Newly-remodeled Victorian with ample common spaces, reading nook, traditional moldings and custom carvings, and five nature- and culture-themed guest rooms, each furnished with antiques and having its own glass or stone-tiled bathroom.

$95–$150
5 rooms, 5 pb
Most CC Cash
C-ltd/S-no/P-ltd/HC-no

BB | Full breakfast

Bluebird Guesthouse
3517 SE Division St

503-238-4333 | 866-717-4333
info@bluebirdguesthouse.com | www.bluebirdguesthouse.com

Charming, friendly & reasonably priced, the Bluebird Guesthouse is located in the heart of Southeast Portland. Visit our website to see an availability calendar and to make reservations.

$60–$105
7 rooms, 2 pb
Visa MC
C-ltd/S-no/P-no/HC-no

BB | Simple Continental Breakfast
A full kitchen guests can use to prepare meals
In-room A/C & heat controls. Complementary: wi-fi, internet computer, local phone, maps.

Britannia at Terwilliger Vista
515 SW Westwood Dr

503-244-0602 | 888-244-0602 | *Carl & Irene*
terwilligervista@gmail.com | www.terwilligervista.com

An elegant Georgian Colonial located in the West Hills of Portland. Situated on over a 1/2 acre of gardens, manicured lawns, and mature trees. This inn features blonde Honduran mahogany woodwork and Waterford crystal chandeliers throughout.

$110–$200
5 rooms, 5 pb
Visa MC
C-ltd/S-no/P-no/HC-ltd

BB | Full breakfast
Complimentary sodas & water
Sitting room, library, suites, fireplaces, cable TV, wireless Internet

Clinton Street Guesthouse
4220 SE Clinton Street

503-234-8752 | *Ann Skvarek & Jason Fayen*
everettandclintonstreet@gmail.com | www.clintonstreetguesthouse.com/

A lovely 1913 craftsman style B&B that offers authentic residential ambiance in a casual setting. Located in southeast Portland.

$70–$115
4 rooms, 2 pb
Most CC Cash Checks
C-ltd/S-ltd/P-no/HC-ltd

BB | Continental plus breakfast
Coffee & tea, special diets and early risers accommodated with prior notice
Front porch, living room, dining room, WiFi, books & DVDs, luxury linens, 20 minutes from airport

Evermore Guesthouse
3860 SE Clinton St
Portland

503-206-6509 | *Chris & Cecily*
info@evermoreguesthouse.com | www.evermoreguesthouse.com

Charming and relaxed accommodations in the heart of Southeast Portland. Furnished comfortably and simply - just enough of what you'd like without the clutter. Minutes to city attractions and a short walk to some of the best restaurants, cafes & shops

$90–$150
5 rooms, 5 pb
C-ltd/S-no/P-no/HC-no

BB |Continental Breakfast
Included: off-street parking, fast internet computer/wi-fi, area maps, local & long distance calls

PORTLAND

Hostess House
5758 NE Emerson St

503-282-7892 | 877-760-7799 | *Milli Laughlin*
hostess@hostesshouse.com | www.hostesshouse.com

An affordable tranquil getaway (since 1988). Gourmet breakfasts. Our inn is not for the conspicuous consumer but for the lower-maintenance person who is looking for quality accommodations with a smile. You'll not be disappointed.

$75–$85
2 rooms, 0 pb
Most CC
C-yes/S-ltd/P-no/HC-ltd

BB | Full gourmet breakfast
Afternoon tea
Outstanding hospitality since 1988, sitting rm, fireplace, park like backyard

Lion & the Rose
Victorian B&B
1810 NE 15th Ave

503-287-9245 | 800-955-1647 | Steven Unger
innkeeper@lionrose.com | www.lionrose.com

Exceptional B&B on the National Register of Historic Places, this majestic 1906 Queen Anne Victorian mansion takes you to another time. Seven unique guestrooms, with private baths, emanate Victorian charm.

$99–$224
7 rooms, 7 pb
Most CC
C-ltd/S-no/P-no/HC-no

BB | Full breakfast
Complimentary beverages, light refreshments
Telephones, free local & long distance, cable TV, data ports, high-speed wireless Internet access

Mt. Scott Manor
12570 SE Callahan Rd

503-477-4949 | *Virgil and Della*
mt.scottmanorbandb@comcast.net | http://mtscottmanor.com/

Mt. Scott Manor is a three-story modern home with 6,000sq.ft. guest area. Inspired by the grand old Tudor manor houses of England, you would think you were there. Placed between a breathtaking mountain view and a private forest complete with resident deer

$90–$150
4 rooms, 4 pb
Visa MC   Cash Checks
C-yes/S-no/P-ltd/HC-no

BB | Family style
Minutes from surrounding attractions, but located in a peaceful setting of nature and serenity

PROSPECT

Prospect Historic
Hotel-Motel
and Dinner House
391 Mill Creek Drive

541-560-3664 | 800-944-6490 | *Fred & Karen*
info@prospecthotel.com | www.prospecthotel.com

This spectacular Crater Lake lodging is located just 28 miles from Crater Lake National Park and 1/4 mile from the Rogue River, offering warm and inviting accommodations in the natural beauty of Oregon.

$70–$150
24 rooms, 24 pb
Visa MC Disc Cash
C-yes/S-no/P-yes/HC-yes

BB | Hearty breakfast
Dinner House offers superb American Cuisine from May through October. Prime Rib, Salmon, Shrimp, etc
Closest Historic Hotel B&B to Crater Lake. Modern Motel & Restaurant

SAINT PAUL

Inn at Champoeg
8899 Champoeg Rd NE

503-678-6088 | *Paterese & West Livaudais*
info@innatchampoeg.com | *www.innatchampoeg.com*

Located among the rolling hills and fields of the north Willamette Valley, The Inn at Champoeg is uniquely suited as a destination of quiet repose. The spacious elegance of the Inn welcomes each visitor with open arms.

$149–$169
2 rooms, 2 pb
Visa MC AmEx   Cash
C-ltd/S-no/P-no/HC-no

BB | Full breakfast

SEAL ROCK

Caledonia House B&B
6575 NW Pacific
Coast Hwy

541-563-7337 | *Dee Brodie & Belinda Goody*
caledoniabnb@peak.org | http://caledoniabb.com

Our Scotland-inspired B&B is perfectly located between the Pacific Ocean and the temperate coastal rain forests that encompass over 2 acres of our certified wildlife habitat and nature trails. We are also centrally located on the scenic Oregon coast.

$119–$169
5 rooms, 5 pb
Visa MC   Cash
C-ltd/S-no/P-no/HC-no

BB | Full breakfast
In room coffee or tea and "Welcome" treats.
luxurious linens, flat screen TVs, in room temp. control, WiFi or PC, guest kitchen, Tub for Two...

SEASIDE

Gilbert Inn
341 Beach Drive

503-738-9770 | **800-410-9770** | *Gilbert Inn LLC*
gilbertinn@seasurf.net | www.gilbertinn.com

Enjoy a unique opportunity to stay in the Historic Home of Alexandre Gilbert. This Queen Anne Victorian is located in Seaside, Oregon. One block from the beach and downtown, this Seaside oasis is quiet and relaxed, offering guests a home away from home.

$69–$229
6 rooms, 6 pb
Most CC Cash
S-no/P-no/HC-no

EP |
In-room coffee. Many restaurants within 5 minute walk from the Inn
Sitting room, games, books

SOUTH BEACH

**Stone Crest Cellar
Bed & Breakfast**
9556 South Coast Hwy.

541-867-6621 | *Judy & Craig Joubert*
jjoubert@charter.net | www.stonecrestbb.com

A spectacular ocean front Inn & venue for relaxing get-aways, weddings, elopements & receptions. Full service wedding packages for all budgets. Voted 2010 Bride's Choice Award Wedding Wire.

$145–$195
2 rooms, 2 pb
Most CC Cash Checks
C-ltd/S-ltd/P-no/HC-ltd

BB | Full breakfast
Evening wine & appetizers
Ocean views, private baths, sitting room, deck

ST. HELENS
Nob Hill Riverview B&B 503-396-5555 | *Matthew & Tana Phemester*
285 S 2nd St   stay@nobhillbb.com | www.nobhillbb.com

Nob Hill Riverview Bed and Breakfast loves to pamper our guests! The home is newly restored, fresh and beautiful. Listed on historical places. A true 1900 Arts and Craft home. Beautiful views of the river from most rooms. Upscale and luxury.

$110–$210   BB | Full Hot Organic Gourmet Breakfast
3 rooms, 3 pb   In the late afternoon guests can enjoy a complimentary Afternoon Tea and
Most CC Cash Checks   appetizers upon request
C-ltd/S-no/P-no/HC-ltd   Gathering rooms, wood-burning fireplace, sunroom filled with flowers, TV, business
                 accommodations

SUN RIVER
DiamondStone   **541-536-6263** | *Doug & Gloria Watt*
Guest Lodges   diamond@diamondstone.com | www.diamondstone.com/

DiamondStone manages several luxurious, comfy, rural Vacation Rentals. DS B&B offers private baths, TV/DVD/VCRs/phones, outdoor spa. Featured in "Northwest Best Places" it is at the heart of the recreational mecca that is Central Oregon—golf, fish, ski!

$99–$139   BB | Full breakfast
10 rooms, 10 pb   Coffee, tea, complimentary beverages - beer, wine, juices.
Most CC Cash Checks   Western art, hot tub, outdoor BBQ, free movie library.
C-yes/S-ltd/P-yes/HC-no

WALDPORT
Cliff House B&B   **541-563-2506** | *Sharon Robinson*
1450 SW Adahi Rd   innkeeper@cliffhouseoregon.com | www.cliffhouseoregon.com

Cliff House Bed and Breakfast, a luxuriously restored historic home, overlooks the Pacific Ocean and Alsea Bay on the Central Oregon Coast. Experience a renaissance of elegance and old world charm transposed into the 21st century.

$125–$225   BB | Full breakfast
4 rooms, 4 pb   Afternoon tea, coffee, fresh lemonade, cookies
Visa MC   Cash Checks   Sitting room, hot tubs, decks, ocean gazing, wireless Internet, massage services,
C-ltd/S-no/P-no/HC-no   outdoor weddings

WHEELER
Wheeler On The   **503-368-5858** | **800-469-3204** | *Pat Scribner*
Bay Lodge   WheelerLodge@nehalemtel.net | www.wheeleronthebay.com
580 Marine Dr

Two hours west of Portland is a rare find on the Oregon Coast. Wheeler on the Bay Lodge on Nehalem Bay Estuary has water & mountain views. Services include free WiFi, spas, massages, movies,kayaks and a private boat dock. Charter boat, fishing or crabbing

$85–$225   BB | Limited breakfast
11 rooms, 11 pb   Complimentary teas, coffee, spiced cider, cocoa
Visa MC Disc Cash Checks Spa, fireplace, TV, DVD/VHS movies, massage, fridge, micro, coffee maker,
C-yes/S-ltd/P-no/HC-yes   telephones, kayaks, WiFi

SeaQuest Inn
95354 Highway 101

541-547-3782 | **800-341-4878** | *Kelley Essoe & Nerina Perez*
info@seaquestinn.com | www.seaquestinn.com

As our most welcomed guest — indulgent comfort, ocean views, the crashing surf, and your own warm, inviting Jacuzzi tub await your arrival at the oceanfront SeaQuest Inn Bed and Breakfast in Yachats, Oregon.

$150–$275
7 rooms, 7 pb
Most CC Cash
C-ltd/S-no/P-no/HC-ltd

BB | Full Gourmet Breakfast
All day home-baked goodies, coffee, tea, hot cocoa & cider, fresh fruit, cheese & crackers
Jacuzzi tubs, private decks, ocean views, great room, sitting room, 2 ponds, sandy beach, vast lawn

OREGON STATE ANIMAL: BEAVER

Washington

OLYMPIC MOUNTAINS,
WASHINGTON

● Seattle

ABERDEEN

A Harbor View Inn
111 W 11th St

360-533-7996 | 877-533-7996 | *Cindy Lonn*
info@aharborview.com | www.aharborview.com

Historic Colonial Revival home, antiques, every room with waterview, located in a historic district, walking homes tour included with your stay and breakfast in the sunroom overlooking the harbor.

$119–$225
5 rooms, 5 pb
Visa MC AmEx
C-ltd/S-no/P-no/HC-ltd

BB | Full Country Breakfast
Huge selection of afternoon tea, organic snacks & coffee
Sitting room, tennis court, suites, fireplace, cable TV, accommodates business travelers

ASHFORD

Alexander's Country Inn, Restaurant & Day Spa
37515 State Rd 706 E

360-569-2300 | 800-654-7615 | *Bernadette Ronan/Jerry Harnish*
info@alexanderscountryinn.com | www.alexanderscountryinn.com

One mile from Mount Rainier National Park. Retains its historic charm and character while providing modern amenities. Full breakfast, evening wine, media room and hot tub are included in the daily rate. 2 self-catered vacation cabins. Popular Restaurant.

$99–$175
12 rooms, 12 pb
Visa MC Disc Cash
C-yes/S-no/P-no/HC-ltd

BB | Full breakfast
Complimentary wine & seasonal fresh fruits, acclaimed restaurant
Day Spa offering massage. Parlor with fireplace. Hot tub, Media Room w/big cable TV. Free WiFi

BAINBRIDGE ISLAND

Holly Lane Gardens
9432 Holly Farm Ln

206-842-8959 | *Patti Dusbabek*
patty.dusbabek@comcast.net | www.hollylanegardens.com

Olympic Mountain views, flowers, woodlands. Cottage and Suite offer bedroom, front room, kitchen and bath. Clerestory Room on the 2nd floor of the house, has a spectacular mountain & garden view as does the 3rd floor bedroom.

$90–$135
5 rooms, 4 pb
Most CC Cash Checks
C-yes/S-ltd/P-ltd/HC-ltd

BB | Full breakfast
Beverages, homemade international desserts, organic eggs/vegetables/fruit/herbs
Reading, entertainment center, libraries, hot tub, 8.6 acres, private cottage, fire pit, gardens

BELFAIR

Selah Inn on Hood Canal
130 NE Dulalip Landing

360-275-0916 | 877-232-7941 | *Bonnie & Pat McCullough*
innkeeper@selahinn.com | www.selahinn.com

An elegant NW lodge with a majestic view of the Hood Canal. Access to the beach for digging clams; we'll steam them for your first of five courses at dinner. A perfect spot for a destination wedding! Small groups and business travelers are welcome.

$95–$195
4 rooms, 4 pb
Visa MC
C-ltd/S-no/P-no/HC-ltd

BB | Full breakfast
Lunch & dinner available, bar service
Conference room, sitting room, library, Jacuzzi, fireplaces, cable TV, ensuite massage, deck hot tub

BELLEVUE

A Cascade View
13425 NE 27th St

425-883-7078 | 888-883-7078 | *Marianne & Bill Bundren*
innkeepers@acascadeview.com | www.acascadeview.com

Panoramic views of the Cascade Mountains with extensive colorful and fragrant gardens. 2 beautiful rooms with private baths and extra amenities, fireplace, TV/VCR, sitting room, full breakfasts. The perfect location for the tourist or business traveler

$130–$150
2 rooms, 2 pb
Visa MC AmEx   Cash Checks
C-yes/S-ltd/P-no/HC-no

BB | Full breakfast
Afternoon tea if requested
Sitting room, library, fireplaces, cable TV, accommodate business travelers, wireless home

BIRCH BAY

Cottages by the Beach
4813 Lora Lane

425-339-8081 | *Kelvin & Patti Barton*
info@ilovecottages.com | www.ilovecottages.com

Two fully furnished cottages beautifully decorated with full kitchens in the heart of Birch Bay, a resort area for over 100 years. Romantic lace and French Country adorn the 2 bedroom "Lora's Cottage" while "Seashell Cottage" is great for golfing getaways

$150–$285
2 rooms, 3 pb
Visa MC Disc
C-yes/S-no/P-no/HC-no

BB | Brioche, cinnamon rolls, fruit
Cheese & egg layer casserole baked in a brioche shell, cinnamon rolls, fruit, coffee & tea
Firewood & firestarters provided, custom soaps, dishwasher, full kitchen, washer/dryer, RV parking

CAMANO ISLAND

Inn at Barnum Point
464 S Barnum Rd

360-387-2256 | 800-910-2256 | *Carolin Barnum*
barnumpoint@camano.net | www.innatbarnumpoint.com

All rooms have spectacular water and mountain views. Enjoy our spacious 900 sq ft suite. A Cape Cod house on a bluff overlooking Port Susan Bay and the Cascade Mountains. Private bath and fireplaces. A tranquil place to relax, beachcomb, enjoy the birds.

$125–$225
3 rooms, 3 pb
Visa MC Disc Cash Checks
C-yes/S-no/P-no/HC-no

BB |Full breakfast brunch
Complimentary beverages
books,VCR tapes, sidewalks, landscaping, outside lighting, waterfront views from every window

CAMAS

Camas Hotel
405 NE 4th Avenue

360-834-5722 | *Thomas and Karen Hall*
reservations@camashotel.com | www.camashotel.com

Situated near Portland & the Columbia River Gorge! 100 year old hotel set amidst historic tree-lined shopping district of Camas. Restored to its original 1911 charm with added comfort of European style hospitality & American warmth.

$79–$130
10 rooms, 10 pb
Most CC Cash
C-ltd/S-no/P-ltd/HC-no

BB | Continental plus breakfast
On site restaurant
Free wifi, free parking, concierge service

COLVILLE

Lazy Bee B&B
3651 Deep Lake
Boundary Rd

509-732-8917 | *Bud Budinger & Joann Bender*
budinger.bender@plix.com | www.travelguides.com/home/Lazy_Bee/

The Lazy Bee is a rustic lodge nestled at the base of Red Mountain with a view of Stone Mountain near the Canadian border. We've deliberately slowed the pace of life in order to give guests less stress and a sense of tranquility.

$129
2 rooms, 0 pb
Visa MC
C-ltd/S-ltd/P-ltd/HC-ltd

BB | Continental breakfast
Lunch, dinner, afternoon tea, snacks
Library, bicycles, fireplaces,   accommodate business travelers, new outdoor romantic bedroom

COUPEVILLE

Anchorage Inn
807 N Main St

360-678-5581 | **877-230-1313** | *Dave & Dianne Binder*
crowsnest@anchorage-inn.com | www.anchorage-inn.com

Awarded the best B&B in the Pacific NW, the Victorian Anchorage Inn B&B is located on beautiful Whidbey Island, in the historic town of Coupeville, Washington. Perfect for privacy, group retreats, weddings, anniversaries and as an escape for lovers.

$89–$149
7 rooms, 7 pb
Visa MC   Cash Checks
C-ltd/S-ltd/P-ltd/HC-ltd

BB | Full breakfast
Cookies, popcorn, coffee, tea, cider, hot chocolate & cold beverages
WiFi, cable TV, VCR, DVD, telephone, dinner reservations, porch & patio, maps, umbrellas

The Blue Goose Inn
702 N Main St

360-678-4284 | **877-678-4284** | *Sue & Marty*
stay@bluegooseinn.com | www.bluegooseinn.com

Named "Best in the West 2010–2011"—for the second year in a row! The Blue Goose Inn graciously combines history and comfort in neighboring 1880's Victorian homes.

 Dreams Do Come True participating inn—Valid anytime; will offer a room upgrade

$119–$149
6 rooms, 6 pb
Visa MC   Cash Checks
S-no/P-no/HC-ltd

BB | Scrumptious full breakfast
Fresh baked cookies & hot beverages all day; cheese platters, wine & champagne available on request
Centrally located on Whidbey Island just a short walk to Coupeville's waterfront shops & restaurants

DEER HARBOR

**The Place at
Cayou Cove**
161 Olympic Lane

360-376-3199 | **888-596-7222** | *Charles & Valerie Binford*
stay@cayoucove.com | www.cayoucove.com/

Nestled on the shore of Deer Harbor between Cayou Valley's two mountain ridges at the southwest tip of Orcas Island, The Place At Cayou Cove takes full advantage of the southerly views across the Harbor to the Olympic Mountains in the distance.

$125–$495
3 rooms, 3 pb
Visa MC   Cash
C-yes/S-no/P-yes/HC-yes

BB | Full Breakfast
Coffee & teas, wine & hors d'oeuvres are offered each evening during the summer season
Complimentary ferry & airport pickup, organic garden, private hot tubs, self-service rates available

EASTSOUND

Kangaroo House B&B
on Orcas Island
1459 North Beach Rd

360-376-2175 | **888-371-2175** | *Charles & Jill*
innkeeper@KangarooHouse.com | www.KangarooHouse.com

1907 Craftsman B&B near Eastsound on beautiful Orcas Island in WA state's San Juan Islands. Offering comfortable beds, delicious full breakfasts, and a relaxing atmosphere. This stately Orcas Island landmark has been hosting guests for over 100 years.

$100–$195
5 rooms, 5 pb
Most CC Cash
C-ltd/S-no/P-no/HC-no

BB | Full delicious 3 course breakfast
Early risers get breakfast to go if you can't sit down with us in the morning
Special diets on request, living room fireplace, sitting room, hot tub in garden

FORKS

Miller Tree Inn
654 E Division St

360-374-6806 | **800-943-6563** | *Bill & Susan Brager*
millertreeinn@centurytel.net | www.millertreeinn.com

Come and share our beautiful 1916 farmhouse, located on the edge of town and bordered by trees and pasture lands. We offer a warm welcome, hearty breakfasts, spacious common areas, and quiet, comfortable rooms for a reasonable price.

 Dreams Do Come True participating inn—Valid October 1–May 15

$115–$215
8 rooms, 8 pb
Most CC Cash Checks
C-ltd/S-no/P-ltd/HC-ltd

BB | Full breakfast
Lemonade, coffee, tea, cocoa and cookies, pre-dawn breakfast during fishing season available
Off-street parking, TV, DVDs, books, piano, board games, fireplace, wireless net, some jetted tubs

FRIDAY HARBOR

Bird Rock Hotel
35 First St

360-378-5848 | **800-352-2632** | *Laura Saccio*
stay@birdrockhotel.com | www.birdrockhotel.com

An exquisitely crafted, eco-intelligent collection of stylishly modern rooms ranging from simple, European-style sleeping rooms to deluxe, harbor-view suites.

$87–$345
15 rooms, 11 pb
Visa MC AmEx   Cash
C-yes/S-no/P-no/HC-yes

BB | Gourmet breakfast delivered to you
Afternoon snacks and refreshments
Rooms have ipod-docking radio, beach cruiser bikes for use, free wifi, flat-panel hdtv

**Harrison House
Suites B&B**
235 C St

360-378-3587 | 800-407-7933
Anna Maria de Freitas & David Pass
innkeeper@harrisonhousesuites.com | www.harrisonhousesuites.com

*A hillside retreat conveniently located 1½ blocks from the ferry terminal
and historic downtown Friday Harbor. Old world charm combined with
contemporary conveniences offer one of a kind accommodations in this
historic residence.*

 Dreams Do Come True participating inn—Valid October–May (except holidays)

$99–$395
6 rooms, 6 pb
Most CC Cash Checks
C-yes/S-ltd/P-yes/HC-ltd

BB | Full breakfast
On-site catering & dinner at Coho Restaurant, cookies, cooking classes & wine dinner
Use of bikes, kayaks, laundry facilities, off-street parking, reading and movie library,
massages

GIG HARBOR

Bear's Lair B&B
13706 92nd Ave Ct NW

253-857-8877 | 877-855-9768 | *Giulio & Jenny Santori*
bearslairbb@aol.com | www.bearslairbb.com

*Come enjoy our luxurious five acre country estate-style B&B. Stay at the
private carriage house, perfect for romantic getaways or one of the three
luxurious rooms in the main house. Breathtaking gardens, island
gazebo, duck pond and minutes from downtown.*

$115–$215
4 rooms, 4 pb
Visa MC   Cash Checks
C-ltd/S-ltd/P-no/HC-yes

BB | Full breakfast
Homemade baked goods throughout the day, self-service coffee & tea 24 hours
Upscale accommodations, private cottage, gardens, suites, fireplaces, video library

Waterfront Inn
9017 N Harborview Dr

253-857-0770 | *Steve & Janis Denton*
info@waterfront-inn.com | www.waterfront-inn.com

*Located at the head of Gig Harbor Bay, the Waterfront Inn offers private,
luxurious rooms in a beautiful historic home. Each room has a private
entrance, a large bath with Jacuzzi tub, & many rooms have a fireplace
with a sitting area & awesome views.*

$140–$229
7 rooms, 7 pb
Visa MC
C-ltd/S-no/P-no/HC-ltd

BB | Continental breakfast
Complimentary tea, hot chocolate & popcorn to go with free DVDs, catering available
Huge over-the-water sitting pier, complimentary kayak use, lovely garden, Jacuzzi
tub, Internet

GREENBANK

**Guest House
Log Cottages**
24371 SR 525

360-678-3115 | 800-997-3115 | *Peggy Walker*
stay@guesthouselogcottages.com | www.guesthouselogcottages.com

*Spark and rekindle your romance at Guest House Log Cottages B&B, a
place where your pleasure and comfort are a priority. These beautifully
furnished, cozy cottages are scattered on 25 acres of forest on Whidbey
Island in Puget Sound.*

 *Dreams Do Come True participating inn—Valid October 15, 2011–April 30, 2012;
Sunday–Thursday mid-week winter*

$125–$350
6 rooms, 6 pb
Visa MC Disc
C-ltd/S-no/P-no/HC-ltd

BB | Generous continental breakfast
TV/DVD/VCR, CD player, exercise room, pool, spa, retreat & honeymoon spot,
free WiFi, fireplaces

ILWACO

**China Beach
Retreat Inn**
222 Robert Gray Dr

360-642-5660 | 800-INN-1896
David Campiche & Laurie Anderson
innkeeper@chinabeachretreat.com | www.chinabeachretreat.com

China Beach Retreat is a nest of delights, where your senses receive all that they can demand of nature. This B&B retreat is elegantly and comfortably furnished in antiques. The decor is an eclectic enhancement of the beautiful views.

$179–$299
4 rooms, 4 pb
Visa MC AmEx   Cash
S-no/P-no/HC-ltd

BB | Full breakfast
Coffee & tea service available all day. Freshly baked cookies upon arrival.
Group retreats, weddings, views, spa tubs. Audubon Cottage is perfect for honeymoons and anniversary

LA CONNER

La Conner Country Inn
107 S. 2nd St.

360-466-3101 | 888-466-4113 | *Cindy Nelson*
reservations@laconnerlodging.com |
www.laconnerlodging.com/laconner-country-inn.php

Spacious and cozy guest rooms feature fireplace, wooden accents and charm. Wireless Internet and full service conference facilities available. Expansive breakfast includes fresh fruit, pastries, home made granola, hard boiled eggs and much more.

$109–$189
28 rooms, 28 pb
Most CC Cash
C-yes/S-no/P-yes/HC-yes

BB | Continental plus breakfast
Freshly baked cookies, coffee & tea served in the library every afternoon
Business Center, Wireless Internet, meeting facilities

LAKEWOOD

Thornewood Castle Inn
8601 N Thorne Lane SW

253-584-4393 | *Deanna Robinson, J B Douglas*
info@thornewoodcastle.com | www.thornewoodcastle.com

Thornewood Castle is World Class, Historic & One of a Kind. Experience another time, another space with an overnight visit to this magnificent estate. Perfect for a honeymoon, romantic evening with someone special, or to treat yourself to rest & renew.

$250–$550
8 rooms, 8 pb
Most CC Cash Checks
C-ltd/S-no/P-no/HC-ltd

BB | Full breakfast
In room refrigerator & microwave, TV/VCR, jetted tubs, fireplaces,
murder mystery evenings

WASHINGTON
STATE MARINE MAMMAL:
ORCA WHALE

LANGLEY

Country Cottage
of Langley
215 6th St

360-221-8709 | 800-713-3860 | *Jacki Stewart*
stay@acountrycottage.com | www.acountrycottage.com

A classic, 1920 farmhouse with 5 romantic & distinctly designed cottages with private decks on 2 acres of beautiful gardens. Amazing view of Puget Sound, 2-person Jacuzzis, fireplaces, gourmet breakfast delivered to cottage, short walk to the village.

$139–$189
5 rooms, 5 pb
Visa MC AmEx   Cash Checks
C-yes/S-no/P-ltd/HC-ltd

BB | Full gourmet breakfast
A full, hot breakfast served in your cottage, on the deck, or in our four seasons dining room
Scenic dining room, WiFi, view, deck, living room, gardens, gazebo, croquet & bocce ball

Saratoga Inn
201 Cascade Ave

360-221-5801 | 800-698-2910 | *Kayce Nakamura*
info@saratogainnwhidbeyisland.com | www.saratogainnwhidbeyisland.com/

The stunning beauty of Puget Sound and its many islands is the setting for the Saratoga Inn. Your journey begins with a scenic, 20 minute, car-ferry ride from the mainland to Whidbey Island.

$145–$325
16 rooms, 16 pb
Most CC Cash
C-yes/S-no/P-no/HC-yes

BB | Full breakfast
Afternoon wine, tea & hors d' oeuvres, freshly-baked cookies, drinks available throughout the day
Porch with rocking chairs, bicycles to borrow, sitting room, conference room

LEAVENWORTH

Abendblume Pension
12570 Ranger Rd

509-548-4059 | 800-669-7634 | *Randy & Renee Sexauer*
info@abendblume.com | www.abendblume.com

Inspired by fine European country inns, Abendblume is one of Leavenworth's finest award-winning bed and breakfasts. "A very private world

to escape and rejuvenate."

$145–$269
7 rooms, 7 pb
Visa MC Disc Cash Checks
S-no/P-no/HC-ltd

BB | Full breakfast
Fireplaces, down comforters, balconies, whirlpool tubs

All Seasons River Inn
8751 Icicle Rd

509-548-1425 | 800-254-0555 | *Susan & Dale Wells*
info@allseasonsriverinn.com | www.allseasonsriverinn.com

Set on a quiet wooded riverbank, this gracious inn offers spacious riverview suites with jetted tubs, private bath, comfortable riverview seating; decks, and some fireplace. And oh, what a breakfast!

$165–$230
7 rooms, 7 pb
Visa MC
C-ltd/S-no/P-no/HC-yes

BB | Full breakfast
Dessert
Game table area, TV room, bicycles, Jacuzzis, suites, fireplaces, refrigerators, wireless Internet

LEAVENWORTH

Enchanted River Inn
9700 E Leavenworth Rd

509-548-9797 | **877-548-9797** | *Bill & Kathy Lynn*
river.inn@verizon.net | www.enchantedriverinn.com

Situated on a rapidly flowing river with awesome views of nature encircled by tall mountains yet only a short walk to the Bavarian Village of Leavenworth. Sleep to the peaceful sounds of the river and awaken to the aroma of a gourmet breakfast.

$230–$250
3 rooms, 3 pb
Visa MC AmEx   Cash Checks
S-no/P-no/HC-no

BB | 3 course gourmet breakfast
Pillow top king beds, binoculars for watching the area wild life and river features, guest robes

Haus Rohrbach
Pension
12882 Ranger Rd

509-548-7024 | **800-548-4477** | *Carol & Mike Wentink*
info@hausrohrbach.com | www.hausrohrbach.com

A European-style Country Inn overlooking the beautiful Leavenworth Valley celebrating 34 years of service in 2008. Where hospitality, recreation and relaxation are a tradition.

$105–$200
10 rooms, 8 pb
Most CC Cash Checks
C-yes/S-no/P-no/HC-ltd

BB | Full country breakfast!
Wine dinner series, Theatre dinners
Seasonal pool and year-round spa, and incredible gardens, scrapbooking weekends

Mountain Home Lodge
8201 Mountain Home Rd

509-548-7077 | **800-414-2378** | *Kathy & Brad Schmidt*
info@mthome.com | www.mthome.com

On a secluded 20 acre meadow overlooking the Cascades, & surrounded by forest, our luxurious 12 guestroom lodge & cabins combine superb cuisine, year-round outdoor activities and total pampered relaxation.

$130–$530
12 rooms, 12 pb
Visa MC Disc
C-ltd/S-no/P-no/HC-ltd

BB | Full breakfast
Four course dinner, gourmet breakfast & lunch included in winter
Fireplace, Jacuzzi, robes, stereo systems, heated pool, hot tub, tennis court, weddings, plasma TVs

River Haus
in the Pines
9690 E Leavenworth Rd

509-548-9690 | *Mike & Cindy Hendricks*
info@riverhausinthepines.com | www.riverhausinthepines.com

River Haus in the Pines B&B is a craftsman style home beautifully situated on the Wenatchee River with seasonal shoreline access. Ideal setting for both peaceful relaxation and outdoor adventures.

$189–$225
3 rooms, 3 pb
Visa MC
C-ltd/S-no/P-no/HC-ltd

BB | Full breakfast
River & mountain views, fireplace, private decks, private bathrooms with soaking tub, TV/DVD/CD

LEAVENWORTH

Run of the River
9308 E Leavenworth Rd

509-548-7171 | **800-288-6491** | *Steve & Jan Bollinger*
info@runoftheriver.com | www.runoftheriver.com

As Washington's only 4-star inn rated by NW Best Places, Run of the River Inn has earned its distinction for peaceful romance and luxury surroundings. Six suites offer a haven of privacy, with fireplaces, Jacuzzi tubs and decks to view the refuge.

$230–$265
6 rooms, 6 pb
Visa MC Disc Cash
S-no/P-no/HC-yes

BB | Hearty, healthy and fresh!
Afternoon tea, treats
Complimentary tandem, mountain bikes & snowshoes, expert tips on discovering the magic of the Valley

LONG BEACH

Boreas B&B Inn
607 N Ocean Beach Blvd

360-642-8069 | **888-642-8069** | *Susie Goldsmith & Bill Verner*
info@boreasinn.com | www.boreasinn.com

If you love three-course gourmet breakfasts created from local delicacies, glorious ocean vistas, beautiful surroundings, and award-winning gracious service, Boreas Inn is your getaway. The ambiance at Boreas entices you to never go home again!

$179–$199
5 rooms, 5 pb
Most CC Cash Checks
C-ltd/S-no/P-no/HC-no

BB | Full 3 course gourmet breakfast
Triple chocolate brownies, organic Boreas coffee, extensive tea selection, pistachios & chocolates!
Concierge service, two living rooms with fireplaces, glorious ocean views, hot tub by the sand dunes

LOPEZ ISLAND

Edenwild Inn
132 Lopez Rd

360-468-3238 | **800-606-0662** | *Kris Weinshilboum*
edenwild@rockisland.com | www.edenwildinn.com/

Experience friendly service and the warm atmosphere of Lopez Island from our premium accommodations, nestled in the heart of Lopez Village.

$170–$195
8 rooms, 8 pb
Visa MC
C-ltd/S-no/P-no/HC-yes

BB | Self serve breakfast
Patio, living room, dining room, unique decor, comfortable accommodations, marina views, fireplaces

LUMMI ISLAND

Full Bloom Farm
2330 Tuttle Ln

360-758-7173 | *Elisabeth Marshall*
info@fullbloomfarmpeonies.com | www.fullbloomfarmpeonies.com/vacation

At Full Bloom Farm, enjoy the relaxing ambiance of our lovely cottage and apartment in our beautiful, award-winning garden setting. We raise herbaceous and intersectional peonies—in Spring, the fields are a stunning sight in full bloom.

$120–$150
2 rooms, 2 pb
Cash Checks
C-ltd/S-no/P-ltd/HC-yes

EP |
Deck, full kitchen, fireplaces, bicycles, award-winning gardens, cottage & apartment rentals

LUMMI ISLAND

The Celtic Mariner B&B
1611 Seacrest Dr.

360-758-2270 | *James & Tammy Strong*
jmtbstrong@msn.com | www.thecelticmarinerbandb.com/

The Celtic Mariner offers you an escape from urban intensity! Our B&B has a picnic and relaxation area on the seacliff with splendid views of Hale Passage, Mt Baker, The Sisters, Portage Island and incredible sunrises.

$100–$120
1 rooms, 1 pb
Visa MC   Cash
C-ltd/S-no/P-no/HC-no

BB | Full breakfast
Private entrance, queen sized bed, leather sofa, kitchenette with mini refrigerator, fireplace

MT. BAKER

Mt. Baker Lodging, Inc.
7463 Mt Baker Hwy

360-599-2453 | **800-709-SNOW (7669)** | *Guest Services*
reservations@mtbakerlodging.com | www.mtbakerlodging.com

A delightful alternative to the traditional Mt. Baker area bed & breakfast or inn, Mt. Baker Lodging proudly offers private, self-catered, fully equipped vacation home rentals, located in Glacier and Maple Falls at the gateway to Mount Baker, Washington.

$109–$509
95 rooms, 95 pb
Most CC
C-yes/S-ltd/P-ltd/HC-ltd

EP |
Fully equipped kitchens with cookware. Catering available upon request!
All bed & bath linens provided

MUKILTEO

Hogland House B&B
917 Webster St

425-742-7639 | **888-681-5101** | *Kay Scheller*
romance@hoglandhouse.com | www.hoglandhouse.com

A National Historic Register waterfront home with Old World finishes, overlooking Puget Sound in Old Mukilteo. Includes a hot tub, collectibles, wooded trails on five acres at the end of a quiet road.

$85–$125
2 rooms, 2 pb
Visa MC
C-yes/S-ltd/P-yes/HC-no

BB | Full breakfast or "On Your Own"
Hot tub, porches, sitting room, TV/DVD, wireless Internet, in-room coffee

NORTH BEND

Roaring River B&B
46715 SE 129th St

425-888-4834 | **877-627-4647** | *Herschel & Peggy Backues*
roaringriver@comcast.net | www.theroaringriver.com

Choose a hot tub, sauna, or Jacuzzi room. Very romantic, very private, wonderful restaurants and incredible views of mountains, rivers, forests and occasional wildlife.

$109–$195
5 rooms, 5 pb
Most CC
C-ltd/S-no/P-no/HC-no

BB | Full breakfast
Warm full breakfast baskets delivered to the door each morning
Jacuzzis, WiFi, fireplaces, cable TV, business travelers, private entrances, sitting areas, decks

OCEAN PARK

Charles Nelson
Guest House
26205 Sandridge Rd

360-665-3016 | 888-862-9756 | *Ginger Bish*
cnbandb@charlesnelsonbandb.com | www.charlesnelsonbandb.com

On the edge of Ocean Park and just within the boundaries of Nachotta, our inn overlooks Willapa Bay and the Wildlife Refuge of Long Island.

 Dreams Do Come True participating inn—Valid September–June 30th; will offer a room upgrade

$160–$180
3 rooms, 3 pb
Visa MC AmEx   Cash Checks
C-yes/S-no/P-yes/HC-no

BB | Full breakfast
Smoked oyster or salmon with seasonal fruit, cheese & fruit plate
Sunroom, fireplace, hammocks, freshly pressed sheets, soft robes & thirsty towels,
wine @ 5:00 pm

George Johnson
House B&B
26301 'N' Place

360-665-6993 | 866-665-6993 | *Charlotte Killien*
stay@georgejohnsonhouse.com | www.georgejohnsonhouse.com

Experience the Peninsula's historic spirit in this beautiful 1913 Crafts-man home. Nestled on a quiet street, it's just a short walk to the ocean beach or to nearby attractions. Each of the three guestrooms offer private bathrooms and wireless Internet.

$125–$165
3 rooms, 3 pb
Visa MC   Cash Checks
C-ltd/S-no/P-no

BB | Full Country Breakfast
Antique accessories, high-speed wireless Internet, wraparound porch, library &
perennial gardens

PORT ANGELES

Colette's B&B
339 Finn Hall Rd

360-457-9197 | 877-457-9777 | *Karen & Richard Fields*
colettes@colettes.com | www.colettes.com

Breathtaking 10-acre oceanfront estate, nestled between the Olympic Range and the Strait of Juan de Fuca. Luxury oceanfront king suites w/Jacuzzi spas for two and romantic fireplaces. Fodors "Top Choice". Best Places to Kiss-"Utopian Oceanfront Hideaway".

$195–$395
5 rooms, 5 pb
Visa MC
S-no/P-no/HC-ltd

BB | Multi-Course Gourmet Breakfast
Afternoon Tea, evening wine & hors d'oeuvres
Romantic getaway, concierge services, Jacuzzis, fireplaces, king suites, DVD library,
very private

Domaine Madeleine
146 Wildflower Ln

360-457-4174 | 888-811-8376 | *Jeri Weinhold*
stay@domainemadeleine.com | www.domainemadeleine.com

Serene, romantic, contemporary estate with panoramic mountain and waterviews. Exquisite gardens, Monet garden replica, European/Asian antiques, fireplace, Jacuzzi, private entrance, renowned 5-course breakfast.

$150–$310
5 rooms, 5 pb
Most CC Cash Checks
C-ltd/S-ltd/P-no/HC-no

BB | Full breakfast
24 hour coffee, tea, hot chocolate, cider, cookies, candy
Sitting room, library, Jacuzzi, games, fireplaces, cable TV, DVDs, maps, guidebooks,
panoramic views

PORT ANGELES

Eden by the Sea
1027 Finn Hall Rd.

360-452-6021 | *David & Evelyn Brown*
info@edenbythesea.net | www.edenbythesea.net/index.html

A unique Eden by the Sea experience awaits you, secluded on the Olympic Peninsula, in the land of the Great Northwest. This waterfront property will provide you with a peaceful rest in rooms with private baths and views of the water and mountains.

$150–$185
3 rooms, 3 pb
Visa MC   Cash Checks
C-ltd/S-no/P-no/HC-ltd

BB | Multiple course gourmet breakfast
Afternoon Tea, lemonade & cookies, fruit, fresh veggies, crackers, chips, nuts
Great room & library downstairs, large conversation room with TV upstairs

Inn at Rooster Hill
112 Reservoir Rd

360-452-4933 | **877-221-0837** | *Peggy Frehner*
info@innatroosterhill.com | www.innatroosterhill.com

Inn at Rooster Hill is a quiet, French-country bed and breakfast set on a 2½ acre piece of wooded property in Port Angeles, Washington. All of our rooms have great amenities and with all new, high-quality bedding, you are assured of a good night's sleep

$119–$189
7 rooms, 7 pb
Visa MC Disc Cash Checks
C-ltd/S-ltd/P-ltd/HC-no

BB | Full breakfast
Jacuzzi tub, antique beds, luxury bedding, TV,fridge, coffee, wireless

Sea Cliff Gardens
Bed & Breakfast
397 Monterra Dr

360-452-2322 | **800-880-1332** | *Bonnie & Phillip Kuchler*
info@SeaCliffGardens.com | www.seacliffgardens.com

Quiet waterfront luxury near Olympic National Park. Roam through two acres brimming with oceanfront flower gardens and towering cedars, then relax on a bench-for-two and watch the sunset over the Salish Sea. Spacious rooms feature spectacular water views.

$135–$245
5 rooms, 5 pb
Visa MC Disc Cash
S-no/P-no/HC-ltd

BB | Full breakfast
Breakfast-to-go is available for early-starters, daily fresh-baked cookies, coffee, teas, hot cocoa
Fireplace, two-person Jacuzzi or hot tub, TV, DVD, CD, hi-speed wireless internet access

PORT ORCHARD

Reflections—A B&B
3878 Reflection Lane East

360-871-5582 | *Cathy Hall*
jimreflect@wavecable.com | www.reflectionsbnb.com

Just a short distance from downtown Port Orchard, Reflections Bed & Breakfast Inn is a perfect place for an overnight or weekend stay.

free *Dreams Do Come True participating inn—Valid anytime*

$65–$110
4 rooms, 2 pb
Visa MC
C-ltd/S-no/P-no/HC-no

BB | Full breakfast
evening snack, wine or tea on arrival
TV/VCR, fireplace, ceiling fans, meeting rooms, washer/dryer, library.

Commander's
Beach House
400 Hudson St

360-385-1778 | 888-385-1778 | *Gail Dionne Oldroyd*
stay@commandersbeachhouse.com | www.commandersbeachhouse.com

This quiet and relaxing Cape Cod style beach house offers the best of both worlds. We are located on the water with miles of beach to explore And.. just three blocks from downtown shops and restaurants. "Come relax and solve nothing."

$99–$225
4 rooms, 3 pb
Visa MC
C-ltd/S-no/P-no/HC-ltd

BB | Full breakfast
Gourmet hot chocolate, teas, coffee, and spiced cider with biscottis for dunking
Ocean views, living room, fireplaces, verandah, weddings

Holly Hill House B&B
611 Polk Street

360-385-5619 | 800-435-1454 | *Nina & Greg Dortch*
info@hollyhillhouse.com | www.hollyhillhouse.com

Holly Hill House is an 1872 Victorian B&B in the historic uptown district. Providing comfortable and relaxing accommodations that pamper our guests.

$99–$178
5 rooms, 5 pb
Visa MC
C-ltd/S-ltd/P-no/HC-no

BB | Full breakfast at 9:00am
Tea, cocoa, homemade marshmallows, snacks, wine
Parlor with TV, DVD & video, gardens, views, patio, packages

Quimper Inn
1306 Franklin St

360-385-1060 | 800-557-1060 | *Sue & Ron Ramage*
rooms@quimperinn.com | www.quimperinn.com

Since 1991 our guests have enjoyed staying in our home. Our 4 guest rooms reflect unique, elegant, uncluttered decor, beautiful woodwork, high ceilings and period fixtures.

$98–$160
4 rooms, 4 pb
Visa MC   Cash Checks
C-ltd/S-no/P-no/HC-ltd

BB | Full breakfast
Please inform us if you have special dietary requirements or restrictions.

POULSBO

Morgan Hill Retreat
1921 Northeast Sawdust
Hill Rd

360-598-4930 | 800-598-3926 | *Marcia Breece*
marcia@morganhillretreat.com | www.morganhillretreat.com/

Morgan Hill Retreat features comfortably sophisticated accommodations created to inspire relaxation and renewal. With an emphasis on privacy, this refuge will indulge visitors craving rest, solitude and inspiration.

$125–$175
3 rooms, 3 pb
Visa MC   Checks
C-ltd/S-no/P-ltd/HC-yes

BB | Full breakfast
We'll stock the refrigerator—just let us know in advance! (however, additional charges apply)
Labyrinth, trout pond, fly fishing or lavender cooking lessons, in-room massage, free WiFi, wildlife

PUYALLUP

Hedman House
502 9th St SW

253-848-2248 | **866-433-6267** | *Neil & Normajean Hedman*
hedman-house@msn.com | www.hedmanhouse.com

Hedman House, a B&B, located in Puyallup, Washington is a comfortable and romantic lodging alternative to the hotels and motels in Seattle and Tacoma. Perfect for romantic weekend getaways, antiquing, the Fair or business.

$105–$145
2 rooms, 1 pb
Visa MC   Cash Checks
C-ltd/S-no/P-no/HC-no

BB | Full breakfast
Covered porch, courtyard, spa tub, fireplace, wireless Internet, central air

REDMOND

A Cottage Creek Inn
12525 Avondale Rd NE

425-881-5606 | *Steve & Jeanette Wynecoop*
innkeepers@cottagecreekinn.com | www.cottagecreekinn.com

Romantic English Tudor in beautiful, tranquil garden setting. Five lovely rooms/suites w/ private baths & cable TV. Many fine wineries & restaurants nearby. Phones & high speed WiFi are comp. Private nature trail, Hot Tub, Full Breakfast included.

$110–$160
5 rooms, 5 pb
Visa MC AmEx Cash Checks
C-ltd/S-ltd/P-no/HC-no

BB | Full breakfast
Afternoon tea on request
Sitting room, Jacuzzis, suites, hot tub, pond, creek, conference facilities, WiFi, phones, wineries

Meritage Meadows Inn
21407 NE Union Hill Rd

425-487-4019 | **888-613-4223** | *Bob and Karen Spencer*
innkeeper@meritagemeadows.com | www.meritagemeadows.com/

Meritage Meadows Inn is in the heart of Washington Wine Country. Just 3 miles from downtown Redmond and 10 miles from Seattle, it feels completely secluded on our 14 acre property. Complimentary wine tasting daily for guests.

$150–$185
5 rooms, 5 pb
Most CC Checks
C-ltd/S-ltd/P-no/HC-no

BB | Full breakfast
Complimentary wine tasting daily. Cookies and treats are available around the clock.
Common Areas, heated floors, jetted tubs, flat screen LCD TVs, exercise room, home theater, library

SEATTLE

**11th Avenue Inn
Bed & Breakfast**
121 11th Avenue E

206-720-7161 | **800-720-7161** | *David Williams*
info@11thavenueinn.com | www.11thavenueinn.com

Walk to the Pike Place Market and to the other downtown Seattle attractions from a charming 1906 Seattle bed and breakfast on a tree-lined side street in Seattle's Capitol Hill neighborhood. We're near dozens of restaurants, shops, a popular park, and bus

$69–$169
8 rooms, 8 pb
Most CC
C-ltd/S-no/P-no/HC-no

BB | Full breakfast
50 restaurants within a 15 minute walk
Free parking, free WiFi & guest Internet computers & printer, TV/DVD, living room, den, front porch.

B&B on Broadway
722 Broadway Ave E

206-329-8933 | *Russel Lyons & Don Fabian*
info@bbonbroadway.com | www.bbonbroadway.com/

First, you notice the finely carved banister and staircase, then the oversize stained glass window over the landing. Facing the stairway, block glass panels frame the doorway in the roomy foyer. Welcome to the B&B on Broadway, your B&B on Capitol Hill.

$145–$175
4 rooms, 4 pb
Most CC Cash Checks
S-no/P-no/HC-no

BB | Continental breakfast

Bacon Mansion B&B
959 Broadway E

206-329-1864 | **800-240-1864** | *Daryl J. King*
info@baconmansion.com | www.baconmansion.com

Stay in Seattle's leading Bed and Breakfast and enjoy the charm and comfort of yesterday, with all the convenience of today. One of Capitol Hill's gracious mansions c. 1909.

$99–$234
11 rooms, 9 pb
Most CC Cash
C-ltd/S-no/P-ltd/HC-ltd

BB | Continental plus breakfast
Tea & cookies in the afternoon
Sitting room, library, conference room, cable TV, hairdryer, private telephone,
bathrobe, free WiFi

Bed & Breakfast Inn Seattle
1808 E Denny Way

206-412-REST | *Seleima Silikula, Shannon Seth*
Stay@BnBInnSeattle.com | www.SeattleBednBreakfast.com

An Urban Inn for the savvy traveler. Located just 10 blocks from downtown Seattle. 10 minute bus ride to Space Needle and Waterfront. Your home away from home.

$85–$165
14 rooms, 1 pb
Visa MC Disc Cash Checks
C-ltd/S-no/P-ltd/HC-ltd

BB | Full Breakfast
Access to our gourmet kitchen, wireless, off-street parking, laundry facility and
bike rental

Chambered Nautilus Bed and Breakfast Inn
5005 22nd Ave NE

206-522-2536 | **800-545-8459** | *Joyce Schulte*
stay@chamberednautilus.com | www.chamberednautilus.com

An elegant Inn near the University of campus. Minutes from downtown. Features spacious, quiet and comfortable rooms with amazing breakfasts and homemade cookies! Fireplaces in winter, gardens for spring and summer. WiFi throughout.

$104–$204
10 rooms, 10 pb
Visa MC AmEx
C-ltd/S-no/P-ltd/HC-no

BB |Full 3-course breakfast
Tea, coffee, fruit & cookies
Fireplaces, porches, A/C, private baths, robes, HDTV, hairdryer, in room WiFi,
guest computer

Chelsea Station
Inn B&B
4915 Linden Ave N

206-547-6077 | *Bennett, Lauren, Maureen and Toni*
info@chelseastationinn.com | http://chelseastationinn.com/

Located just 10 minutes from downtown Seattle and right across the street from the Woodland Park Zoo, Chelsea Station Inn B&B features four luxurious suites, each can accommodate up to four guests!

$159–$275
4 rooms, 4 pb
Visa MC
C-yes/S-ltd/P-no/HC-no

BB | Full breakfast
Kitchenette stocked with treats
Suites with living room, dining room, kitchenette, powder room & sumptuous master suite

Gaslight Inn
1727 15th Ave

206-325-3654 | *Stephen Bennett*
innkeepr@gaslight-inn.com | www.gaslight-inn.com

In restoring Gaslight Inn, we have brought out this bed and breakfast's original turn-of-the-century ambiance and warmth, while keeping in mind the additional conveniences and contemporary style needed by today's travelers.

$98–$168
8 rooms, 6 pb
Visa MC AmEx   Cash Checks
C-ltd/S-no/P-no/HC-ltd

BB | Seasonal Continental Breakfast
A wet bar, microwave and under counter refrigerator are the only food storage/ preparation facilities
Heated pool, sun deck, living room, fireplace, library

Greenlake Guest House
7630 E Green Lake Dr N

206-729-8700 | **866-355-8700** | *Blayne & Julie McAferty*
stay@greenlakeguesthouse.com | www.greenlakeguesthouse.com

1920 Craftsman style B&B, located across the street from Green Lake. All rooms include private bath with Jacuzzi tub/shower & heated tile floors, lake views or gas fireplace, TV/DVD, wireless Internet, full breakfast. 10 minute drive to downtown Seattle.

$134–$214
4 rooms, 4 pb
Visa MC Disc Cash Checks
C-ltd/S-no/P-no/HC-no

BB | Full breakfast
Tea, coffee, homemade cookies, guest refrigerator with sodas & bottled water
Dining room, fireplace, living room, sunroom, wireless Internet, TV/DVD, large DVD library

Inn at Harbor Steps
1221 First Ave

206-748-0973 | **888-728-8910** | *David Huynh*
innatharborsteps@foursisters.com | www.innatharborsteps.com

Nestled in the heart of Seattle's sleek arts and business district and crowned by the glamorous Harbor Steps Park, the Inn at Harbor Steps is perfectly located to the best Seattle has to offer.

$175–$250
28 rooms, 28 pb
Most CC Cash
C-yes/S-no/P-no/HC-yes

BB | Full breakfast
Afternoon wine, tea & hors d' oeuvres, freshly-baked cookies, drinks available throughout the day
High speed internet, fireplaces, jetted tubs, on-site parking, indoor pool, basketball court, gym

Inn of Twin Gables
3258 14th Ave W

206-284-3979 | **866-466-3979** | *Katie Frame*
innkeepers@innoftwingables.com | www.innoftwingables.com

The Inn of Twin Gables offers 3 comfortable guest rooms and a Garden Suite with 2 BRs, bath, full kitchen, private entrance; and a substantial gourmet breakfast. Personal attention and an ambiance of welcome and comfort make it your home away from home.

$100–$250
4 rooms, 4 pb
Visa MC AmEx   Cash Checks
C-ltd/S-no/P-ltd/HC-ltd

BB | Full gourmet breakfast
We serve a full gourmet breakfast using herbs from our garden.
Enclosed sun porch, living room, fireplace, convenient to attractions, dining, shopping, WiFi

Mildred's
1202 15th Ave E

206-325-6072 | **800-327-9692** | *Melodee Sarver*
innkeeper@mildredsbnb.com | www.mildredsbnb.com

1890 Victorian. Wraparound veranda, lace curtains, red carpets. City location near bus, electric trolley, park, art museum, flower conservatory.

$125–$225
4 rooms, 4 pb
Visa MC AmEx   Cash Checks
C-yes/S-ltd/P-no/HC-no

BB | Full breakfast
Afternoon tea or coffee, homemade cookies
Sitting room, fireplace, library, veranda, grand piano, queen beds, front yard putting green

Olympic View Bed & Breakfast Cottage
2705 SW 164th Pl

206-200-8801 | *Dave & Eileen Schmidt*
innkeeper@olympicviewbb.com | http://olympicviewbb.com

Awarded "Most Scenic View" & "Best Kept Secret". Private cottage with hot tub overlooking spectacular water and mountain views. Full kitchen, breakfast, king bed, living area, TV, DVD, stereo, private bath, walk to beach and close to Seattle attractions.

$165–$220
1 rooms, 1 pb
Visa MC
C-ltd/S-ltd/P-no/HC-no

BB | Full breakfast
Sodas, snacks, fresh fruit, afternoon tea, requests are taken for special meals in the cottage
Private cottage & hot tub, king bed, free WiFi, laundry facilities, cable TV, CD/DVD, videos

Shafer Baillie Mansion
907 14th Ave E

206-322-4654 | **800-985-4654** | *Mark Mayhle & Ana Lena Melka*
sbmansion@gmail.com | www.sbmansion.com/

Magnificent 1914 Tudor Revival 14,000 sq ft mansion on Seattle's original Millionaires' Row. Capitol Hill location, central to all major attractions and amenities: downtown, waterfront, Pike Place Market, Seattle Center, Washington Convention Center.

$139–$219
8 rooms, 8 pb
Most CC Cash Checks
C-yes/S-no/P-no/HC-no

BB | Expanded Continental breakfast
Coffee & tea available all day
Sitting room, fireplaces, weddings hosted

SEATTLE

Sleeping Bulldog B&B
816 19th Ave. South

206-325-0202 | *Korby Kencayd and Randal Potter*
innkeepers@sleepingbulldog.com | www.sleepingbulldog.com/

We are an intimate B&B located in a quiet neighborhood close to Downtown and Seattle's Sports Stadiums. Enjoy the dramatic view of Downtown, Puget Sound, Qwest Field and the Olympic Mountain. A Full Gourmet breakfast awaits you in the morning.

$116–$206
3 rooms, 3 pb
Most CC Cash Checks
C-ltd/S-no/P-no/HC-no

BB | Full breakfast
fresh baked cookies, or cupcakes
flat-screen TVs, DVD players, iHome radios, and Keurig coffee makers.

Soundview Cottage B&B
17600 Sylvester Rd SW

206-244-5209 | **888-244-5209** | *Annie Phillips*
annie@soundviewcottage.com | www.seattlecottage.net

Soundview Cottage Bed & Breakfast is a self-contained, absolutely private, charming guest house. With amazing views of Puget Sound, islands, and mountains from your cozy, intimate hideaway, you will be assured of a memorable visit.

$190–$200
1 rooms, 1 pb
Most CC Cash Checks
C-ltd/S-no/P-no/HC-ltd

BB |Self-prepared breakfast
Stereo, DVD, CD player, Cable TV, hi-speed Internet connection,
and an outdoor deck and hot tub

Three Tree Point
17026 33rd Ave SW
Seattle

206-669-7646 | **888-369-7696** | *Penny & Doug Whisler*
whislers@comcast.net | www.3treepointbnb.com

Escape to one of Seattle's most enjoyable bed and breakfast getaways. Located on a quiet hillside overlooking Puget Sound and Three Tree Point, this is a true Northwest retreat.

$150–$250
2 rooms, 2 pb
Visa MC AmEx   Cash Checks
C-yes/S-ltd/P-yes/HC-ltd

BB | Full breakfast
Snacks
A/C, terry robes & slippers, stereo w/CD player, in-room cable TV/VCR, morning paper

Villa Heidelberg B&B
4845 45th Ave SW
Seattle

206-938-3658 | **800-671-2942** | *Judy Burbrink*
info@villaheidelberg.com | www.villaheidelberg.com

1909 Craftsman home, just minutes from the airport & downtown Seattle. Two blocks to shops, bus & a variety of ethnic restaurants. Great view of Puget Sound and Olympic Mountains with marvelous sunsets. Close to Lincoln Park and Alki Beach.

$100–$250
6 rooms, 2 pb
Visa MC AmEx
C-ltd/S-no/P-no/HC-no

BB |F ull breakfast
Cable TV, WiFi & fax access, each bathroom has Noevir products, a hairdryer & bathrobes in each room

Shelburne Inn
4415 Pacific Way

360-642-2442 | 800-INN-1896
Laurie Anderson & David Campiche
innkeeper@theshelburneinn.com | www.theshelburneinn.com

The oldest surviving hotel in Washington state, with the time-honored tradition of superb service, decor and cuisine. Can accommodate small meetings of up to 30. The restaurant serves breakfast, lunch and dinner making creative use of local ingredients.

$115–$195
15 rooms, 15 pb
Visa MC AmEx Cash
C-yes/S-no/P-no/HC-ltd

BB | Full country breakfast
Freshly baked cookies upon arrival. Shelburne Restaurant and Pub serve breakfast, lunch and dinner.
Lobby and main dining room have fireplaces. Guest computer available in library. Wireless Internet.

SEQUIM

Groveland Cottage B&B
4861 Sequim-
Dungeness Way

360-683-3565 | 800-879-8859 | *Simone Nichols*
simone@olypen.com | www.grovelandcottage.com/

Groveland Cottage is located in the Sequim-Dungeness Valley along the Strait of Juan de Fuca on Washington's beautiful North Olympic Peninsula. Sequim offers convenient access to Olympic National Park, Dungeness Spit National Wildlife Refuge, & the ferry.

$125–$155
5 rooms, 5 pb
Most CC Cash Checks
C-ltd/S-no/P-ltd/HC-no

BB | Full breakfast
Snacks in the afternoon. Breakfast to go if early departure is needed
High speed wireless Internet, Cable TV and lush gardens

Juan de Fuca Cottages
182 Marine Dr

360-683-4433 | 866-683-4433 | *Missy & Tom Rief*
juandefuca@olypen.com | www.juandefuca.com

Charming, completely equipped cottages and suites perched on a 50-foot bluff overlooking Dungeness Spit. We have our own private beach on Dungeness Bay. Prepare your own breakfast in cozy kitchens.

(free) *Dreams Do Come True participating inn—Valid September 15–June 15, Sunday–Thursday (not valid with any other specials); will offer a room upgrade*

$99–$315
14 rooms, 14 pb
Visa MC Disc Cash Checks
C-yes/S-no/P-ltd/HC-ltd

EP |
Complimentary coffee & tea
Whirlpool tub, CabTV/VCR/DVD/CD, robes, slippers, 2 fireplace suites, kayak rentals, 200 movies free

Lost Mountain Lodge
303 Sunny View Dr

360-683-2431 | 888-683-2431 | *Dwight & Lisa Hostvedt*
getaway@lostmountainlodge.com | www.lostmountainlodge.com

Discover why newest Best Places to Kiss gave us their only, highest 4-kisses rating on the Olympic Peninsula. 9+ acres of mountain views & idyllic ponds. Romantic fireplace suites, king beds & superb amenities. Gourmet breakfast, lattes, hydrotherapy spa.

$189–$349
5 rooms, 5 pb
Visa MC AmEx Cash
C-ltd/S-no/P-no/HC-ltd

BB | Farmer's Market Gourmet Breakfast
Complimentary lattes & espresso, welcome tray of wine & hors d'oeuvres, evening treats, free popcorn
Free Wi-Fi, spa services, hydrotherapy spa, free movies & DVDs, library

SEQUIM

Red Caboose
Getaway B&B
24 Old Coyote Way

360-683-7350 | *Charlotte & Olaf*
info@redcaboosegetaway.com | www.redcaboosegetaway.com

Stay in one of six themed luxury cabooses in the beautiful town of Sequim, in the shadow of the Olympic mountains & minutes away from John Wayne Marina. Our gourmet breakfast are elegantly served in our private 1937 Zephyr dining car, "The Silver Eagle".

$155–$210
6 rooms, 6 pb
Most CC
S-no/P-no/HC-no

BB | Full gourmet breakfast
Vegan, vegetarian,etc. just let us know when making reservations
Queen featherbed, large whirlpool tubs, robes, hairdryer, fireplace, mini-fridge, TV/DVD, WIFI

SNOHOMISH

Pillows & Platters B&B **360-862-8944** | *Shirley & Dennis Brindle*
502 Avenue C
pillowsandplatters@gmail.com | www.pillowsandplatters.com

Welcome to this cheery house, built in 1892 as the original Methodist Parsonage for the city of Snohomish. Three intriguing rooms available, one with private bath, friendly hosts, and a romantic and relaxing atmosphere. Enjoy your trip!

$80–$100
3 rooms, 1 pb
Visa MC   Cash Checks
C-ltd/S-no/P-no/HC-ltd

BB | Full breakfast
High speed wireless internet access, porch swing

Roberts' Mansion
1923 W 1st Ave
Spokane

509-456-8839 | *Mary Moltke*
manager@ejrobertsmansion.com | www.ejrobertsmansion.com

Nestled proudly in Spokane's historic Browne's Addition, the meticulously restored Roberts Mansion celebrates its Victorian heritage in grand style. Suited as a Bed & Breakfast and Event facility, consider holding your wedding, or other event with us.

$140–$200
5 rooms, 5 pb
Visa MC   Cash Checks
C-yes/S-no/P-no/HC-no

BB | Full breakfast
Wireless Internet service, weddings & events, gardens, parlor, billiard room, library, sunroom

Branch Colonial House **253-752-3565** | **877-752-3565** | *Robin Korobkin*
2420 N 21st St
Tacoma
stay@branchcolonialhouse.com | www.branchcolonialhouse.com

Nestled above Tacoma's historical Old Town district and over looking Commencement Bay, the Branch Colonial House offers romantic views, antique furnishings, and easy access to all of Puget Sound area dinning and attractions.

$135–$209
6 rooms, 6 pb
Visa MC AmEx   Cash
C-yes/S-no/P-no/HC-no

BB | Full or continental breakfast
Sitting room, jetted tubs, fireplace, cable TV, Bose Wave radio/CD, DVD players, wireless Internet

TACOMA

Plum Duff House
619 North K St

253-627-6916 | **888-627-1920** | *Peter & Robin Stevens*
plumduffhouse@gmail.com | www.plumduff.com

Built in 1900 and listed on the Tacoma Historic Register, this unique, charming home has high ceilings, arches, and lovely gardens. We invite you to relax and enjoy genuine hospitality in a casual, leisurely atmosphere.

$90–$150
4 rooms, 4 pb
Most CC Cash
C-ltd/S-no/P-ltd/HC-no

BB | Full breakfast
Tea, coffee, hot chocolate, cookies, cold drinks, fruit
Gardens, sitting room, sun room, Jacuzzi, fireplaces, WiFi, cable TV/videos, local phones

VASHON ISLAND

Artist's Studio
Loft B&B
16529 91st Ave SW

206-463-2583 | *Jacqueline Clayton*
info@vashonbedandbreakfast.com | www.vashonbedandbreakfast.com

An enchanting, romantic getaway nestled on five acres with flower gardens & hot tub, on beautiful Vashon Island, minutes from Seattle. Cottages with fireplaces & Jacuzzis. Healing, serene atmosphere, private entrances & baths. Rated 3 diamonds by AAA.

$119–$215
5 rooms, 5 pb
Most CC Cash Checks
C-ltd/S-no/P-no/HC-no

BB | Full or expanded continental
Bicycles, Jacuzzi, suites, fireplace, conference facilities, kitchenette, hot tub

Swallow's Nest
Guest Cottages
6030 SW 248th St

206-463-2646 | **800-269-6378** | *Bob Keller*
anynest@vashonislandcottages.com | www.vashonislandcottages.com

The Swallow's Nest affords travelers the opportunity to sojourn to a private country retreat on Vashon Island. There are 7 charming cottages in 3 separate locations each furnished in a comfortable & warm manner, some with views.

$105–$145
7 rooms, 7 pb
Most CC
C-yes/S-no/P-ltd/HC-ltd

EP |
Cottages with kitchens; coffee, tea, cocoa
Some hot tubs, fireplaces, golf, boating nearby

YAKIMA

A Touch of Europe
220 N 16th Ave

509-454-9775 | **888-438-7073** | *Chef Erika & James A. Cenci*
atoeurope@msn.com | www.winesnw.com/toucheuropeb&b.htm

Pamper yourself with luxurious surroundings, enjoy a signature, candlelit breakfast included in rates, arrange optional three course candlelit signature dinner prepared fresh by 3-time cookbook author-award winning chef/owner—unforgettable flavors

2011 Lanier Best West Coast Award Winner:
Best for Nearby Winery

$129–$137
2 rooms, 2 pb
Most CC Cash
S-no/P-no/HC-no

BB | Full breakfast
Afternoon high tea, fine dining onsite with prior arrangement for multi-course luncheons & dinners
Nearby Wineries-Golfing-Museums-Farms-Markets-Antiques-Hiking-Fishing-Birding-Skiing-Rafting

In California in the
early Spring, there
are pale yellow morn-
ings, when the mist
burns slowly into
day...I have dreamed
this coast myself.

ROBERT HASS